MznLnx

Missing Links Exam Preps

Exam Prep for

Early Transcendental Single Variable Calculus

Stewart, 5th Edition

The MznLnx Exam Prep is your link from the texbook and lecture to your exams.
The MznLnx Exam Preps are unauthorized and comprehensive reviews of your textbooks.

All material provided by MznLnx and Rico Publications (c) 2010
Textbook publishers and textbook authors do not particpate in or contribute to these reviews.

MznLnx

Rico
Publications

Exam Prep for Early Transcendental Single Variable Calculus
5th Edition
Stewart

Publisher: Raymond Houge
Assistant Editor: Michael Rouger
Text and Cover Designer: Lisa Buckner
Marketing Manager: Sara Swagger
Project Manager, Editorial Production: Jerry Emerson
Art Director: Vernon Lowerui

Product Manager: Dave Mason
Editorial Assitant: Rachel Guzmanji
Pedagogy: Debra Long
Cover Image: Jim Reed/Getty Images
Text and Cover Printer: City Printing, Inc.
Compositor: Media Mix, Inc.

(c) 2010 Rico Publications

ALL RIGHTS RESERVED. No part of this work covered by the copyright may be reproduced or used in any form or by an means--graphic, electronic, or mechanical, including photocopying, recording, taping, Web distribution, information storage, and retrieval systems, or in any other manner--without the written permission of the publisher.

Printed in the United States
ISBN:

For more information about our products, contact us at:
Dave.Mason@RicoPublications.com

For permission to use material from this text or product, submit a request online to:
Dave.Mason@RicoPublications.com

Contents

CHAPTER 1
Functions and Models — 1

CHAPTER 2
Limits and Derivatives — 21

CHAPTER 3
Differentiation Rules — 37

CHAPTER 4
Applications of Differentiation — 62

CHAPTER 5
Integrals — 88

CHAPTER 6
Applications of Integration — 105

CHAPTER 7
Techniques of Integration — 117

CHAPTER 8
Further Applications of Integration — 135

CHAPTER 9
Differential Equations — 152

CHAPTER 10
Parametric Equations and Polar Coordinates — 167

CHAPTER 11
Infinite Sequences and Series — 174

ANSWER KEY — 183

TO THE STUDENT

COMPREHENSIVE

The *MznLnx* Exam Prep series is designed to help you pass your exams. Editors at MznLnx review your textbooks and then prepare these practice exams to help you master the textbook material. Unlike study guides, workbooks, and practice tests provided by the texbook publisher and textbook authors, *MznLnx* gives you **all** of the material in each chapter in exam form, not just samples, so you can be sure to nail your exam.

MECHANICAL

The MznLnx Exam Prep series creates exams that will help you learn the subject matter as well as test you on your understanding. Each question is designed to help you master the concept. Just working through the exams, you gain an understanding of the subject--its a simple mechanical process that produces success.

INTEGRATED STUDY GUIDE AND REVIEW

MznLnx is not just a set of exams designed to test you, its also a comprehensive review of the subject content. Each exam question is also a review of the concept, making sure that you will get the answer correct without having to go to other sources of material. You learn as you go! Its the easiest way to pass an exam.

HUMOR

Studying can be tedious and dry. MznLnx's instructional design includes moderate humor within the exam questions on occassion, to break the tedium and revitalize the brain

Chapter 1. Functions and Models

1. _____, usually denoted symbolically by the Greek letter phi, ϕ, gives the location of a place on Earth north or south of the equator. _____ is an angular measurement in degrees (marked with Â°) ranging from 0Â° at the Equator (low _____) to 90Â° at the poles (90Â° N for the North Pole or 90Â° S for the South Pole; high _____). The complementary angle of a _____ is called the colatitude.
   a. Thing
   b. Latitude0
   c. Undefined
   d. Undefined

2. The mathematical concept of a _____ expresses the intuitive idea of deterministic dependence between two quantities, one of which is viewed as primary and the other as secondary. A _____ then is a way to associate a unique output for each input of a specified type, for example, a real number or an element of a given set.
   a. Function0
   b. Thing
   c. Undefined
   d. Undefined

3. _____ is a mathematical subject that includes the study of limits, derivatives, integrals, and power series and constitutes a major part of modern university curriculum.
   a. Calculus0
   b. Thing
   c. Undefined
   d. Undefined

4. In Euclidean geometry, a _____ is the set of all points in a plane at a fixed distance, called the radius, from a given point, the center.
   a. Thing
   b. Circle0
   c. Undefined
   d. Undefined

5. In classical geometry, a _____ of a circle or sphere is any line segment from its center to its boundary. By extension, the _____ of a circle or sphere is the length of any such segment. The _____ is half the diameter. In science and engineering the term _____ of curvature is commonly used as a synonym for _____.
   a. Radius0
   b. Thing
   c. Undefined
   d. Undefined

6. _____ the expected value of a random variable displays the average or central value of the variable.It is a summary value of the distribution of the variable.
   a. Thing
   b. Determining0
   c. Undefined
   d. Undefined

7. In mathematics, the _____ of a function is the set of all "output" values produced by that function. Given a function $f : A \to B$, the _____ of f, is defined to be the set $\{x \in B : x = f(a)$ for some $a \in A\}$.
   a. Thing
   b. Range0
   c. Undefined
   d. Undefined

8. In mathematics, a _____ of a k-place relation $L \subseteq X_1 \times \ldots \times X_k$ is one of the sets X_j, $1 \leq j \leq k$. In the special case where $k = 2$ and $L \subseteq X_1 \times X_2$ is a function $L : X_1 \to X_2$, it is conventional to refer to X_1 as the _____ of the function and to refer to X_2 as the codomain of the function.
   a. Domain0
   b. Thing
   c. Undefined
   d. Undefined

9. A _____ is a symbolic representation denoting a quantity or expression. It often represents an "unknown" quantity that has the potential to change.

Chapter 1. Functions and Models

a. Variable0
b. Thing
c. Undefined
d. Undefined

10. In mathematics, an _____ is any of the arguments, i.e. "inputs", to a function. Thus if we have a function f(x), then x is a _____.
   a. Thing
   b. Independent variable0
   c. Undefined
   d. Undefined

11. In a function the _____, is the variable which is the value, i.e. the "output", of the function.
   a. Dependent variable0
   b. Thing
   c. Undefined
   d. Undefined

12. An _____ or member of a set is an object that when collected together make up the set.
   a. Element0
   b. Thing
   c. Undefined
   d. Undefined

13. A _____ is a simplified and structured visual representation of concepts, ideas, constructions, relations, statistical data, anatomy etc used in all aspects of human activities to visualize and clarify the topic.
   a. Thing
   b. Diagram0
   c. Undefined
   d. Undefined

14. In mathematics, the _____ f is the collection of all ordered pairs . In particular, graph means the graphical representation of this collection, in the form of a curve or surface, together with axes, etc. Graphing on a Cartesian plane is sometimes referred to as curve sketching.
   a. Thing
   b. Graph of a function0
   c. Undefined
   d. Undefined

15. _____ is often used to describe the measurement of the steepness, incline, gradient, or grade of a straight line. The _____ is defined as the ratio of the "rise" divided by the "run" between two points on a line, or in other words, the ratio of the altitude change to the horizontal distance between any two points on the line.
   a. Thing
   b. Slope0
   c. Undefined
   d. Undefined

16. _____ is a synonym for information.
   a. Thing
   b. Data0
   c. Undefined
   d. Undefined

17. A _____, scatter diagram or scatter graph is a chart that uses Cartesian coordinates to display values for two variables.
   a. Scatter plot0
   b. Thing
   c. Undefined
   d. Undefined

18. A _____ is an abstract model that uses mathematical language to describe the behavior of a system. Eykhoff defined a _____ as 'a representation of the essential aspects of an existing system which presents knowledge of that system in usable form'.

Chapter 1. Functions and Models

   a. Thing
   c. Undefined
   b. Mathematical model0
   d. Undefined

19. In sociology and biology a _____ is the collection of people or organisms of a particular species living in a given geographic area or space, usually measured by a census.
   a. Thing
   c. Undefined
   b. Population0
   d. Undefined

20. _____ is change in population over time, and can be quantified as the change in the number of individuals in a population per unit time.
   a. Population growth0
   c. Undefined
   b. Thing
   d. Undefined

21. _____ are the basic objects of study in graph theory. Informally speaking, a graph is a set of objects called points, nodes, or vertices connected by links called lines or edges.
   a. Thing
   c. Undefined
   b. Graphs0
   d. Undefined

22. In logic and mathematics, logical _____ (usual symbol and) is a two-place logical operation that results in a value of true if both of its operands are true, otherwise a value of false.
   a. Concept
   c. Undefined
   b. Conjunction0
   d. Undefined

23. _____ is defined as the rate of change or derivative with respect to time of velocity.
   a. Thing
   c. Undefined
   b. Acceleration0
   d. Undefined

24. An _____ is the result from the sudden release of stored energy in the Earth's crust that creates seismic waves.
   a. Earthquake0
   c. Undefined
   b. Thing
   d. Undefined

25. A _____ is 360° or 2ð radians.
   a. Turn0
   c. Undefined
   b. Thing
   d. Undefined

26. _____ is a physical property of a system that underlies the common notions of hot and cold; something that is hotter has the greater _____.
   a. Thing
   c. Undefined
   b. Temperature0
   d. Undefined

27. Initial objects are also called _____, and terminal objects are also called final.
   a. Coterminal0
   c. Undefined
   b. Thing
   d. Undefined

28. In mathematics and the mathematical sciences, a _____ is a fixed, but possibly unspecified, value. This is in contrast to a variable, which is not fixed.

a. Constant0
b. Thing
c. Undefined
d. Undefined

29. In the scientific method, an _____ (Latin: ex-+-periri, "of (or from) trying"), is a set of actions and observations, performed in the context of solving a particular problem or question, in order to support or falsify a hypothesis or research concerning phenomena.
    a. Thing
    b. Experiment0
    c. Undefined
    d. Undefined

30. In finance, a _____ is collateral that the holder of a position in securities, options, or futures contracts has to deposit to cover the credit risk of his counterparty.
    a. Thing
    b. Margin0
    c. Undefined
    d. Undefined

31. _____ are a measure of time.
    a. Minutes0
    b. Thing
    c. Undefined
    d. Undefined

32. The _____ of a solid object is the three-dimensional concept of how much space it occupies, often quantified numerically.
    a. Thing
    b. Volume0
    c. Undefined
    d. Undefined

33. In plane geometry, a _____ is a polygon with four equal sides, four right angles, and parallel opposite sides. In algebra, the _____ of a number is that number multiplied by itself.
    a. Thing
    b. Square0
    c. Undefined
    d. Undefined

34. The metre (or _____, see spelling differences) is a measure of length. It is the basic unit of length in the metric system and in the International System of Units (SI), used around the world for general and scientific purposes.
    a. Meter0
    b. Concept
    c. Undefined
    d. Undefined

35. Mathematical _____ is used to represent ideas.
    a. Notation0
    b. Thing
    c. Undefined
    d. Undefined

36. A _____ is a number that is less than zero.
    a. Thing
    b. Negative number0
    c. Undefined
    d. Undefined

37. In mathematics, a _____ may be described informally as a number that can be given by an infinite decimal representation.
    a. Real number0
    b. Thing
    c. Undefined
    d. Undefined

Chapter 1. Functions and Models

38. In mathematics, a _____ of a number x is a number r such that $r^2 = x$, or in words, a number r whose square (the result of multiplying the number by itself) is x.
    a. Square root0
    b. Thing
    c. Undefined
    d. Undefined

39. In mathematics, the concept of a _____ tries to capture the intuitive idea of a geometrical one-dimensional and continuous object. A simple example is the circle.
    a. Curve0
    b. Thing
    c. Undefined
    d. Undefined

40. Equivalence is the condition of being _____ or essentially equal.
    a. Equivalent0
    b. Thing
    c. Undefined
    d. Undefined

41. In mathematics, a _____ of a complex-valued function f is a member x of the domain of f such that f(x) vanishes at x, that is, x : f (x) = 0.
    a. Root0
    b. Thing
    c. Undefined
    d. Undefined

42. In elementary algebra, an _____ is a set that contains every real number between two indicated numbers and may contain the two numbers themselves.
    a. Interval0
    b. Thing
    c. Undefined
    d. Undefined

43. _____ is the notation in which permitted values for a variable are expressed as ranging over a certain interval; "5 < x < 9" is an example of the application of _____.
    a. Thing
    b. Interval notation0
    c. Undefined
    d. Undefined

44. _____ is a test to determine if a relation or its graph is a function or not
    a. Vertical line test0
    b. Thing
    c. Undefined
    d. Undefined

45. Acid _____ ratio measures the ability of a company to use its near cash or quick assets to immediately extinguish its current liabilities.
    a. Test0
    b. Thing
    c. Undefined
    d. Undefined

46. There are two main approaches to _____ in mathematics. They are the model theory of _____ and the proof theory of _____.
    a. Thing
    b. Truth0
    c. Undefined
    d. Undefined

47. In mathematics, the term _____ is applied to certain functions. There are two common ways it is applied: these are related historically, but diverged somewhat during the twentieth century.

Chapter 1. Functions and Models

    a. Functional0   b. Thing
    c. Undefined   d. Undefined

48. In mathematics, the _____ is a conic section generated by the intersection of a right circular conical surface and a plane parallel to a generating straight line of that surface. It can also be defined as locus of points in a plane which are equidistant from a given point.
    a. Parabola0   b. Thing
    c. Undefined   d. Undefined

49. A _____ is a one-dimensional picture in which the integers are shown as specially-marked points evenly spaced on a line.
    a. Number line0   b. Thing
    c. Undefined   d. Undefined

50. In mathematics, the _____ (or modulus) of a real number is its numerical value without regard to its sign.
    a. Thing   b. Absolute value0
    c. Undefined   d. Undefined

51. In mathematics, the _____ of a coordinate system is the point where the axes of the system intersect.
    a. Origin0   b. Thing
    c. Undefined   d. Undefined

52. A _____ is a unit of length, usually used to measure distance, in a number of different systems, including Imperial units, United States customary units and Norwegian/Swedish mil. Its size can vary from system to system, but in each is between 1 and 10 kilometers. In contemporary English contexts _____ refers to either:
    a. Thing   b. Mile0
    c. Undefined   d. Undefined

53. In business, particularly accounting, a _____ is the time intervals that the accounts, statement, payments, or other calculations cover.
    a. Thing   b. Period0
    c. Undefined   d. Undefined

54. In astronomy, geography, geometry and related sciences and contexts, a plane is said to be _____ at a given point if it is locally perpendicular to the gradient of the gravity field, i.e., with the direction of the gravitational force at that point.
    a. Horizontal0   b. Thing
    c. Undefined   d. Undefined

55. In geometry, an _____ of a triangle is a straight line through a vertex and perpendicular to (i.e. forming a right angle with) the opposite side or an extension of the opposite side.
    a. Altitude0   b. Concept
    c. Undefined   d. Undefined

56. In mathematics, a _____ is a two-dimensional manifold or surface that is perfectly flat.

Chapter 1. Functions and Models

a. Thing
b. Plane0
c. Undefined
d. Undefined

57. _____ of an object is its speed in a particular direction.
a. Thing
b. Velocity0
c. Undefined
d. Undefined

58. _____ is a kind of property which exists as magnitude or multitude. It is among the basic classes of things along with quality, substance, change, and relation.
a. Thing
b. Amount0
c. Undefined
d. Undefined

59. An _____ is a combination of numbers, operators, grouping symbols and/or free variables and bound variables arranged in a meaningful way which can be evaluated..
a. Expression0
b. Thing
c. Undefined
d. Undefined

60. In geometry, a _____ is defined as a quadrilateral where all four of its angles are right angles.
a. Rectangle0
b. Thing
c. Undefined
d. Undefined

61. _____ is the distance around a given two-dimensional object. As a general rule, the _____ of a polygon can always be calculated by adding all the length of the sides together. So, the formula for triangles is P = a + b + c, where a, b and c stand for each side of it. For quadrilaterals the equation is P = a + b + c + d. For equilateral polygons, P = na, where n is the number of sides and a is the side length.
a. Thing
b. Perimeter0
c. Undefined
d. Undefined

62. A _____ is one of the basic shapes of geometry: a polygon with three vertices and three sides which are straight line segments.
a. Triangle0
b. Thing
c. Undefined
d. Undefined

63. In geometry, an _____ polygon is a polygon which has all sides of the same length.
a. Equilateral0
b. Thing
c. Undefined
d. Undefined

64. An _____ is a triangle in which all sides are of equal length.
a. Equilateral triangle0
b. Thing
c. Undefined
d. Undefined

65. A _____ is a three-dimensional solid object bounded by six square faces, facets, or sides, with three meeting at each vertex.
a. Cube0
b. Thing
c. Undefined
d. Undefined

Chapter 1. Functions and Models

66. A function on the real numbers is called a _____ if it can be written as a finite linear combination of indicator functions of half-open intervals.
    a. Thing
    b. Step function0
    c. Undefined
    d. Undefined

67. _____ means "constancy", i.e. if something retains a certain feature even after we change a way of looking at it, then it is symmetric.
    a. Symmetry0
    b. Thing
    c. Undefined
    d. Undefined

68. In mathematics, a _____ is the result of multiplying, or an expression that identifies factors to be multiplied.
    a. Product0
    b. Thing
    c. Undefined
    d. Undefined

69. In mathematics, _____ refers to the rewriting of an expression into a simpler form.
    a. Thing
    b. Reduction0
    c. Undefined
    d. Undefined

70. _____ is a statistical measure of the average length of survival of a living thing.
    a. Life expectancy0
    b. Thing
    c. Undefined
    d. Undefined

71. The _____, the average in everyday English, which is also called the arithmetic _____ (and is distinguished from the geometric _____ or harmonic _____). The average is also called the sample _____. The expected value of a random variable, which is also called the population _____.
    a. Mean0
    b. Thing
    c. Undefined
    d. Undefined

72. In economics, supply and _____ describe market relations between prospective sellers and buyers of a good.
    a. Demand0
    b. Thing
    c. Undefined
    d. Undefined

73. A _____ is a statement or claimt that a particular event will occur in the future in more certain terms than a forecast.
    a. Thing
    b. Prediction0
    c. Undefined
    d. Undefined

74. A _____ is a deliberate process for transforming one or more inputs into one or more results.
    a. Calculation0
    b. Thing
    c. Undefined
    d. Undefined

75. In a mathematical proof or a syllogism, a _____ is a statement that is the logical consequence of preceding statements.
    a. Conclusion0
    b. Concept
    c. Undefined
    d. Undefined

Chapter 1. Functions and Models

76. The _____ of a ring R is defined to be the smallest positive integer n such that n a = 0, for all a in R.
    a. Thing
    b. Characteristic0
    c. Undefined
    d. Undefined

77. A _____ is a special kind of ratio, indicating a relationship between two measurements with different units, such as miles to gallons or cents to pounds.
    a. Thing
    b. Rate0
    c. Undefined
    d. Undefined

78. In geographic information systems, a _____ comprises an entity with a geographic location, typically determined by points, arcs, or polygons. Carriageways and cadastres exemplify _____ data.
    a. Feature0
    b. Thing
    c. Undefined
    d. Undefined

79. The word _____ comes from the Latin word linearis, which means created by lines.
    a. Thing
    b. Linear0
    c. Undefined
    d. Undefined

80. A _____ is a first degree polynomial mathematical function of the form: f(x) = mx + b where m and b are real constants and x is a real variable.
    a. Linear function0
    b. Thing
    c. Undefined
    d. Undefined

81. A _____ is a unit of length in the metric system, equal to one thousand metres, the current SI base unit of length
    a. Kilometer0
    b. Thing
    c. Undefined
    d. Undefined

82. A _____ signifies a point or points of probability on a subject e.g., the _____ of creativity, which allows for the formation of rule or norm or law by interpretation of the phenomena events that can be created.
    a. Principle0
    b. Thing
    c. Undefined
    d. Undefined

83. A central concept in science and the scientific method is that all evidence must be _____, or empirically based, that is, dependent on evidence or consequences that are observable by the senses.
    a. Empirical0
    b. Thing
    c. Undefined
    d. Undefined

84. In mathematics, an _____, mean, or central tendency of a data set refers to a measure of the "middle" or "expected" value of the data set.
    a. Concept
    b. Average0
    c. Undefined
    d. Undefined

85. _____ is a method of constructing new data points from a discrete set of known data points.
    a. Thing
    b. Interpolation0
    c. Undefined
    d. Undefined

Chapter 1. Functions and Models

86. In mathematics, an _____ is a statement about the relative size or order of two objects.
    a. Inequality0
    b. Thing
    c. Undefined
    d. Undefined

87. In mathematics, a _____ is a constant multiplicative factor of a certain object. The object can be such things as a variable, a vector, a function, etc. For example, the _____ of $9x^2$ is 9.
    a. Thing
    b. Coefficient0
    c. Undefined
    d. Undefined

88. In mathematics, there are several meanings of _____ depending on the subject.
    a. Degree0
    b. Thing
    c. Undefined
    d. Undefined

89. In mathematics, a _____ is an expression that is constructed from one or more variables and constants, using only the operations of addition, subtraction, multiplication, and constant positive whole number exponents. is a _____. Note in particular that division by an expression containing a variable is not in general allowed in polynomials. [1]
    a. Thing
    b. Polynomial0
    c. Undefined
    d. Undefined

90. A _____ is a polynomial function of the form $f(x) = ax^2 + bx + c$, where a, b, c are real numbers and a , 0.
    a. Event
    b. Quadratic function0
    c. Undefined
    d. Undefined

91. _____ is a function of the form
    a. Thing
    b. Cubic function0
    c. Undefined
    d. Undefined

92. In mathematics, a _____ is a polynomial equation of the second degree. The general form is $ax^2 + bx + c = 0$.
    a. Thing
    b. Quadratic equation0
    c. Undefined
    d. Undefined

93. A quadratic equation with real solutions, called roots, which may be real or complex, is given by the _____ : $x = \frac{-b \pm \sqrt{b^2 - 4ac}}{2a}$.
    a. Thing
    b. Quadratic formula0
    c. Undefined
    d. Undefined

94. _____ has many meanings, most of which simply .
    a. Thing
    b. Power0
    c. Undefined
    d. Undefined

95. In mathematics, _____ is an elementary arithmetic operation. When one of the numbers is a whole number, _____ is the repeated sum of the other number.
    a. Thing
    b. Multiplication0
    c. Undefined
    d. Undefined

Chapter 1. Functions and Models

96. In mathematics, a _____ number is a number which can be expressed as a ratio of two integers. Non-integer _____ numbers (commonly called fractions) are usually written as the vulgar fraction a / b, where b is not zero.
    a. Thing
    b. Rational0
    c. Undefined
    d. Undefined

97. In mathematics, a _____ is any function which can be written as the ratio of two polynomial functions.
    a. Thing
    b. Rational function0
    c. Undefined
    d. Undefined

98. In mathematics, the multiplicative inverse of a number x, denoted $1/x$ or x^{-1}, is the number which, when multiplied by x, yields 1. The multiplicative inverse of x is also called the _____ of x.
    a. Thing
    b. Reciprocal0
    c. Undefined
    d. Undefined

99. _____ is informally a function which satisfies a polynomial equation whose coefficients are themselves polynomials.
    a. Algebraic function0
    b. Thing
    c. Undefined
    d. Undefined

100. _____ are external two-dimensional outlines, with the appearance or configuration of some thing - in contrast to the matter or content or substance of which it is composed.
    a. Thing
    b. Shapes0
    c. Undefined
    d. Undefined

101. The _____ in a vacuum is an important physical constant denoted by the letter c for constant or the Latin word celeritas meaning "swiftness
    a. Speed of light0
    b. Thing
    c. Undefined
    d. Undefined

102. _____ is electromagnetic radiation with a wavelength that is visible to the eye (visible _____) or, in a technical or scientific context, electromagnetic radiation of any wavelength.
    a. Thing
    b. Light0
    c. Undefined
    d. Undefined

103. _____ is the property of a physical object that quantifies the amount of matter and energy it is equivalent to.
    a. Thing
    b. Mass0
    c. Undefined
    d. Undefined

104. _____ is the process in which an unstable atomic nucleus loses energy by emitting radiation in the form of particles or electromagnetic waves.
    a. Thing
    b. Radioactive decay0
    c. Undefined
    d. Undefined

105. In mathematics, _____ growth occurs when the growth rate of a function is always proportional to the function's current size.

Chapter 1. Functions and Models

a. Exponential0
b. Thing
c. Undefined
d. Undefined

106. _____ is one of the most important functions in mathematics. A function commonly used to study growth and decay
   a. Exponential function0
   b. Thing
   c. Undefined
   d. Undefined

107. _____ element of an element x with respect to a binary operation * with identity element e is an element y such that x * y = y * x = e. In particular,
   a. Inverse0
   b. Thing
   c. Undefined
   d. Undefined

108. An _____ is a function which does the reverse of a given function.
   a. Thing
   b. Inverse function0
   c. Undefined
   d. Undefined

109. In mathematics, a _____ number is a real or complex number which is not algebraic, that is, not a solution of a non-zero polynomial equation, with rational coefficients.
   a. Thing
   b. Transcendental0
   c. Undefined
   d. Undefined

110. In mathematics, the _____ functions are functions of an angle; they are important when studying triangles and modeling periodic phenomena, among many other applications.
   a. Trigonometric0
   b. Thing
   c. Undefined
   d. Undefined

111. _____ is a set, with some particular properties and usually some additional structure, such as the operations of addition or multiplication, for instance.
   a. Space0
   b. Thing
   c. Undefined
   d. Undefined

112. _____ is a temperature scale named after the German physicist Daniel Gabriel _____ , who proposed it in 1724.
   a. Fahrenheit0
   b. Thing
   c. Undefined
   d. Undefined

113. _____ is, or relates to, the _____ temperature scale .
   a. Celsius0
   b. Thing
   c. Undefined
   d. Undefined

114. In Euclidean geometry, a uniform _____ is a linear transformation that enlargers or diminishes objects, and whose _____ factor is the same in all directions. This is also called homothethy.
   a. Scale0
   b. Thing
   c. Undefined
   d. Undefined

Chapter 1. Functions and Models

115. In botany, _____ are above-ground plant organs specialized for photosynthesis. Their characteristics are typically analyzed by using Fiobonacci's sequences.
    a. Leaves0
    b. Thing
    c. Undefined
    d. Undefined

116. _____ is the pressure at some point withig the fluid
    a. Thing
    b. Water pressure0
    c. Undefined
    d. Undefined

117. In regression analysis, _____, also known as ordinary _____ analysis is a method for linear regression that determines the values of unknown quantities in a statistical model by minimizing the sum of the residuals difference between the predicted and observed values squared.
    a. Thing
    b. Least squares0
    c. Undefined
    d. Undefined

118. _____, in economics and political economy, are the distributions or payments awarded to the various suppliers of the factors of production.
    a. Returns0
    b. Thing
    c. Undefined
    d. Undefined

119. According to _____ relationship, in a production system with fixed and variable inputs, beyond some point, each additional unit of variable input yields less and less additional output.
    a. Thing
    b. Diminishing returns0
    c. Undefined
    d. Undefined

120. In mathematics, a _____ in elementary terms is any of a variety of different functions from geometry, such as rotations, reflections and translations.
    a. Thing
    b. Transformation0
    c. Undefined
    d. Undefined

121. The _____ of measurement are a globally standardized and modernized form of the metric system.
    a. Units0
    b. Thing
    c. Undefined
    d. Undefined

122. _____ is a trigonemtric function that is important when studying triangles and modeling periodic phenomena, among other applications.
    a. Sine0
    b. Thing
    c. Undefined
    d. Undefined

123. A _____ is the result of the addition of a set of numbers. The numbers may be natural numbers, complex numbers, matrices, or still more complicated objects. An infinite _____ is a subtle procedure known as a series.
    a. Sum0
    b. Thing
    c. Undefined
    d. Undefined

124. In mathematics, a _____ is the end result of a division problem. It can also be expressed as the number of times the divisor divides into the dividend.

a. Thing
c. Undefined
b. Quotient0
d. Undefined

125. _____ is a branch of mathematics concerning the study of structure, relation and quantity.
   a. Algebra0
   b. Concept
   c. Undefined
   d. Undefined

126. In mathematics, the _____ of two sets A and B is the set that contains all elements of A that also belong to B (or equivalently, all elements of B that also belong to A), but no other elements.
   a. Thing
   b. Intersection0
   c. Undefined
   d. Undefined

127. In mathematics, _____ is a part of the set theoretic notion of function.
   a. Image0
   b. Thing
   c. Undefined
   d. Undefined

128. A _____ number is a positive integer which has a positive divisor other than one or itself.
   a. Composite0
   b. Thing
   c. Undefined
   d. Undefined

129. A _____, formed by the composition of one function on another, represents the application of the former to the result of the application of the latter to the argument of the composite.
   a. Composite function0
   b. Thing
   c. Undefined
   d. Undefined

130. In mathematics, a _____ of a positive integer n is a way of writing n as a sum of positive integers.
   a. Thing
   b. Composition0
   c. Undefined
   d. Undefined

131. The _____ of an angle is the ratio of the length of the adjacent side to the length of the hypotenuse.
   a. Cosine0
   b. Concept
   c. Undefined
   d. Undefined

132. A _____ is a negotiable instrument instructing a financial institution to pay a specific amount of a specific currency from a specific demand account held in the maker/depositor's name with that institution. Both the maker and payee may be natural persons or legal entities.
   a. Thing
   b. Check0
   c. Undefined
   d. Undefined

133. In _____ algebra, a *-ring is an associative ring with an antilinear, antiautomorphism * : A ¨ A which is an involution.
   a. Thing
   b. Star0
   c. Undefined
   d. Undefined

134. In mathematics, defined and _____ are used to explain whether or not expressions have meaningful, sensible, and unambiguous values.

a. Thing
b. Undefined0
c. Undefined
d. Undefined

135. _____ is the transport of people on a trip/journey or the process or time involved in a person or object moving from one location to another.
a. Thing
b. Travel0
c. Undefined
d. Undefined

136. _____ is the difference of electrical potential between two points of an electrical or electronic circuit, expressed in volts
a. Voltage0
b. Thing
c. Undefined
d. Undefined

137. In physics, _____ is the rate of change of acceleration; more precisely, the derivative of acceleration with respect to time, the second derivative of velocity, or the third derivative of displacement. _____ is described by the following equation:
a. Jerk0
b. Thing
c. Undefined
d. Undefined

138. The deductive-nomological model is a formalized view of scientific _____ in natural language.
a. Explanation0
b. Thing
c. Undefined
d. Undefined

139. In statistics, _____ means the most frequent value assumed by a random variable, or occurring in a sampling of a random variable.
a. Concept
b. Mode0
c. Undefined
d. Undefined

140. In geometry, a line _____ is a part of a line that is bounded by two end points, and contains every point on the line between its end points.
a. Concept
b. Segment0
c. Undefined
d. Undefined

141. A _____ is a part of a line that is bounded by two end points, and contains every point on the line between its end points.
a. Line segment0
b. Thing
c. Undefined
d. Undefined

142. _____ variables are variables other than the independent variable that may bear any effect on the behavior of the subject being studied.
a. Thing
b. Extraneous0
c. Undefined
d. Undefined

143. A _____ of a number is a number a such that $a^3 = x$.

a. Cube root0
b. Thing
c. Undefined
d. Undefined

144. In mathematics, a _____ of a number x is the exponent y of the power by such that $x = b^y$. The value used for the base b must be neither 0 nor 1, nor a root of 1 in the case of the extension to complex numbers, and is typically 10, e, or 2.
   a. Thing
   b. Logarithm0
   c. Undefined
   d. Undefined

145. In mathematics, _____ are the intuitive idea of a geometrical one-dimensional and continuous object.
   a. Thing
   b. Curves0
   c. Undefined
   d. Undefined

146. In mathematics, an _____ .
   a. Ellipse0
   b. Thing
   c. Undefined
   d. Undefined

147. In mathematics, a _____ is a type of conic section defined as the intersection between a right circular conical surface and a plane which cuts through both halves of the cone.
   a. Hyperbola0
   b. Thing
   c. Undefined
   d. Undefined

148. In mathematics, an _____ number is any real number that is not a rational number- that is, it is a number which cannot be expressed as a fraction m/n, where m and n are integers.
   a. Irrational0
   b. Thing
   c. Undefined
   d. Undefined

149. In mathematics, an _____ is any real number that is not a rational number ¡ª that is, it is a number which cannot be expressed as m/n, where m and n are integers.
   a. Thing
   b. Irrational number0
   c. Undefined
   d. Undefined

150. In mathematics, _____ are any real number that is not a rational number ¡ª that is, it is a number which cannot be expressed as m/n, where m and n are integers.
   a. Thing
   b. Irrational numbers0
   c. Undefined
   d. Undefined

151. An _____ is a straight line or curve A to which another curve B approaches closer and closer as one moves along it. As one moves along B, the space between it and the _____ A becomes smaller and smaller, and can in fact be made as small as one could wish by going far enough along. A curve may or may not touch or cross its _____. In fact, the curve may intersect the _____ an infinite number of times.
   a. Thing
   b. Asymptote0
   c. Undefined
   d. Undefined

152. In mathematics, a _____ is a number which can be expressed as a ratio of two integers. Non-integer rational numbers (commonly called fractions) are usually written as the vulgar fraction a / b, where b is not zero.

Chapter 1. Functions and Models

a. Concept
b. Rational Number0
c. Undefined
d. Undefined

153. In mathematics, a _____ is a demonstration that, assuming certain axioms, some statement is necessarily true.
    a. Proof0
    b. Thing
    c. Undefined
    d. Undefined

154. _____ is a mathematical operation, written a^n, involving two numbers, the base a and the exponent n.
    a. Thing
    b. Exponentiating0
    c. Undefined
    d. Undefined

155. _____ is a mathematical operation, written a^n, involving two numbers, the base a and the exponent n.
    a. Thing
    b. Exponentiation0
    c. Undefined
    d. Undefined

156. A recession (i.e. _____) is traditionally defined in macroeconomics as a decline in a country's real Gross Domestic Product (GDP) for two or more successive quarters of a year (equivalently, two consecutive quarters of negative real economic growth).
    a. Depression0
    b. Thing
    c. Undefined
    d. Undefined

157. _____ is a subset of a population.
    a. Sample0
    b. Thing
    c. Undefined
    d. Undefined

158. In trigonometry, the _____ is a function defined as $\tan x = \sin x / \cos x$. The function is so-named because it can be defined as the length of a certain segment of a _____ (in the geometric sense) to the unit circle. In plane geometry, a line is _____ to a curve, at some point, if both line and curve pass through the point with the same direction.
    a. Tangent0
    b. Thing
    c. Undefined
    d. Undefined

159. _____ has two distinct but etymologically-related meanings: one in geometry and one in trigonometry.
    a. Thing
    b. Tangent line0
    c. Undefined
    d. Undefined

160. A _____ is a function that assigns a number to subsets of a given set.
    a. Thing
    b. Measure0
    c. Undefined
    d. Undefined

161. In mathematics, the notion of _____ is a generalization of the notion of invertible.
    a. Cancellation0
    b. Thing
    c. Undefined
    d. Undefined

162. A _____ is a set of numbers that designate location in a given reference system, such as x,y in a planar _____ system or an x,y,z in a three-dimensional _____ system.

Chapter 1. Functions and Models

a. Coordinate0
b. Thing
c. Undefined
d. Undefined

163. An _____ is when two lines intersect somewhere on a plane creating a right angle at intersection
   a. Thing
   b. Axes0
   c. Undefined
   d. Undefined

164. _____ is a test used to determine if a function is injective, surjective or bijective.
   a. Horizontal line test0
   b. Thing
   c. Undefined
   d. Undefined

165. _____ is the logarithm to the base e, where e is an irrational constant approximately equal to 2.718281828459.
   a. Natural logarithm0
   b. Thing
   c. Undefined
   d. Undefined

166. _____ is a relation in Euclidean geometry among the three sides of a right triangle.
   a. Thing
   b. Pythagorean Theorem0
   c. Undefined
   d. Undefined

167. In mathematics, a _____ (also spelled reflexion) is a map that transforms an object into its mirror image.
   a. Concept
   b. Reflection0
   c. Undefined
   d. Undefined

168. _____ has one 90° internal angle a right angle.
   a. Thing
   b. Right triangle0
   c. Undefined
   d. Undefined

169. In mathematics, a _____ is a statement that can be proved on the basis of explicitly stated or previously agreed assumptions.
   a. Thing
   b. Theorem0
   c. Undefined
   d. Undefined

170. _____ is a straight line or curve A to which another curve B the one being studied approaches closer and closer as one moves along it.
   a. Vertical asymptote0
   b. Thing
   c. Undefined
   d. Undefined

171. In mathematics, the _____(e) for L-functions are a class of summation formulae, expressing sums taken over the complex number zeroes of a given L-function, typically in terms of quantities studied by number theory by use of the theory of special functions.
   a. Thing
   b. Explicit formula0
   c. Undefined
   d. Undefined

172. In common philosophical language, a proposition or _____, is the content of an assertion, that is, it is true-or-false and defined by the meaning of a particular piece of language.

Chapter 1. Functions and Models

a. Statement0
b. Concept
c. Undefined
d. Undefined

173. In geometry, the _____ of an object is a point in some sense in the middle of the object.
    a. Center0
    b. Thing
    c. Undefined
    d. Undefined

174. _____ is the ability to hold, receive or absorb, or a measure thereof, similar to the concept of volume.
    a. Concept
    b. Capacity0
    c. Undefined
    d. Undefined

175. _____ usually refers to the biological _____ of a population level that can be supported for an organism, given the quantity of food, habitat, water and other life infrastructure present.
    a. Carrying capacity0
    b. Thing
    c. Undefined
    d. Undefined

176. _____ are objects, characters, or other concrete representations of ideas, concepts, or other abstractions.
    a. Thing
    b. Symbols0
    c. Undefined
    d. Undefined

177. _____ is bother the congnitive process of transferring information from a particular subject, and a linguistic expression corresponding to such a process.
    a. Analogy0
    b. Thing
    c. Undefined
    d. Undefined

178. In mathematics, science including computer science, linguistics and engineering, an _____ is, generally speaking, an independent variable or input to a function.
    a. Argument0
    b. Thing
    c. Undefined
    d. Undefined

179. Deductive _____ is the kind of _____ in which the conclusion is necessitated by, or reached from, previously known facts (the premises).
    a. Reasoning0
    b. Thing
    c. Undefined
    d. Undefined

180. In logic, Modus tollens (or Modus ponendo tollens) means to affirm by denying. It is the formal name for _____ proof or proof by contrapositive (contrapositive inference), often abbreviated to MT.
    a. Indirect0
    b. Thing
    c. Undefined
    d. Undefined

181. _____ is a type of logical argument where one assumes a claim for the sake of argument, derives an absurd or ridiculous outcome, and then concludes that the original assumption must have been wrong as it led to an absurd result. It makes use of the law of non-contradiction - a statement cannot be both true and false. In some cases it may also make use of the law of excluded middle - a statement must be either true or false. The phrase is traceable back to the Greek ç åéò ÜôïðïÞ áðáãùãÞ , meaning "reduction to the impossible", often used by Aristotle.

Chapter 1. Functions and Models

    a. Thing
    c. Undefined
    b. Reductio ad absurdum0
    d. Undefined

182. _____ is a method of mathematical proof typically used to establish that a given statement is true of all natural numbers
    a. Mathematical induction0
    c. Undefined
    b. Thing
    d. Undefined

183. _____ forms part of thinking. Considered the most complex of all intellectual functions, _____ has been defined as higher-order cognitive process that requires the modulation and control of more routine or fundamental skills.
    a. Thing
    c. Undefined
    b. Problem solving0
    d. Undefined

184. The _____ of a right triangle is the triangle's longest side; the side opposite the right angle.
    a. Thing
    c. Undefined
    b. Hypotenuse0
    d. Undefined

185. In a right triangle, the _____ of the triangle are the two sides that are perpendicular to each other, as opposed to the hypotenuse.
    a. Legs0
    c. Undefined
    b. Thing
    d. Undefined

186. In geometry, two lines or planes if one falls on the other in such a way as to create congruent adjacent angles. The term may be used as a noun or adjective. Thus, referring to Figure 1, the line AB is the _____ to CD through the point B.
    a. Thing
    c. Undefined
    b. Perpendicular0
    d. Undefined

187. In mathematics, a _____ of an integer n, also called a factor of n, is an integer which evenly divides n without leaving a remainder.
    a. Divisor0
    c. Undefined
    b. Thing
    d. Undefined

Chapter 2. Limits and Derivatives

1. _____ is a mathematical subject that includes the study of limits, derivatives, integrals, and power series and constitutes a major part of modern university curriculum.
   a. Calculus0
   b. Thing
   c. Undefined
   d. Undefined

2. When _____ symmetry one can determine whether or not an object is symmetric with respect to a given mathematical operation, if, when applied to the object, this operation does not change the object or its appearance.
   a. Investigating0
   b. Thing
   c. Undefined
   d. Undefined

3. _____ of an object is its speed in a particular direction.
   a. Thing
   b. Velocity0
   c. Undefined
   d. Undefined

4. _____ is an adjective usually refering to being in the centre.
   a. Thing
   b. Central0
   c. Undefined
   d. Undefined

5. In trigonometry, the _____ is a function defined as $\tan x = \sin x / \cos x$. The function is so-named because it can be defined as the length of a certain segment of a _____ (in the geometric sense) to the unit circle. In plane geometry, a line is _____ to a curve, at some point, if both line and curve pass through the point with the same direction.
   a. Thing
   b. Tangent0
   c. Undefined
   d. Undefined

6. The _____ is a measurement of how a function changes when the values of its inputs change.
   a. Thing
   b. Derivative0
   c. Undefined
   d. Undefined

7. A _____ is traditionally an infinitesimally small change in a variable.
   a. Thing
   b. Differential0
   c. Undefined
   d. Undefined

8. _____, a field in mathematics, is the study of how functions change when their inputs change. The primary object of study in _____ is the derivative.
   a. Differential calculus0
   b. Thing
   c. Undefined
   d. Undefined

9. The _____, the average in everyday English, which is also called the arithmetic _____ (and is distinguished from the geometric _____ or harmonic _____). The average is also called the sample _____. The expected value of a random variable, which is also called the population _____.
   a. Mean0
   b. Thing
   c. Undefined
   d. Undefined

10. _____ is often used to describe the measurement of the steepness, incline, gradient, or grade of a straight line. The _____ is defined as the ratio of the "rise" divided by the "run" between two points on a line, or in other words, the ratio of the altitude change to the horizontal distance between any two points on the line.

a. Thing
b. Slope0
c. Undefined
d. Undefined

11. _____ has two distinct but etymologically-related meanings: one in geometry and one in trigonometry.
    a. Tangent line0
    b. Thing
    c. Undefined
    d. Undefined

12. In mathematics, the _____ is a conic section generated by the intersection of a right circular conical surface and a plane parallel to a generating straight line of that surface. It can also be defined as locus of points in a plane which are equidistant from a given point.
    a. Thing
    b. Parabola0
    c. Undefined
    d. Undefined

13. _____ is a trigonometric function that is the reciprocal of cosine.
    a. Thing
    b. Secant0
    c. Undefined
    d. Undefined

14. _____ of a curve is a line that intersects two or more points on the curve.
    a. Secant line0
    b. Thing
    c. Undefined
    d. Undefined

15. In mathematics, the concept of a _____ tries to capture the intuitive idea of a geometrical one-dimensional and continuous object. A simple example is the circle.
    a. Thing
    b. Curve0
    c. Undefined
    d. Undefined

16. _____ is a synonym for information.
    a. Thing
    b. Data0
    c. Undefined
    d. Undefined

17. The mathematical concept of a _____ expresses the intuitive idea of deterministic dependence between two quantities, one of which is viewed as primary and the other as secondary. A _____ then is a way to associate a unique output for each input of a specified type, for example, a real number or an element of a given set.
    a. Thing
    b. Function0
    c. Undefined
    d. Undefined

18. In mathematics, two quantities are called _____ if they vary in such a way that one of the quantities is a constant multiple of the other, or equivalently if they have a constant ratio.
    a. Thing
    b. Proportional0
    c. Undefined
    d. Undefined

19. In plane geometry, a _____ is a polygon with four equal sides, four right angles, and parallel opposite sides. In algebra, the _____ of a number is that number multiplied by itself.
    a. Thing
    b. Square0
    c. Undefined
    d. Undefined

Chapter 2. Limits and Derivatives

20. In the scientific method, an _____ (Latin: ex-+-periri, "of (or from) trying"), is a set of actions and observations, performed in the context of solving a particular problem or question, in order to support or falsify a hypothesis or research concerning phenomena.
    a. Thing
    b. Experiment0
    c. Undefined
    d. Undefined

21. _____ was an Italian physicist, mathematician, astronomer, and philosopher who is closely associated with the scientific revolution.
    a. Galileo Galilei0
    b. Person
    c. Undefined
    d. Undefined

22. In elementary algebra, an _____ is a set that contains every real number between two indicated numbers and may contain the two numbers themselves.
    a. Thing
    b. Interval0
    c. Undefined
    d. Undefined

23. The metre (or _____, see spelling differences) is a measure of length. It is the basic unit of length in the metric system and in the International System of Units (SI), used around the world for general and scientific purposes.
    a. Meter0
    b. Concept
    c. Undefined
    d. Undefined

24. In mathematics, an _____, mean, or central tendency of a data set refers to a measure of the "middle" or "expected" value of the data set.
    a. Average0
    b. Concept
    c. Undefined
    d. Undefined

25. In business, particularly accounting, a _____ is the time intervals that the accounts, statement, payments, or other calculations cover.
    a. Period0
    b. Thing
    c. Undefined
    d. Undefined

26. U.S. liquid _____ is legally defined as 231 cubic inches, and is equal to 3.785411784 litres or abotu 0.13368 cubic feet. This is the most common definition of a _____. The U.S. fluid ounce is defined as 1/128 of a U.S. _____.
    a. Thing
    b. Gallon0
    c. Undefined
    d. Undefined

27. A _____ is a special kind of ratio, indicating a relationship between two measurements with different units, such as miles to gallons or cents to pounds.
    a. Rate0
    b. Thing
    c. Undefined
    d. Undefined

28. A _____ is a function that assigns a number to subsets of a given set.
    a. Thing
    b. Measure0
    c. Undefined
    d. Undefined

Chapter 2. Limits and Derivatives

29. _____ are a measure of time.
    a. Thing
    b. Minutes0
    c. Undefined
    d. Undefined

30. Mathematical _____ is used to represent ideas.
    a. Notation0
    b. Thing
    c. Undefined
    d. Undefined

31. A _____ is a deliberate process for transforming one or more inputs into one or more results.
    a. Calculation0
    b. Thing
    c. Undefined
    d. Undefined

32. In linear algebra, the _____ of an n-by-n square matrix A is defined to be the sum of the elements on the main diagonal of A,
    a. Trace0
    b. Thing
    c. Undefined
    d. Undefined

33. _____ are the basic objects of study in graph theory. Informally speaking, a graph is a set of objects called points, nodes, or vertices connected by links called lines or edges.
    a. Thing
    b. Graphs0
    c. Undefined
    d. Undefined

34. In statistics, _____ means the most frequent value assumed by a random variable, or occurring in a sampling of a random variable.
    a. Concept
    b. Mode0
    c. Undefined
    d. Undefined

35. In mathematics, defined and _____ are used to explain whether or not expressions have meaningful, sensible, and unambiguous values.
    a. Undefined0
    b. Thing
    c. Undefined
    d. Undefined

36. _____ was a self-taught English electrical engineer, mathematician, and physicist who adapted complex numbers to the study of electrical circuits, developed techniques for applying Laplace transforms to the solution of differential equations, reformulated Maxwell's field equations in terms of electric and magnetic forces and energy flux, and independently co-formulated vector analysis.
    a. Person
    b. Oliver Heaviside0
    c. Undefined
    d. Undefined

37. An _____ is a combination of numbers, operators, grouping symbols and/or free variables and bound variables arranged in a meaningful way which can be evaluated..
    a. Thing
    b. Expression0
    c. Undefined
    d. Undefined

38. _____ is the state of being greater than any finite real or natural number, however large.

Chapter 2. Limits and Derivatives

a. Infinite0
b. Thing
c. Undefined
d. Undefined

39. _____ is the state of being greater than any finite number, however large.
   a. Infinity0
   b. Thing
   c. Undefined
   d. Undefined

40. _____ is a straight line or curve A to which another curve B the one being studied approaches closer and closer as one moves along it.
   a. Vertical asymptote0
   b. Thing
   c. Undefined
   d. Undefined

41. An _____ is a straight line or curve A to which another curve B approaches closer and closer as one moves along it. As one moves along B, the space between it and the _____ A becomes smaller and smaller, and can in fact be made as small as one could wish by going far enough along. A curve may or may not touch or cross its _____. In fact, the curve may intersect the _____ an infinite number of times.
   a. Thing
   b. Asymptote0
   c. Undefined
   d. Undefined

42. In physics, a _____ may refer to the scalar _____ or to the vector _____.
   a. Potential0
   b. Thing
   c. Undefined
   d. Undefined

43. Deductive _____ is the kind of _____ in which the conclusion is necessitated by, or reached from, previously known facts (the premises).
   a. Reasoning0
   b. Thing
   c. Undefined
   d. Undefined

44. _____ is a kind of property which exists as magnitude or multitude. It is among the basic classes of things along with quality, substance, change, and relation.
   a. Amount0
   b. Thing
   c. Undefined
   d. Undefined

45. In mathematics, _____ growth occurs when the growth rate of a function is always proportional to the function's current size.
   a. Thing
   b. Exponential0
   c. Undefined
   d. Undefined

46. _____ is one of the most important functions in mathematics. A function commonly used to study growth and decay
   a. Exponential function0
   b. Thing
   c. Undefined
   d. Undefined

47. In geometry, a _____ is defined as a quadrilateral where all four of its angles are right angles.

Chapter 2. Limits and Derivatives

   a. Thing
   c. Undefined
   b. Rectangle0
   d. Undefined

48. The _____ in a vacuum is an important physical constant denoted by the letter c for constant or the Latin word celeritas meaning "swiftness
   a. Thing
   c. Undefined
   b. Speed of light0
   d. Undefined

49. _____ is electromagnetic radiation with a wavelength that is visible to the eye (visible _____) or, in a technical or scientific context, electromagnetic radiation of any wavelength.
   a. Thing
   c. Undefined
   b. Light0
   d. Undefined

50. _____ is the property of a physical object that quantifies the amount of matter and energy it is equivalent to.
   a. Mass0
   c. Undefined
   b. Thing
   d. Undefined

51. A _____ of a number is the product of that number with any integer.
   a. Multiple0
   c. Undefined
   b. Thing
   d. Undefined

52. In mathematics and the mathematical sciences, a _____ is a fixed, but possibly unspecified, value. This is in contrast to a variable, which is not fixed.
   a. Thing
   c. Undefined
   b. Constant0
   d. Undefined

53. In mathematics, a _____ is the result of multiplying, or an expression that identifies factors to be multiplied.
   a. Product0
   c. Undefined
   b. Thing
   d. Undefined

54. In mathematics, a _____ is the end result of a division problem. It can also be expressed as the number of times the divisor divides into the dividend.
   a. Quotient0
   c. Undefined
   b. Thing
   d. Undefined

55. A _____ is the part of a fraction that tells how many equal parts make up a whole, and which is used in the name of the fraction: "halves", "thirds", "fourths" or "quarters", "fifths" and so on.
   a. Concept
   c. Undefined
   b. Denominator0
   d. Undefined

56. A _____ is a numeral used to indicate a count. The most common use of the word today is to name the part of a fraction that tells the number or count of equal parts.
   a. Thing
   c. Undefined
   b. Numerator0
   d. Undefined

57. In mathematics, a _____ of a complex-valued function f is a member x of the domain of f such that f(x) vanishes at x, that is, x : f (x) = 0.
   a. Thing
   b. Root0
   c. Undefined
   d. Undefined

58. Sir Isaac _____, was an English physicist, mathematician, astronomer, natural philosopher, and alchemist, regarded by many as the greatest figure in the history of science
   a. Person
   b. Newton0
   c. Undefined
   d. Undefined

59. _____, also known as _____ of Alexandria, was a Greek mathematician. His Elements is the most successful textbook in the history of mathematics. In it, the principles of geometry are deduced from a small set of axioms. His method of proving mathematical theorems by logical reasoning from accepted first principles remains the backbone of mathematics and is responsible for the field's characteristic rigor
   a. Person
   b. Euclid0
   c. Undefined
   d. Undefined

60. _____ was a highly influential French philosopher, mathematician, scientist, and writer. Dubbed the "Founder of Modern Philosophy", and the "Father of Modern Mathematics". His theories provided the basis for the calculus of Newton and Leibniz, by applying infinitesimal calculus to the tangent line problem, thus permitting the evolution of that branch of modern mathematics
   a. Person
   b. Descartes0
   c. Undefined
   d. Undefined

61. _____ was an English divine, scholar and mathematician who is generally given minor credit for his role in the development of modern calculus; in particular, for his work regarding the tangent; for example, Barrow is given credit for being the first to calculate the tangents of the kappa curve. Isaac Newton was a student of Barrow's. Lunar crater Barrow is named after him.
   a. Thing
   b. Isaac Barrow0
   c. Undefined
   d. Undefined

62. A _____ is the sum of the elements of a sequence.
   a. Thing
   b. Series0
   c. Undefined
   d. Undefined

63. _____ algebra (sometimes called General algebra) is the field of mathematics that studies the ideas common to all algebraic structures.
   a. Thing
   b. Universal0
   c. Undefined
   d. Undefined

64. A _____ is the result of the addition of a set of numbers. The numbers may be natural numbers, complex numbers, matrices, or still more complicated objects. An infinite _____ is a subtle procedure known as a series.
   a. Sum0
   b. Thing
   c. Undefined
   d. Undefined

65. In mathematics, the _____ is an important formula giving the expansion of powers of sums.

28   *Chapter 2. Limits and Derivatives*

    a. Thing   b. Binomial Theorem0
    c. Undefined   d. Undefined

66. _____ is often represented as the sum of a sequence of terms.
    a. Thing   b. Infinite series0
    c. Undefined   d. Undefined

67. The _____ of a function is an extension of the concept of a sum, and are identified or found through the use of integration.
    a. Integral0   b. Thing
    c. Undefined   d. Undefined

68. In mathematics, a _____ is a statement that can be proved on the basis of explicitly stated or previously agreed assumptions.
    a. Thing   b. Theorem0
    c. Undefined   d. Undefined

69. In elementary algebra, a _____ is a polynomial with two terms: the sum of two monomials. It is the simplest kind of polynomial except for a monomial.
    a. Thing   b. Binomial0
    c. Undefined   d. Undefined

70. The _____ of a solid object is the three-dimensional concept of how much space it occupies, often quantified numerically.
    a. Thing   b. Volume0
    c. Undefined   d. Undefined

71. _____ of Syracuse was an ancient Greek mathematician, physicist and engineer. In addition to making important discoveries in the field of mathematics and geometry, he is credited with producing machines that were well ahead of their time.
    a. Archimedes0   b. Person
    c. Undefined   d. Undefined

72. Sir _____ was an English physicist, mathematician, astronomer, natural philosopher, and alchemist, regarded by many as the greatest figure in the history of science.
    a. Isaac Newton0   b. Person
    c. Undefined   d. Undefined

73. _____ is a branch of mathematics concerning the study of structure, relation and quantity.
    a. Concept   b. Algebra0
    c. Undefined   d. Undefined

74. In calculus, the _____ is a theorem regarding the limit of a function. The theorem asserts that if two functions approach the same limit at a point, and if a third function is "squeezed" between those functions, then the third function also approaches that limit at that point.

Chapter 2. Limits and Derivatives

a. Thing
b. Squeeze Theorem0
c. Undefined
d. Undefined

75. In mathematics, a _____ number is a number which can be expressed as a ratio of two integers. Non-integer _____ numbers (commonly called fractions) are usually written as the vulgar fraction a / b, where b is not zero.
    a. Rational0
    b. Thing
    c. Undefined
    d. Undefined

76. In mathematics, a _____ is any function which can be written as the ratio of two polynomial functions.
    a. Rational function0
    b. Thing
    c. Undefined
    d. Undefined

77. In mathematics, a _____ is an expression that is constructed from one or more variables and constants, using only the operations of addition, subtraction, multiplication, and constant positive whole number exponents. is a _____. Note in particular that division by an expression containing a variable is not in general allowed in polynomials. [1]
    a. Thing
    b. Polynomial0
    c. Undefined
    d. Undefined

78. In mathematics, a _____ of a k-place relation $L \subseteq X_1 \times \ldots \times X_k$ is one of the sets X_j, $1 \leq j \leq k$. In the special case where k = 2 and $L \subseteq X_1 \times X_2$ is a function $L : X_1 \to X_2$, it is conventional to refer to X_1 as the _____ of the function and to refer to X_2 as the codomain of the function.
    a. Domain0
    b. Thing
    c. Undefined
    d. Undefined

79. In mathematics, an _____ number is any real number that is not a rational number- that is, it is a number which cannot be expressed as a fraction m/n, where m and n are integers.
    a. Thing
    b. Irrational0
    c. Undefined
    d. Undefined

80. In geometry, the _____ of an object is a point in some sense in the middle of the object.
    a. Center0
    b. Thing
    c. Undefined
    d. Undefined

81. In Euclidean geometry, a _____ is the set of all points in a plane at a fixed distance, called the radius, from a given point, the center.
    a. Thing
    b. Circle0
    c. Undefined
    d. Undefined

82. In classical geometry, a _____ of a circle or sphere is any line segment from its center to its boundary. By extension, the _____ of a circle or sphere is the length of any such segment. The _____ is half the diameter. In science and engineering the term _____ of curvature is commonly used as a synonym for _____.
    a. Thing
    b. Radius0
    c. Undefined
    d. Undefined

83. In mathematics, the _____ of a coordinate system is the point where the axes of the system intersect.

30   **Chapter 2. Limits and Derivatives**

   a. Thing   b. Origin0
   c. Undefined   d. Undefined

84. Equivalence is the condition of being _____ or essentially equal.
   a. Thing   b. Equivalent0
   c. Undefined   d. Undefined

85. In astronomy, geography, geometry and related sciences and contexts, a plane is said to be _____ at a given point if it is locally perpendicular to the gradient of the gravity field, i.e., with the direction of the gravitational force at that point.
   a. Horizontal0   b. Thing
   c. Undefined   d. Undefined

86. In mathematics, a _____ is a countable collection of open covers of a topological space that satisfies certain separation axioms.
   a. Thing   b. Development0
   c. Undefined   d. Undefined

87. In mathematics, a _____ is a demonstration that, assuming certain axioms, some statement is necessarily true.
   a. Thing   b. Proof0
   c. Undefined   d. Undefined

88. Mathematical _____ are demonstrations that, assuming certain axioms, some statement is necessarily true.
   a. Thing   b. Proofs0
   c. Undefined   d. Undefined

89. Leonhard _____ was a pioneering Swiss mathematician and physicist, who spent most of his life in Russia and Germany.
   a. Euler0   b. Person
   c. Undefined   d. Undefined

90. _____ has many meanings, most of which simply .
   a. Thing   b. Power0
   c. Undefined   d. Undefined

91. A _____ is a symbolic representation denoting a quantity or expression. It often represents an "unknown" quantity that has the potential to change.
   a. Variable0   b. Thing
   c. Undefined   d. Undefined

92. In mathematics, an _____ is a statement about the relative size or order of two objects.
   a. Thing   b. Inequality0
   c. Undefined   d. Undefined

93. _____ is a set, with some particular properties and usually some additional structure, such as the operations of addition or multiplication, for instance.

a. Thing
b. Space0
c. Undefined
d. Undefined

94. In mathematics, in the field of group theory, a _____ of a group is a quasisimple subnormal subgroup.
    a. Concept
    b. Component0
    c. Undefined
    d. Undefined

95. In common philosophical language, a proposition or _____, is the content of an assertion, that is, it is true-or-false and defined by the meaning of a particular piece of language.
    a. Concept
    b. Statement0
    c. Undefined
    d. Undefined

96. A _____ is a simplified and structured visual representation of concepts, ideas, constructions, relations, statistical data, anatomy etc used in all aspects of human activities to visualize and clarify the topic.
    a. Diagram0
    b. Thing
    c. Undefined
    d. Undefined

97. In mathematics, a _____ is a polynomial equation of the third degree.
    a. Cubic equation0
    b. Thing
    c. Undefined
    d. Undefined

98. In mathematics, science including computer science, linguistics and engineering, an _____ is, generally speaking, an independent variable or input to a function.
    a. Argument0
    b. Thing
    c. Undefined
    d. Undefined

99. A _____ function is a function for which, intuitively, small changes in the input result in small changes in the output.
    a. Event
    b. Continuous0
    c. Undefined
    d. Undefined

100. Continuous functions are of utmost importance in mathematics and applications. However, not all functions are continuous. If a function is not continuous at a point in its domain, one says that it has a _____ there. The set of all points of _____ of a function may be a discrete set, a dense set, or even the entire domain of the function.
    a. Thing
    b. Discontinuity0
    c. Undefined
    d. Undefined

101. In mathematics, the _____ f is the collection of all ordered pairs . In particular, graph means the graphical representation of this collection, in the form of a curve or surface, together with axes, etc. Graphing on a Cartesian plane is sometimes referred to as curve sketching.
    a. Thing
    b. Graph of a function0
    c. Undefined
    d. Undefined

102. _____ is a function whose values do not vary and thus are constant.

Chapter 2. Limits and Derivatives

a. Thing
c. Undefined
b. Constant function0
d. Undefined

103. A _____ is 360° or 2δ radians.
a. Turn0
c. Undefined
b. Thing
d. Undefined

104. _____ is a trigonemtric function that is important when studying triangles and modeling periodic phenomena, among other applications.
a. Sine0
c. Undefined
b. Thing
d. Undefined

105. The _____ of an angle is the ratio of the length of the adjacent side to the length of the hypotenuse.
a. Concept
c. Undefined
b. Cosine0
d. Undefined

106. A _____ number is a positive integer which has a positive divisor other than one or itself.
a. Thing
c. Undefined
b. Composite0
d. Undefined

107. A _____, formed by the composition of one function on another, represents the application of the former to the result of the application of the latter to the argument of the composite.
a. Thing
c. Undefined
b. Composite function0
d. Undefined

108. The _____ implies that on any great circle around the world, the temperature, pressure, elevation, carbon dioxide concentration, or anything else that varies continuously, there will always exist two antipodal points that share the same value for that variable.
a. Thing
c. Undefined
b. Intermediate Value Theorem0
d. Undefined

109. In mathematics, a set is called _____ if there is a bijection between the set and some set of the form {1, 2, ..., n} where n is a natural number.
a. Finite0
c. Undefined
b. Thing
d. Undefined

110. _____ means in succession or back-to-back
a. Thing
c. Undefined
b. Consecutive0
d. Undefined

111. In geometry, an _____ of a triangle is a straight line through a vertex and perpendicular to (i.e. forming a right angle with) the opposite side or an extension of the opposite side.
a. Concept
c. Undefined
b. Altitude0
d. Undefined

Chapter 2. Limits and Derivatives

112. _____ is a physical property of a system that underlies the common notions of hot and cold; something that is hotter has the greater _____.
   a. Temperature0
   b. Thing
   c. Undefined
   d. Undefined

113. _____ is the weakest of the four fundamental forces of bature, as described by Issac Newton
   a. Thing
   b. Gravitational force0
   c. Undefined
   d. Undefined

114. A _____, as defined by the International Astronomical Union, is a celestial body orbiting a star or stellar remnant that is massive enough to be rounded by its own gravity, not massive enough to cause thermonuclear fusion in its core, and has cleared its neighboring region of planetesimals.
   a. Planet0
   b. Thing
   c. Undefined
   d. Undefined

115. In physics, _____ is an influence that may cause an object to accelerate. It may be experienced as a lift, a push, or a pull. The actual acceleration of the body is determined by the vector sum of all forces acting on it, known as net _____ or resultant _____.
   a. Thing
   b. Force0
   c. Undefined
   d. Undefined

116. In mathematics, a _____ may be described informally as a number that can be given by an infinite decimal representation.
   a. Real number0
   b. Thing
   c. Undefined
   d. Undefined

117. In mathematics, the _____ (or modulus) of a real number is its numerical value without regard to its sign.
   a. Thing
   b. Absolute value0
   c. Undefined
   d. Undefined

118. In geometry, an _____ polygon is a polygon which has all sides of the same length.
   a. Thing
   b. Equilateral0
   c. Undefined
   d. Undefined

119. In mathematics, a _____ is a type of conic section defined as the intersection between a right circular conical surface and a plane which cuts through both halves of the cone.
   a. Thing
   b. Hyperbola0
   c. Undefined
   d. Undefined

120. In mathematics, a _____ is a number which can be expressed as a ratio of two integers. Non-integer rational numbers (commonly called fractions) are usually written as the vulgar fraction a / b, where b is not zero.
   a. Concept
   b. Rational Number0
   c. Undefined
   d. Undefined

121. A _____ is a quantity that denotes the proportional amount or magnitude of one quantity relative to another.

a. Ratio0   b. Thing
c. Undefined   d. Undefined

122. An _____ is a straight line around which a geometric figure can be rotated.
   a. Axis0   b. Thing
   c. Undefined   d. Undefined

123. In mathematics, factorization (British English: factorisation) or factoring is the decomposition of an object (for example, a number, a polynomial, or a matrix) into a product of other objects, or _____, which when multiplied together give the original.
   a. Thing   b. Factors0
   c. Undefined   d. Undefined

124. Any point where a graph makes contact with an coordinate axis is called an _____ of the graph
   a. Thing   b. Intercept0
   c. Undefined   d. Undefined

125. A _____ is a negotiable instrument instructing a financial institution to pay a specific amount of a specific currency from a specific demand account held in the maker/depositor's name with that institution. Both the maker and payee may be natural persons or legal entities.
   a. Check0   b. Thing
   c. Undefined   d. Undefined

126. The act of _____ is the calculated approximation of a result which is usable even if input data may be incomplete, uncertain, or noisy.
   a. Estimating0   b. Thing
   c. Undefined   d. Undefined

127. _____ is defined as the rate of change or derivative with respect to time of velocity.
   a. Thing   b. Acceleration0
   c. Undefined   d. Undefined

128. The _____ of measurement are a globally standardized and modernized form of the metric system.
   a. Units0   b. Thing
   c. Undefined   d. Undefined

129. _____ is the change in total cost that arises when the quantity produced changes by one unit.
   a. Thing   b. Marginal cost0
   c. Undefined   d. Undefined

130. In mathematics, a _____ number (or a _____) is a natural number that has exactly two (distinct) natural number divisors, which are 1 and the _____ number itself.
   a. Prime0   b. Thing
   c. Undefined   d. Undefined

131. _____ is a statistical measure of the average length of survival of a living thing.

Chapter 2. Limits and Derivatives

a. Life expectancy0
b. Thing
c. Undefined
d. Undefined

132. There are two simple _____ the greatest common factor and least common multiple: standard factorization and prime factorization.
   a. Thing
   b. Methods for finding0
   c. Undefined
   d. Undefined

133. A frame of _____ is a particular perspective from which the universe is observed.
   a. Reference0
   b. Thing
   c. Undefined
   d. Undefined

134. _____ was an American mathematician, known for his work in geometry and the history of mathematics.
   a. Howard Eves0
   b. Person
   c. Undefined
   d. Undefined

135. _____ Any process by which a specified characteristic usually amplitude of the output of a device is prevented from exceeding a predetermined value.
   a. Limiting0
   b. Thing
   c. Undefined
   d. Undefined

136. In mathematics, _____ expressions is used to reduce the expression into the lowest possible term.
   a. Simplifying0
   b. Thing
   c. Undefined
   d. Undefined

137. In mathematics, the notion of _____ is a generalization of the notion of invertible.
   a. Cancellation0
   b. Thing
   c. Undefined
   d. Undefined

138. In mathematics, the _____ of a function is the set of all "output" values produced by that function. Given a function $f : A \to B$, the _____ of f, is defined to be the set $\{x \in B : x = f(a) \text{ for some } a \in A\}$.
   a. Thing
   b. Range0
   c. Undefined
   d. Undefined

139. A _____ is a set whose members are members of another set or a set contained within another set.
   a. Subset0
   b. Thing
   c. Undefined
   d. Undefined

140. The _____ is an imaginary line on the Earth's surface equidistant from the North Pole and South Pole.
   a. Thing
   b. Equator0
   c. Undefined
   d. Undefined

141. In mathematics, the additive inverse, or _____ of a number n is the number that, when added to n, yields zero. The additive inverse of n is denoted −n. For example, 7 is −7, because 7 + (−7) = 0, and the additive inverse of −0.3 is 0.3, because −0.3 + 0.3 = 0.

a. Thing
b. Opposite0
c. Undefined
d. Undefined

142. In mathematics, the _____ of a number n is the number that, when added to n, yields zero. The _____ of n is denoted −n. For example, 7 is −7, because 7 + (−7) = 0, and the _____ of −0.3 is 0.3, because −0.3 + 0.3 = 0.
   a. Thing
   b. Additive inverse0
   c. Undefined
   d. Undefined

Chapter 3. Differentiation Rules

1. In mathematics and the mathematical sciences, a _____ is a fixed, but possibly unspecified, value. This is in contrast to a variable, which is not fixed.
   a. Thing
   b. Constant0
   c. Undefined
   d. Undefined

2. _____ is a function whose values do not vary and thus are constant.
   a. Constant function0
   b. Thing
   c. Undefined
   d. Undefined

3. The mathematical concept of a _____ expresses the intuitive idea of deterministic dependence between two quantities, one of which is viewed as primary and the other as secondary. A _____ then is a way to associate a unique output for each input of a specified type, for example, a real number or an element of a given set.
   a. Thing
   b. Function0
   c. Undefined
   d. Undefined

4. In mathematics, a _____ is a demonstration that, assuming certain axioms, some statement is necessarily true.
   a. Proof0
   b. Thing
   c. Undefined
   d. Undefined

5. Mathematical _____ is used to represent ideas.
   a. Notation0
   b. Thing
   c. Undefined
   d. Undefined

6. _____ is often used to describe the measurement of the steepness, incline, gradient, or grade of a straight line. The _____ is defined as the ratio of the "rise" divided by the "run" between two points on a line, or in other words, the ratio of the altitude change to the horizontal distance between any two points on the line.
   a. Slope0
   b. Thing
   c. Undefined
   d. Undefined

7. _____ was a German mathematician and philosopher. He invented calculus independently of Newton, and his notation is the one in general use since.
   a. Person
   b. Leibniz0
   c. Undefined
   d. Undefined

8. _____ named in honor of the 17th century German philosopher and mathematician Gottfried Wilhelm Leibniz, was originally the use of expressions such as dx and dy and to represent "infinitely small" or infinitesimal increments of quantities x and y, just as Äx and Äy represent finite increments of x and y respectively.
   a. Leibniz notation0
   b. Thing
   c. Undefined
   d. Undefined

9. In astronomy, geography, geometry and related sciences and contexts, a plane is said to be _____ at a given point if it is locally perpendicular to the gradient of the gravity field, i.e., with the direction of the gravitational force at that point.
   a. Horizontal0
   b. Thing
   c. Undefined
   d. Undefined

10. The _____ is a measurement of how a function changes when the values of its inputs change.

Chapter 3. Differentiation Rules

a. Derivative0
c. Undefined
b. Thing
d. Undefined

11. A _____ is 360° or 2ð radians.
a. Turn0
c. Undefined
b. Thing
d. Undefined

12. In mathematics, a _____ may be described informally as a number that can be given by an infinite decimal representation.
a. Real number0
c. Undefined
b. Thing
d. Undefined

13. _____ has many meanings, most of which simply .
a. Thing
c. Undefined
b. Power0
d. Undefined

14. _____ is a method for differentiating expressions involving exponentiation the power operation.
a. Power rule0
c. Undefined
b. Thing
d. Undefined

15. In trigonometry, the _____ is a function defined as $\tan x = \sin x / \cos x$. The function is so-named because it can be defined as the length of a certain segment of a _____ (in the geometric sense) to the unit circle. In plane geometry, a line is _____ to a curve, at some point, if both line and curve pass through the point with the same direction.
a. Thing
c. Undefined
b. Tangent0
d. Undefined

16. _____ has two distinct but etymologically-related meanings: one in geometry and one in trigonometry.
a. Thing
c. Undefined
b. Tangent line0
d. Undefined

17. In mathematics, the concept of a _____ tries to capture the intuitive idea of a geometrical one-dimensional and continuous object. A simple example is the circle.
a. Curve0
c. Undefined
b. Thing
d. Undefined

18. In mathematics, _____ is an elementary arithmetic operation. When one of the numbers is a whole number, _____ is the repeated sum of the other number.
a. Thing
c. Undefined
b. Multiplication0
d. Undefined

19. A _____ of a number is the product of that number with any integer.
a. Thing
c. Undefined
b. Multiple0
d. Undefined

20. In mathematics, a _____ number (or a _____) is a natural number that has exactly two (distinct) natural number divisors, which are 1 and the _____ number itself.

a. Thing
b. Prime0
c. Undefined
d. Undefined

21. A _____ is the result of the addition of a set of numbers. The numbers may be natural numbers, complex numbers, matrices, or still more complicated objects. An infinite _____ is a subtle procedure known as a series.
    a. Sum0
    b. Thing
    c. Undefined
    d. Undefined

22. In calculus, the _____ in differentiation is a method of finding the derivative of a function that is the sum of two other functions for which derivatives exist.
    a. Thing
    b. Sum Rule0
    c. Undefined
    d. Undefined

23. In mathematics, _____ growth occurs when the growth rate of a function is always proportional to the function's current size.
    a. Exponential0
    b. Thing
    c. Undefined
    d. Undefined

24. _____ is one of the most important functions in mathematics. A function commonly used to study growth and decay
    a. Thing
    b. Exponential function0
    c. Undefined
    d. Undefined

25. In mathematics, a _____ is an expression that is constructed from one or more variables and constants, using only the operations of addition, subtraction, multiplication, and constant positive whole number exponents. is a _____. Note in particular that division by an expression containing a variable is not in general allowed in polynomials. [1]
    a. Polynomial0
    b. Thing
    c. Undefined
    d. Undefined

26. _____ are the basic objects of study in graph theory. Informally speaking, a graph is a set of objects called points, nodes, or vertices connected by links called lines or edges.
    a. Graphs0
    b. Thing
    c. Undefined
    d. Undefined

27. _____, a field in mathematics, is the study of how functions change when their inputs change. The primary object of study in _____ is the derivative.
    a. Differential calculus0
    b. Thing
    c. Undefined
    d. Undefined

28. In geometry, a _____ is defined as a quadrilateral where all four of its angles are right angles.
    a. Thing
    b. Rectangle0
    c. Undefined
    d. Undefined

29. A _____ is a set of numbers that designate location in a given reference system, such as x,y in a planar _____ system or an x,y,z in a three-dimensional _____ system.

Chapter 3. Differentiation Rules

a. Thing
b. Coordinate0
c. Undefined
d. Undefined

30. In mathematics, the _____ is a conic section generated by the intersection of a right circular conical surface and a plane parallel to a generating straight line of that surface. It can also be defined as locus of points in a plane which are equidistant from a given point.
    a. Thing
    b. Parabola0
    c. Undefined
    d. Undefined

31. A _____ is a simplified and structured visual representation of concepts, ideas, constructions, relations, statistical data, anatomy etc used in all aspects of human activities to visualize and clarify the topic.
    a. Diagram0
    b. Thing
    c. Undefined
    d. Undefined

32. A _____ is one of the basic shapes of geometry: a polygon with three vertices and three sides which are straight line segments.
    a. Triangle0
    b. Thing
    c. Undefined
    d. Undefined

33. In geometry, a line _____ is a part of a line that is bounded by two end points, and contains every point on the line between its end points.
    a. Segment0
    b. Concept
    c. Undefined
    d. Undefined

34. _____ is a function of the form
    a. Thing
    b. Cubic function0
    c. Undefined
    d. Undefined

35. An _____ is when two lines intersect somewhere on a plane creating a right angle at intersection
    a. Axes0
    b. Thing
    c. Undefined
    d. Undefined

36. In mathematics, a _____ is a type of conic section defined as the intersection between a right circular conical surface and a plane which cuts through both halves of the cone.
    a. Thing
    b. Hyperbola0
    c. Undefined
    d. Undefined

37. A _____ is a part of a line that is bounded by two end points, and contains every point on the line between its end points.
    a. Line segment0
    b. Thing
    c. Undefined
    d. Undefined

38. _____ is the middle point of a line segment.
    a. Thing
    b. Midpoint0
    c. Undefined
    d. Undefined

Chapter 3. Differentiation Rules

39. In mathematics, a _____ is the result of multiplying, or an expression that identifies factors to be multiplied.
    a. Thing
    b. Product0
    c. Undefined
    d. Undefined

40. The _____ governs the differentiation of products of differentiable functions.
    a. Thing
    b. Product rule0
    c. Undefined
    d. Undefined

41. _____ is bother the congnitive process of transferring information from a particular subject , and a linguistic expression corresponding to such a process.
    a. Thing
    b. Analogy0
    c. Undefined
    d. Undefined

42. In mathematics, an _____, mean, or central tendency of a data set refers to a measure of the "middle" or "expected" value of the data set.
    a. Concept
    b. Average0
    c. Undefined
    d. Undefined

43. A _____ is a special kind of ratio, indicating a relationship between two measurements with different units, such as miles to gallons or cents to pounds.
    a. Thing
    b. Rate0
    c. Undefined
    d. Undefined

44. In mathematics, a _____ is the end result of a division problem. It can also be expressed as the number of times the divisor divides into the dividend.
    a. Thing
    b. Quotient0
    c. Undefined
    d. Undefined

45. A _____ function is a function for which, intuitively, small changes in the input result in small changes in the output.
    a. Continuous0
    b. Event
    c. Undefined
    d. Undefined

46. _____ is a kind of property which exists as magnitude or multitude. It is among the basic classes of things along with quality, substance, change, and relation.
    a. Amount0
    b. Thing
    c. Undefined
    d. Undefined

47. In mathematics, _____ expressions is used to reduce the expression into the lowest possible term.
    a. Thing
    b. Simplifying0
    c. Undefined
    d. Undefined

48. The _____ is a method of finding the derivative of a function that is the quotient of two other functions for which derivatives exist.

Chapter 3. Differentiation Rules

a. Thing
c. Undefined
b. Quotient rule0
d. Undefined

49. _____ was an Italian linguist, mathematician, and philosopher.
a. Maria Agnesi0
c. Undefined
b. Thing
d. Undefined

50. In sociology and biology a _____ is the collection of people or organisms of a particular species living in a given geographic area or space, usually measured by a census.
a. Population0
c. Undefined
b. Thing
d. Undefined

51. In mathematics, the multiplicative inverse of a number x, denoted 1/x or x^{-1}, is the number which, when multiplied by x, yields 1. The multiplicative inverse of x is also called the _____ of x.
a. Thing
c. Undefined
b. Reciprocal0
d. Undefined

52. In statistics, a _____ measure is one which is measuring what is supposed to measure.
a. Valid0
c. Undefined
b. Thing
d. Undefined

53. The _____ are the only integral domain whose positive elements are well-ordered, and in which order is preserved by addition. Like the natural numbers, the _____ form a countably infinite set. The set of all _____ is usually denoted in mathematics by a boldface Z .
a. Thing
c. Undefined
b. Integers0
d. Undefined

54. _____ is a trigonometric function that is the reciprocal of cosine.
a. Secant0
c. Undefined
b. Thing
d. Undefined

55. _____ of a curve is a line that intersects two or more points on the curve.
a. Secant line0
c. Undefined
b. Thing
d. Undefined

56. The function difference divided by the point difference is known as the _____
a. Difference quotient0
c. Undefined
b. Thing
d. Undefined

57. In elementary algebra, an _____ is a set that contains every real number between two indicated numbers and may contain the two numbers themselves.
a. Interval0
c. Undefined
b. Thing
d. Undefined

58. The metre (or _____, see spelling differences) is a measure of length. It is the basic unit of length in the metric system and in the International System of Units (SI), used around the world for general and scientific purposes.

Chapter 3. Differentiation Rules 43

a. Concept
b. Meter0
c. Undefined
d. Undefined

59. _____ of an object is its speed in a particular direction.
a. Velocity0
b. Thing
c. Undefined
d. Undefined

60. The _____, the average in everyday English, which is also called the arithmetic _____ (and is distinguished from the geometric _____ or harmonic _____). The average is also called the sample _____. The expected value of a random variable, which is also called the population _____.
a. Mean0
b. Thing
c. Undefined
d. Undefined

61. The _____ or kilogramme is the SI base unit of mass. It is defined as being equal to the mass of the international prototype of the _____.
a. Thing
b. Kilogram0
c. Undefined
d. Undefined

62. The word _____ comes from the Latin word linearis, which means created by lines.
a. Linear0
b. Thing
c. Undefined
d. Undefined

63. _____ is the property of a physical object that quantifies the amount of matter and energy it is equivalent to.
a. Mass0
b. Thing
c. Undefined
d. Undefined

64. _____ is mass m per unit volume V.
a. Density0
b. Thing
c. Undefined
d. Undefined

65. In topology and related areas of mathematics a _____ or Moore-Smith sequence is a generalization of a sequence, intended to unify the various notions of limit and generalize them to arbitrary topological spaces.
a. Net0
b. Thing
c. Undefined
d. Undefined

66. In business, particularly accounting, a _____ is the time intervals that the accounts, statement, payments, or other calculations cover.
a. Period0
b. Thing
c. Undefined
d. Undefined

67. In mathematics, a class _____ is a structure used to organize the various Galois groups and modules that appear in class field theory. They were invented by Emil Artin and John Tate.
a. Thing
b. Formation0
c. Undefined
d. Undefined

Chapter 3. Differentiation Rules

68. The plus and _____ signs are mathematical symbols used to represent the notions of positive and negative as well as the operations of addition and subtraction.
    a. Minus0
    b. Thing
    c. Undefined
    d. Undefined

69. In mathematics, the _____(e) for L-functions are a class of summation formulae, expressing sums taken over the complex number zeroes of a given L-function, typically in terms of quantities studied by number theory by use of the theory of special functions.
    a. Thing
    b. Explicit formula0
    c. Undefined
    d. Undefined

70. _____ is the fee paid on borrowed money.
    a. Thing
    b. Interest0
    c. Undefined
    d. Undefined

71. _____ is a branch of physics that studies the effects of changes in temperature, pressure, and volume on physical systems at the macroscopic scale by analyzing the collective motion of their particles using statistics.
    a. Thing
    b. Thermodynamics0
    c. Undefined
    d. Undefined

72. _____ is a measure of the relative volume change of a fluid or solid as a response to a pressure or mean stress change.
    a. Thing
    b. Compressibility0
    c. Undefined
    d. Undefined

73. Initial objects are also called _____, and terminal objects are also called final.
    a. Thing
    b. Coterminal0
    c. Undefined
    d. Undefined

74. In mathematics, a _____ of a k-place relation $L \subseteq X_1 \times ... \times X_k$ is one of the sets X_j, $1 \leq j \leq k$. In the special case where k = 2 and $L \subseteq X_1 \times X_2$ is a function $L : X_1 \to X_2$, it is conventional to refer to X_1 as the _____ of the function and to refer to X_2 as the codomain of the function.
    a. Domain0
    b. Thing
    c. Undefined
    d. Undefined

75. A _____ signifies a point or points of probability on a subject e.g., the _____ of creativity, which allows for the formation of rule or norm or law by interpretation of the phenomena events that can be created.
    a. Principle0
    b. Thing
    c. Undefined
    d. Undefined

76. _____ is the flow of blood in the cardiovascular system.
    a. Blood flow0
    b. Thing
    c. Undefined
    d. Undefined

77. _____ is an adjective usually refering to being in the centre.

a. Central0
b. Thing
c. Undefined
d. Undefined

78. An _____ is a straight line around which a geometric figure can be rotated.
   a. Thing
   b. Axis0
   c. Undefined
   d. Undefined

79. In geometry, the _____ of an object is a point in some sense in the middle of the object.
   a. Center0
   b. Thing
   c. Undefined
   d. Undefined

80. The _____ of measurement are a globally standardized and modernized form of the metric system.
   a. Units0
   b. Thing
   c. Undefined
   d. Undefined

81. _____ is the change in total cost that arises when the quantity produced changes by one unit.
   a. Thing
   b. Marginal cost0
   c. Undefined
   d. Undefined

82. In business, _____, _____ cost or _____ expense refers to an ongoing expense of operating a business.
   a. Overhead0
   b. Thing
   c. Undefined
   d. Undefined

83. _____, from Latin meaning "to make progress", is defined in two different ways. Pure economic _____ is the increase in wealth that an investor has from making an investment, taking into consideration all costs associated with that investment including the opportunity cost of capital.
   a. Thing
   b. Profit0
   c. Undefined
   d. Undefined

84. _____ is the extra revenue that an additional unit of product will bring a firm. It can also be described as the change in total revenue/change in number of units sold.
   a. Marginal revenue0
   b. Thing
   c. Undefined
   d. Undefined

85. _____ is a business term for the amount of money that a company receives from its activities in a given period, mostly from sales of products and/or services to customers
   a. Revenue0
   b. Thing
   c. Undefined
   d. Undefined

86. In economics, supply and _____ describe market relations between prospective sellers and buyers of a good.
   a. Thing
   b. Demand0
   c. Undefined
   d. Undefined

87. The _____ refers to a relationship between the duration of learning or experience and the resulting progress

Chapter 3. Differentiation Rules

    a. Thing
    b. Learning curve0
    c. Undefined
    d. Undefined

88. _____ is a special mathematical relationship between two quantities. Two quantities are called proportional if they vary in such a way that one of the quantities is a constant multiple of the other, or equivalently if they have a constant ratio.
    a. Thing
    b. Proportionality0
    c. Undefined
    d. Undefined

89. In vector calculus, the _____ of a scalar field is a vector field which points in the direction of the greatest rate of increase of the scalar field, and whose magnitude is the greatest rate of change.
    a. Thing
    b. Gradient0
    c. Undefined
    d. Undefined

90. _____, Greek for "knowledge of nature," is the branch of science concerned with the discovery and characterization of universal laws which govern matter, energy, space, and time.
    a. Thing
    b. Physics0
    c. Undefined
    d. Undefined

91. _____ is a physical property of a system that underlies the common notions of hot and cold; something that is hotter has the greater _____.
    a. Thing
    b. Temperature0
    c. Undefined
    d. Undefined

92. _____ is a mathematical subject that includes the study of limits, derivatives, integrals, and power series and constitutes a major part of modern university curriculum.
    a. Thing
    b. Calculus0
    c. Undefined
    d. Undefined

93. A _____ is traditionally an infinitesimally small change in a variable.
    a. Thing
    b. Differential0
    c. Undefined
    d. Undefined

94. _____ was a French mathematician and physicist who is best known for initiating the investigation of Fourier series and their application to problems of heat flow. The Fourier transform is also named in his honor.
    a. Joseph Fourier0
    b. Person
    c. Undefined
    d. Undefined

95. The _____ is one of the classical simple machines; as the name suggests, it is a flat surface whose endpoints are at different heights. By moving an object up an _____ rather than directly from one height to another, the amount of force required is reduced, at the expense of increasing the distance the object must travel. The mechanical advantage of an _____ is the ratio of the length of the sloped surface to the height it spans; this may also be expressed as the cosecant of the angle between the plane and the horizontal.
    a. Thing
    b. Inclined plane0
    c. Undefined
    d. Undefined

Chapter 3. Differentiation Rules

96. In mathematics, a _____ is a two-dimensional manifold or surface that is perfectly flat.
    a. Plane0
    b. Thing
    c. Undefined
    d. Undefined

97. In plane geometry, a _____ is a polygon with four equal sides, four right angles, and parallel opposite sides. In algebra, the _____ of a number is that number multiplied by itself.
    a. Thing
    b. Square0
    c. Undefined
    d. Undefined

98. _____ is the distance around a given two-dimensional object. As a general rule, the _____ of a polygon can always be calculated by adding all the length of the sides together. So, the formula for triangles is P = a + b + c, where a, b and c stand for each side of it. For quadrilaterals the equation is P = a + b + c + d. For equilateral polygons, P = na, where n is the number of sides and a is the side length.
    a. Perimeter0
    b. Thing
    c. Undefined
    d. Undefined

99. A _____ is a three-dimensional solid object bounded by six square faces, facets, or sides, with three meeting at each vertex.
    a. Cube0
    b. Thing
    c. Undefined
    d. Undefined

100. _____ are of a number n in its third power-the result of multiplying it by itself three times.
    a. Cubes0
    b. Thing
    c. Undefined
    d. Undefined

101. The _____ of a solid object is the three-dimensional concept of how much space it occupies, often quantified numerically.
    a. Volume0
    b. Thing
    c. Undefined
    d. Undefined

102. In Euclidean geometry, a _____ is the set of all points in a plane at a fixed distance, called the radius, from a given point, the center.
    a. Thing
    b. Circle0
    c. Undefined
    d. Undefined

103. In classical geometry, a _____ of a circle or sphere is any line segment from its center to its boundary. By extension, the _____ of a circle or sphere is the length of any such segment. The _____ is half the diameter. In science and engineering the term _____ of curvature is commonly used as a synonym for _____.
    a. Thing
    b. Radius0
    c. Undefined
    d. Undefined

104. _____ is the transport of people on a trip/journey or the process or time involved in a person or object moving from one location to another.
    a. Thing
    b. Travel0
    c. Undefined
    d. Undefined

Chapter 3. Differentiation Rules

105. In mathematics, a _____ is the set of all points in three-dimensional space (R^3) which are at distance r from a fixed point of that space, where r is a positive real number called the radius of the _____. The fixed point is called the center or centre, and is not part of the _____ itself.
    a. Sphere0
    b. Thing
    c. Undefined
    d. Undefined

106. _____ are a measure of time.
    a. Minutes0
    b. Thing
    c. Undefined
    d. Undefined

107. U.S. liquid _____ is legally defined as 231 cubic inches, and is equal to 3.785411784 litres or abotu 0.13368 cubic feet. This is the most common definition of a _____. The U.S. fluid ounce is defined as 1/128 of a U.S. _____.
    a. Gallon0
    b. Thing
    c. Undefined
    d. Undefined

108. Sir Isaac _____, was an English physicist, mathematician, astronomer, natural philosopher, and alchemist, regarded by many as the greatest figure in the history of science
    a. Newton0
    b. Person
    c. Undefined
    d. Undefined

109. Isaac Newton's _____ states the following:Every single point mass attracts every other point mass by a force pointing along the line combining the two.
    a. Thing
    b. Law of gravitation0
    c. Undefined
    d. Undefined

110. The _____ of a mathematical object is its size: a property by which it can be larger or smaller than other objects of the same kind; in technical terms, an ordering of the class of objects to which it belongs.
    a. Magnitude0
    b. Thing
    c. Undefined
    d. Undefined

111. In physics, _____ is an influence that may cause an object to accelerate. It may be experienced as a lift, a push, or a pull. The actual acceleration of the body is determined by the vector sum of all forces acting on it, known as net _____ or resultant _____.
    a. Force0
    b. Thing
    c. Undefined
    d. Undefined

112. _____ is a subset of a population.
    a. Thing
    b. Sample0
    c. Undefined
    d. Undefined

113. _____ is change in population over time, and can be quantified as the change in the number of individuals in a population per unit time.
    a. Thing
    b. Population growth0
    c. Undefined
    d. Undefined

Chapter 3. Differentiation Rules

114. _____ is a synonym for information.
   a. Data0
   b. Thing
   c. Undefined
   d. Undefined

115. _____ is a reaction force applied by a stretched string on the objects which stretch it.
   a. Tension0
   b. Thing
   c. Undefined
   d. Undefined

116. In statistics the _____ of an event i is the number n_i of times the event occurred in the experiment or the study. These frequencies are often graphically represented in histograms.
   a. Concept
   b. Frequency0
   c. Undefined
   d. Undefined

117. _____ is the application of tools and a processing medium to the transformation of raw materials into finished goods for sale.
   a. Thing
   b. Manufacturing0
   c. Undefined
   d. Undefined

118. In mathematics, an inequality is a statement about the relative size or order of two objects. For example 14 > 10, or 14 is _____ 10.
   a. Thing
   b. Greater than0
   c. Undefined
   d. Undefined

119. _____ is electromagnetic radiation with a wavelength that is visible to the eye (visible _____) or, in a technical or scientific context, electromagnetic radiation of any wavelength.
   a. Thing
   b. Light0
   c. Undefined
   d. Undefined

120. The _____ are a set of laws that describe the relationship between thermodynamic temperature T, pressure P and volume V of gases.
   a. Thing
   b. Gas law0
   c. Undefined
   d. Undefined

121. _____ of a population is the number of childbirths per 1,000 persons per year
   a. Thing
   b. Birth rate0
   c. Undefined
   d. Undefined

122. _____ is the ability to hold, receive or absorb, or a measure thereof, similar to the concept of volume.
   a. Concept
   b. Capacity0
   c. Undefined
   d. Undefined

123. _____ usually refers to the biological _____ of a population level that can be supported for an organism, given the quantity of food, habitat, water and other life infrastructure present.
   a. Carrying capacity0
   b. Thing
   c. Undefined
   d. Undefined

Chapter 3. Differentiation Rules

124. In mathematics, the _____ functions are functions of an angle; they are important when studying triangles and modeling periodic phenomena, among many other applications.
   a. Thing
   b. Trigonometric0
   c. Undefined
   d. Undefined

125. The _____ are functions of an angle; they are important when studying triangles and modeling periodic phenomena, among many other applications.
   a. Thing
   b. Trigonometric functions0
   c. Undefined
   d. Undefined

126. _____ is a trigonemtric function that is important when studying triangles and modeling periodic phenomena, among other applications.
   a. Thing
   b. Sine0
   c. Undefined
   d. Undefined

127. The _____ of an angle is the ratio of the length of the adjacent side to the length of the hypotenuse.
   a. Concept
   b. Cosine0
   c. Undefined
   d. Undefined

128. An _____ is an equality that remains true regardless of the values of any variables that appear within it, to distinguish it from an equality which is true under more particular conditions.
   a. Thing
   b. Identity0
   c. Undefined
   d. Undefined

129. In economics, economic _____ is simply a state of the world where economic forces are balanced and in the absence of external influences the values of economic variables will not change.
   a. Equilibrium0
   b. Thing
   c. Undefined
   d. Undefined

130. A _____ is a negotiable instrument instructing a financial institution to pay a specific amount of a specific currency from a specific demand account held in the maker/depositor's name with that institution. Both the maker and payee may be natural persons or legal entities.
   a. Check0
   b. Thing
   c. Undefined
   d. Undefined

131. In mathematics, a _____ is a constant multiplicative factor of a certain object. The object can be such things as a variable, a vector, a function, etc. For example, the _____ of $9x^2$ is 9.
   a. Coefficient0
   b. Thing
   c. Undefined
   d. Undefined

132. _____ is the force that opposes the relative motion or tendency toward such motion of two surfaces in contact.
   a. Friction0
   b. Thing
   c. Undefined
   d. Undefined

133. A _____ number is a positive integer which has a positive divisor other than one or itself.

Chapter 3. Differentiation Rules

a. Composite0
b. Thing
c. Undefined
d. Undefined

134. A _____, formed by the composition of one function on another, represents the application of the former to the result of the application of the latter to the argument of the composite.
   a. Thing
   b. Composite function0
   c. Undefined
   d. Undefined

135. In calculus, the _____ is a formula for the derivative of the composite of two functions.
   a. Chain rule0
   b. Concept
   c. Undefined
   d. Undefined

136. Deductive _____ is the kind of _____ in which the conclusion is necessitated by, or reached from, previously known facts (the premises).
   a. Reasoning0
   b. Thing
   c. Undefined
   d. Undefined

137. _____ is the largest positive integer that divides both numbers without remainder.
   a. Common Factor0
   b. Thing
   c. Undefined
   d. Undefined

138. An _____ is a combination of numbers, operators, grouping symbols and/or free variables and bound variables arranged in a meaningful way which can be evaluated..
   a. Expression0
   b. Thing
   c. Undefined
   d. Undefined

139. In acoustics and telecommunication, the _____ of a wave is a component frequency of the signal that is an integer multiple of the fundamental frequency.
   a. Thing
   b. Harmonic0
   c. Undefined
   d. Undefined

140. Simple _____ is the motion of a simple harmonic oscillator, a motion that is neither driven nor damped. Complex _____ is the superposition — linear combination — of several simultaneous simple harmonic motions.
   a. Thing
   b. Harmonic motion0
   c. Undefined
   d. Undefined

141. A _____ is a symbolic representation denoting a quantity or expression. It often represents an "unknown" quantity that has the potential to change.
   a. Thing
   b. Variable0
   c. Undefined
   d. Undefined

142. In _____ algebra, a *-ring is an associative ring with an antilinear, antiautomorphism * : A ¨ A which is an involution.
   a. Thing
   b. Star0
   c. Undefined
   d. Undefined

Chapter 3. Differentiation Rules

143. _____ is a branch of mathematics concerning the study of structure, relation and quantity.
   a. Algebra0
   b. Concept
   c. Undefined
   d. Undefined

144. _____ is to give an equation R(x,y) = S(x,y) that at least in part has the same graph as y = f(x).
   a. Implicit differentiation0
   b. Thing
   c. Undefined
   d. Undefined

145. _____ are functions which satisfy particular symmetry relations, with respect to taking additive inverses.
   a. Even function0
   b. Thing
   c. Undefined
   d. Undefined

146. In mathematics, a _____ number is a number which can be expressed as a ratio of two integers. Non-integer _____ numbers (commonly called fractions) are usually written as the vulgar fraction a / b, where b is not zero.
   a. Thing
   b. Rational0
   c. Undefined
   d. Undefined

147. In mathematics, a _____ is any function which can be written as the ratio of two polynomial functions.
   a. Thing
   b. Rational function0
   c. Undefined
   d. Undefined

148. _____ is a method of mathematical proof typically used to establish that a given statement is true of all natural numbers
   a. Mathematical induction0
   b. Thing
   c. Undefined
   d. Undefined

149. A _____ is the part of a fraction that tells how many equal parts make up a whole, and which is used in the name of the fraction: "halves", "thirds", "fourths" or "quarters", "fifths" and so on.
   a. Concept
   b. Denominator0
   c. Undefined
   d. Undefined

150. _____ is the symbold used to indicate the nth root of a number
   a. Radical0
   b. Thing
   c. Undefined
   d. Undefined

151. In mathematics, _____ are used to indicate the square root of a number.
   a. Thing
   b. Radicals0
   c. Undefined
   d. Undefined

152. In mathematics, a _____ of a complex-valued function f is a member x of the domain of f such that f(x) vanishes at x, that is, x : f (x) = 0.
   a. Root0
   b. Thing
   c. Undefined
   d. Undefined

153. _____ was a French mathematician born in Bourg-la-Reine.

Chapter 3. Differentiation Rules

a. Evariste Galois0
b. Thing
c. Undefined
d. Undefined

154. Évariste _____ was a French mathematician born in Bourg-la-Reine.
   a. Galois0
   b. Person
   c. Undefined
   d. Undefined

155. In mathematics, the _____ of a coordinate system is the point where the axes of the system intersect.
   a. Thing
   b. Origin0
   c. Undefined
   d. Undefined

156. A _____ is a deliberate process for transforming one or more inputs into one or more results.
   a. Thing
   b. Calculation0
   c. Undefined
   d. Undefined

157. In mathematics, _____ are the intuitive idea of a geometrical one-dimensional and continuous object.
   a. Curves0
   b. Thing
   c. Undefined
   d. Undefined

158. In mathematics, _____ is synonymous with perpendicular when used as a simple adjective that is not part of any longer phrase with a standard definition. It means at right angles. It comes from the Greek á½€Ï Î¸ÏŒÏ, orthos, meaning "straight", used by Euclid to mean right; and Î³Ï‰Î½Î¯Î± gonia, meaning angle. Two streets that cross each other at a right angle are _____ to one another.
   a. Orthogonal0
   b. Thing
   c. Undefined
   d. Undefined

159. In mathematics, a _____ is a family of curves in the plane that intersect a given family of curves at right angles.
   a. Thing
   b. Orthogonal trajectory0
   c. Undefined
   d. Undefined

160. In geometry, two lines or planes if one falls on the other in such a way as to create congruent adjacent angles. The term may be used as a noun or adjective. Thus, referring to Figure 1, the line AB is the _____ to CD through the point B.
   a. Thing
   b. Perpendicular0
   c. Undefined
   d. Undefined

161. In mathematics, the _____ of two sets A and B is the set that contains all elements of A that also belong to B (or equivalently, all elements of B that also belong to A), but no other elements.
   a. Intersection0
   b. Thing
   c. Undefined
   d. Undefined

162. An _____ is a straight line or curve A to which another curve B approaches closer and closer as one moves along it. As one moves along B, the space between it and the _____ A becomes smaller and smaller, and can in fact be made as small as one could wish by going far enough along. A curve may or may not touch or cross its _____. In fact, the curve may intersect the _____ an infinite number of times.

a. Asymptote0
b. Thing
c. Undefined
d. Undefined

163. _____ element of an element x with respect to a binary operation * with identity element e is an element y such that x * y = y * x = e. In particular,
   a. Inverse0
   b. Thing
   c. Undefined
   d. Undefined

164. In mathematics, the _____ are the inverse functions of the trigonometric functions.
   a. Thing
   b. Inverse trigonometric functions0
   c. Undefined
   d. Undefined

165. An _____ is a function which does the reverse of a given function.
   a. Inverse function0
   b. Thing
   c. Undefined
   d. Undefined

166. Mathematical _____ are demonstrations that, assuming certain axioms, some statement is necessarily true.
   a. Proofs0
   b. Thing
   c. Undefined
   d. Undefined

167. In mathematics, an _____ is any of the arguments, i.e. "inputs", to a function. Thus if we have a function f(x), then x is a _____.
   a. Independent variable0
   b. Thing
   c. Undefined
   d. Undefined

168. In mathematics, an _____ .
   a. Thing
   b. Ellipse0
   c. Undefined
   d. Undefined

169. The _____ was studied by the Greek astronomer and mathematician Eudoxus of Cnidus in relation to the classical problem of doubling the cube.
   a. Thing
   b. Kampyle of Eudoxus0
   c. Undefined
   d. Undefined

170. _____ is a particular type of curve: a hypocycloid with four cusps.
   a. Thing
   b. Astroid0
   c. Undefined
   d. Undefined

171. In mathematics, the _____ of Bernoulli is an eight-shaped algebraic curve described by a Cartesian equation
   a. Lemniscate0
   b. Thing
   c. Undefined
   d. Undefined

172. In geometry, the _____ is an epicycloid with one cusp. That is, a _____ is a curve that can be produced as the path of a point on the circumference of a circle as that circle rolls around another fixed circle with the same radius.

Chapter 3. Differentiation Rules

a. Cardioid0
b. Thing
c. Undefined
d. Undefined

173. In mathematics, a _____ is a number which can be expressed as a ratio of two integers. Non-integer rational numbers (commonly called fractions) are usually written as the vulgar fraction a / b, where b is not zero.
    a. Concept
    b. Rational Number0
    c. Undefined
    d. Undefined

174. _____ is defined as the rate of change or derivative with respect to time of velocity.
    a. Acceleration0
    b. Thing
    c. Undefined
    d. Undefined

175. In mathematics, the additive inverse, or _____ of a number n is the number that, when added to n, yields zero. The additive inverse of n is denoted −n. For example, 7 is −7, because 7 + (−7) = 0, and the additive inverse of −0.3 is 0.3, because −0.3 + 0.3 = 0.
    a. Opposite0
    b. Thing
    c. Undefined
    d. Undefined

176. In mathematics, the _____ of a number n is the number that, when added to n, yields zero. The _____ of n is denoted −n. For example, 7 is −7, because 7 + (−7) = 0, and the _____ of −0.3 is 0.3, because −0.3 + 0.3 = 0.
    a. Thing
    b. Additive inverse0
    c. Undefined
    d. Undefined

177. In physics, _____ is the rate of change of acceleration; more precisely, the derivative of acceleration with respect to time, the second derivative of velocity, or the third derivative of displacement. _____ is described by the following equation:
    a. Jerk0
    b. Thing
    c. Undefined
    d. Undefined

178. A _____ is the sum of the elements of a sequence.
    a. Thing
    b. Series0
    c. Undefined
    d. Undefined

179. _____ is the state of being greater than any finite real or natural number, however large.
    a. Thing
    b. Infinite0
    c. Undefined
    d. Undefined

180. _____ is often represented as the sum of a sequence of terms.
    a. Infinite series0
    b. Thing
    c. Undefined
    d. Undefined

181. The _____ is a nonnegative scalar measure of a wave's magnitude of oscillation, that is, the magnitude of the maximum disturbance in the medium during one wave cycle.
    a. Amplitude0
    b. Thing
    c. Undefined
    d. Undefined

Chapter 3. Differentiation Rules

182. A _____ is a mathematical equation for an unknown function of one or several variables which relates the values of the function itself and of its derivatives of various orders.
   a. Thing
   b. Differential equation0
   c. Undefined
   d. Undefined

183. In mathematics, the _____ (or modulus) of a real number is its numerical value without regard to its sign.
   a. Absolute value0
   b. Thing
   c. Undefined
   d. Undefined

184. The _____ of a geographic location is its height above a fixed reference point, often the mean sea level.
   a. Elevation0
   b. Thing
   c. Undefined
   d. Undefined

185. A _____ defined function $f(x)$ of a real variable x is a function whose definition is given differently on disjoint subsets of its domain.
   a. Thing
   b. Piecewise0
   c. Undefined
   d. Undefined

186. In mathematics, a _____ of a number x is the exponent y of the power by such that $x = b^y$. The value used for the base b must be neither 0 nor 1, nor a root of 1 in the case of the extension to complex numbers, and is typically 10, e, or 2.
   a. Logarithm0
   b. Thing
   c. Undefined
   d. Undefined

187. _____ is the logarithm to the base e, where e is an irrational constant approximately equal to 2.718281828459.
   a. Natural logarithm0
   b. Thing
   c. Undefined
   d. Undefined

188. _____ is a mathematical operation, written a^n, involving two numbers, the base a and the exponent n.
   a. Exponentiating0
   b. Thing
   c. Undefined
   d. Undefined

189. _____ is a mathematical operation, written a^n, involving two numbers, the base a and the exponent n.
   a. Thing
   b. Exponentiation0
   c. Undefined
   d. Undefined

190. _____ is the design, analysis, and/or construction of works for practical purposes.
   a. Engineering0
   b. Thing
   c. Undefined
   d. Undefined

191. In mathematics, the _____ of a function is the set of all "output" values produced by that function. Given a function $f : A \to B$, the _____ of f, is defined to be the set $\{x \in B : x = f(a) \text{ for some } a \in A\}$.
   a. Range0
   b. Thing
   c. Undefined
   d. Undefined

192. A _____ is an analog of an ordinary trigonometric, or circular, function.

a. Thing
b. Hyperbolic function0
c. Undefined
d. Undefined

193. _____ is the shape of a hanging flexible chain or cable when supported at its ends and acted upon by a uniform gravitational force. The chain is steepest near the points of suspension because this part of the chain has the most weight pulling down on it. Toward the bottom, the slope of the chain decreases because the chain is supporting less weight.
a. Catenary0
b. Thing
c. Undefined
d. Undefined

194. _____ is a circle with a unit radius, i.e., a circle whose radius is 1.
a. Thing
b. Unit circle0
c. Undefined
d. Undefined

195. The _____ is a unit of plane angle. It is represented by the symbol "rad" or, more rarely, by the superscript c (for "circular measure"). For example, an angle of 1.2 radians would be written "1.2 rad" or "1.2c" (second symbol can produce confusion with centigrads).
a. Radian0
b. Thing
c. Undefined
d. Undefined

196. _____ is a unit of plane angle, equal to 180/δ degrees, or about 57.2958 degrees
a. Radian measure0
b. Thing
c. Undefined
d. Undefined

197. A _____ is a function that assigns a number to subsets of a given set.
a. Measure0
b. Thing
c. Undefined
d. Undefined

198. In differential calculus, _____ problems involve finding the rate at which a quantity is changing by relating that quantity to other quantities whose rates of change are known.
a. Thing
b. Related rates0
c. Undefined
d. Undefined

199. A _____ is a three-dimensional geometric shape formed by straight lines through a fixed point (vertex) to the points of a fixed curve (directrix)
a. Concept
b. Cone0
c. Undefined
d. Undefined

200. _____ are objects, characters, or other concrete representations of ideas, concepts, or other abstractions.
a. Symbols0
b. Thing
c. Undefined
d. Undefined

201. A _____ is a unit of length, usually used to measure distance, in a number of different systems, including Imperial units, United States customary units and Norwegian/Swedish mil. Its size can vary from system to system, but in each is between 1 and 10 kilometers. In contemporary English contexts _____ refers to either:

Chapter 3. Differentiation Rules

    a. Mile0
    c. Undefined
    b. Thing
    d. Undefined

202. _____ is a relation in Euclidean geometry among the three sides of a right triangle.
    a. Pythagorean Theorem0
    c. Undefined
    b. Thing
    d. Undefined

203. In mathematics, a _____ is a statement that can be proved on the basis of explicitly stated or previously agreed assumptions.
    a. Theorem0
    c. Undefined
    b. Thing
    d. Undefined

204. In geometry, an _____ of a triangle is a straight line through a vertex and perpendicular to (i.e. forming a right angle with) the opposite side or an extension of the opposite side.
    a. Altitude0
    c. Undefined
    b. Concept
    d. Undefined

205. In geometry, a _____ (Greek words diairo = divide and metro = measure) of a circle is any straight line segment that passes through the centre and whose endpoints are on the circular boundary, or, in more modern usage, the length of such a line segment. When using the word in the more modern sense, one speaks of the _____ rather than a _____, because all diameters of a circle have the same length. This length is twice the radius. The _____ of a circle is also the longest chord that the circle has.
    a. Diameter0
    c. Undefined
    b. Thing
    d. Undefined

206. An _____ triangle is a triangle with at least two sides of equal length.
    a. Thing
    c. Undefined
    b. Isosceles0
    d. Undefined

207. A _____ is a quadrilateral, which is defined as a shape with four sides, which has a pair of parallel sides.
    a. Thing
    c. Undefined
    b. Trapezoid0
    d. Undefined

208. An _____ (isosceles trapezium in British English) is a quadrilateral with a line of symmetry bisecting one pair of opposite sides, making it automatically a trapezoid. Also, an _____'s base angles are congruent.
    a. Concept
    c. Undefined
    b. Isosceles trapezoid0
    d. Undefined

209. In geometry a _____, or deltoid, is a quadrilateral with two pairs of congruent adjacent sides.
    a. Thing
    c. Undefined
    b. Kite0
    d. Undefined

210. A _____ is a vehicle, missile or aircraft which obtains thrust by the reaction to the ejection of fast moving fluid from within a _____ engine.

Chapter 3. Differentiation Rules

a. Rocket0
b. Thing
c. Undefined
d. Undefined

211. _____ is an approximation of a general function using a linear function more precisely, an affine function.
   a. Thing
   b. Linear approximation0
   c. Undefined
   d. Undefined

212. A _____ is a first degree polynomial mathematical function of the form: f(x) = mx + b where m and b are real constants and x is a real variable.
   a. Thing
   b. Linear function0
   c. Undefined
   d. Undefined

213. In mathematics and its applications, _____ refers to finding the linear approximation to a function at a given point.
   a. Thing
   b. Linearization0
   c. Undefined
   d. Undefined

214. A _____ is an object that is attached to a pivot point so that it can swing freely.
   a. Thing
   b. Pendulum0
   c. Undefined
   d. Undefined

215. In geometry and physics, _____ are half-lines that continue forever in one direction.
   a. Rays0
   b. Thing
   c. Undefined
   d. Undefined

216. _____ is the study of terms and their use — of words and compound words that are used in specific contexts.
   a. Terminology0
   b. Thing
   c. Undefined
   d. Undefined

217. In a function the _____, is the variable which is the value, i.e. the "output", of the function.
   a. Dependent variable0
   b. Thing
   c. Undefined
   d. Undefined

218. The act of _____ is the calculated approximation of a result which is usable even if input data may be incomplete, uncertain, or noisy.
   a. Estimating0
   b. Thing
   c. Undefined
   d. Undefined

219. _____ is the estimation of a physical quantity such as distance, energy, temperature, or time.
   a. Thing
   b. Measurement0
   c. Undefined
   d. Undefined

220. In the mathematical field of numerical analysis, the _____ in some data is the discrepancy between an exact value and some approximation to it.

Chapter 3. Differentiation Rules

  a. Approximation Error0
  b. Thing
  c. Undefined
  d. Undefined

221. The _____ is the distance around a closed curve. _____ is a kind of perimeter.
  a. Thing
  b. Circumference0
  c. Undefined
  d. Undefined

222. In common philosophical language, a proposition or _____, is the content of an assertion, that is, it is true-or-false and defined by the meaning of a particular piece of language.
  a. Concept
  b. Statement0
  c. Undefined
  d. Undefined

223. In mathematics, there are several meanings of _____ depending on the subject.
  a. Degree0
  b. Thing
  c. Undefined
  d. Undefined

224. In mathematics, the _____ is a representation of a function as an infinite sum of terms calculated from the values of its derivatives at a single point.
  a. Thing
  b. Taylor series0
  c. Undefined
  d. Undefined

225. A _____ is a polynomial function of the form $f(x) = ax^2 + bx + c$, where a, b, c are real numbers and a , 0.
  a. Event
  b. Quadratic function0
  c. Undefined
  d. Undefined

226. _____ is a three-dimensional geometric shape formed by straight lines through a fixed point vertex to the points of a fixed curve directrix.
  a. Right circular cone0
  b. Thing
  c. Undefined
  d. Undefined

227. _____ forms part of thinking. Considered the most complex of all intellectual functions, _____ has been defined as higher-order cognitive process that requires the modulation and control of more routine or fundamental skills.
  a. Thing
  b. Problem solving0
  c. Undefined
  d. Undefined

228. In geometry, a _____ is a special kind of point, usually a corner of a polygon, polyhedron, or higher dimensional polytope. In the geometry of curves a _____ is a point of where the first derivative of curvature is zero. In graph theory, a _____ is the fundamental unit out of which graphs are formed
  a. Vertex0
  b. Thing
  c. Undefined
  d. Undefined

229. The _____ rule, also known as a slipstick, is a mechanical analog computer, consisting of at least two finely divided scales , most often a fixed outer pair and a movable inner one, with a sliding window called the cursor.
  a. Slide0
  b. Thing
  c. Undefined
  d. Undefined

Chapter 3. Differentiation Rules

230. A _____ consists of one quarter of the coordinate plane.
 a. Thing
 b. Quadrant0
 c. Undefined
 d. Undefined

231. In physics, the _____ momentum of an object rotating about some reference point is the measure of the extent to which the object will continue to rotate about that point unless acted upon by an external torque.
 a. Thing
 b. Angular0
 c. Undefined
 d. Undefined

232. In physics, the _____ is a vector quantity (more precisely, a pseudovector) which specifies the angular speed at which an object is rotating along with the direction in which it is rotating.
 a. Thing
 b. Angular velocity0
 c. Undefined
 d. Undefined

233. In mathematics, a _____ is a partially ordered set (or poset) in which every pair of elements has a unique supremum (the elements' least upper bound; called their join) and an infimum (greatest lower bound; called their meet).
 a. Concept
 b. Lattice0
 c. Undefined
 d. Undefined

234. In mathematics, a _____ is a quadric surface, with the following equation in Cartesian coordinates: $(x/_a)^2 + (y/_b)^2 = 1$.
 a. Thing
 b. Cylinder0
 c. Undefined
 d. Undefined

235. In mathematics, two quantities are called _____ if they vary in such a way that one of the quantities is a constant multiple of the other, or equivalently if they have a constant ratio.
 a. Proportional0
 b. Thing
 c. Undefined
 d. Undefined

236. _____ was a Greek philosopher, a student of Plato and teacher of Alexander the Great. He wrote on diverse subjects, including physics, metaphysics, poetry, biology and zoology, logic, rhetoric, politics, government, and ethics.
 a. Aristotle0
 b. Person
 c. Undefined
 d. Undefined

Chapter 4. Applications of Differentiation

1. The _____ is a measurement of how a function changes when the values of its inputs change.
   a. Thing
   b. Derivative0
   c. Undefined
   d. Undefined

2. _____, a field in mathematics, is the study of how functions change when their inputs change. The primary object of study in _____ is the derivative.
   a. Thing
   b. Differential calculus0
   c. Undefined
   d. Undefined

3. In mathematics, the _____ f is the collection of all ordered pairs . In particular, graph means the graphical representation of this collection, in the form of a curve or surface, together with axes, etc. Graphing on a Cartesian plane is sometimes referred to as curve sketching.
   a. Thing
   b. Graph of a function0
   c. Undefined
   d. Undefined

4. The mathematical concept of a _____ expresses the intuitive idea of deterministic dependence between two quantities, one of which is viewed as primary and the other as secondary. A _____ then is a way to associate a unique output for each input of a specified type, for example, a real number or an element of a given set.
   a. Function0
   b. Thing
   c. Undefined
   d. Undefined

5. In computer science, an _____ is the problem of finding the best solution from all feasible solutions.
   a. Optimization problem0
   b. Thing
   c. Undefined
   d. Undefined

6. _____ is a mathematical subject that includes the study of limits, derivatives, integrals, and power series and constitutes a major part of modern university curriculum.
   a. Thing
   b. Calculus0
   c. Undefined
   d. Undefined

7. A _____ is traditionally an infinitesimally small change in a variable.
   a. Differential0
   b. Thing
   c. Undefined
   d. Undefined

8. The _____, the average in everyday English, which is also called the arithmetic _____ (and is distinguished from the geometric _____ or harmonic _____). The average is also called the sample _____. The expected value of a random variable, which is also called the population _____.
   a. Thing
   b. Mean0
   c. Undefined
   d. Undefined

9. In mathematics, a _____ of a k-place relation $L \subseteq X_1 \times \ldots \times X_k$ is one of the sets X_j, $1 \leq j \leq k$. In the special case where k = 2 and $L \subseteq X_1 \times X_2$ is a function $L : X_1 \rightarrow X_2$, it is conventional to refer to X_1 as the _____ of the function and to refer to X_2 as the codomain of the function.
   a. Domain0
   b. Thing
   c. Undefined
   d. Undefined

10. The term _____ refers to the largest and the smallest element of a set.

Chapter 4. Applications of Differentiation

a. Thing
b. Extreme value0
c. Undefined
d. Undefined

11. A real-valued function f defined on the real line is said to have a _____ point at the point x∗, if there exists some ε > 0, such that f when x − x∗ < ε.
    a. Local maximum0
    b. Thing
    c. Undefined
    d. Undefined

12. The _____ is the highest point in a certain portion of a graph.
    a. Relative maximum0
    b. Thing
    c. Undefined
    d. Undefined

13. In elementary algebra, an _____ is a set that contains every real number between two indicated numbers and may contain the two numbers themselves.
    a. Interval0
    b. Thing
    c. Undefined
    d. Undefined

14. A _____ function is a function for which, intuitively, small changes in the input result in small changes in the output.
    a. Continuous0
    b. Event
    c. Undefined
    d. Undefined

15. In mathematics, a _____ is a statement that can be proved on the basis of explicitly stated or previously agreed assumptions.
    a. Thing
    b. Theorem0
    c. Undefined
    d. Undefined

16. In mathematics, a _____ is a demonstration that, assuming certain axioms, some statement is necessarily true.
    a. Proof0
    b. Thing
    c. Undefined
    d. Undefined

17. In mathematics, the _____ of a function is the set of all "output" values produced by that function. Given a function $f : A \to B$, the _____ of f, is defined to be the set $\{x \in B : x = f(a) \text{ for some } a \in A\}$.
    a. Range0
    b. Thing
    c. Undefined
    d. Undefined

18. A _____ is a function for which, intuitively, small changes in the input result in small changes in the output.
    a. Event
    b. Continuous function0
    c. Undefined
    d. Undefined

19. Sir Isaac _____, was an English physicist, mathematician, astronomer, natural philosopher, and alchemist, regarded by many as the greatest figure in the history of science
    a. Newton0
    b. Person
    c. Undefined
    d. Undefined

Chapter 4. Applications of Differentiation

20. In trigonometry, the _____ is a function defined as tan x = $\sin x / \cos x$. The function is so-named because it can be defined as the length of a certain segment of a _____ (in the geometric sense) to the unit circle. In plane geometry, a line is _____ to a curve, at some point, if both line and curve pass through the point with the same direction.
    a. Tangent0
    b. Thing
    c. Undefined
    d. Undefined

21. In mathematics, the concept of a _____ tries to capture the intuitive idea of a geometrical one-dimensional and continuous object. A simple example is the circle.
    a. Thing
    b. Curve0
    c. Undefined
    d. Undefined

22. In mathematics, _____ are the intuitive idea of a geometrical one-dimensional and continuous object.
    a. Curves0
    b. Thing
    c. Undefined
    d. Undefined

23. _____ is the study of geometry using the principles of algebra. _____ can be explained more simply: it is concerned with defining geometrical shapes in a numerical way and extracting numerical information from that representation.
    a. Thing
    b. Analytic geometry0
    c. Undefined
    d. Undefined

24. _____ was a highly influential French philosopher, mathematician, scientist, and writer. Dubbed the "Founder of Modern Philosophy", and the "Father of Modern Mathematics". His theories provided the basis for the calculus of Newton and Leibniz, by applying infinitesimal calculus to the tangent line problem, thus permitting the evolution of that branch of modern mathematics
    a. Descartes0
    b. Person
    c. Undefined
    d. Undefined

25. There are two simple _____ the greatest common factor and least common multiple: standard factorization and prime factorization.
    a. Methods for finding0
    b. Thing
    c. Undefined
    d. Undefined

26. In astronomy, geography, geometry and related sciences and contexts, a plane is said to be _____ at a given point if it is locally perpendicular to the gradient of the gravity field, i.e., with the direction of the gravitational force at that point.
    a. Thing
    b. Horizontal0
    c. Undefined
    d. Undefined

27. In geometry, an _____ is a point at which a line segment or ray terminates.
    a. Thing
    b. Endpoint0
    c. Undefined
    d. Undefined

28. In geometry, a _____ is defined as a quadrilateral where all four of its angles are right angles.
    a. Rectangle0
    b. Thing
    c. Undefined
    d. Undefined

Chapter 4. Applications of Differentiation

29. _____ is a point on the domain of a function
    a. Critical point0
    b. Thing
    c. Undefined
    d. Undefined

30. A _____ is a negotiable instrument instructing a financial institution to pay a specific amount of a specific currency from a specific demand account held in the maker/depositor's name with that institution. Both the maker and payee may be natural persons or legal entities.
    a. Check0
    b. Thing
    c. Undefined
    d. Undefined

31. _____ of an object is its speed in a particular direction.
    a. Thing
    b. Velocity0
    c. Undefined
    d. Undefined

32. In mathematics, _____ geometry was the traditional name for the geometry of three-dimensional Euclidean space — for practical purposes the kind of space we live in.
    a. Solid0
    b. Thing
    c. Undefined
    d. Undefined

33. A _____ is a vehicle, missile or aircraft which obtains thrust by the reaction to the ejection of fast moving fluid from within a _____ engine.
    a. Thing
    b. Rocket0
    c. Undefined
    d. Undefined

34. _____ is defined as the rate of change or derivative with respect to time of velocity.
    a. Thing
    b. Acceleration0
    c. Undefined
    d. Undefined

35. In mathematics, maxima and _____, known collectively as extrema, are points in the domain of a function at which the function takes a largest value .
    a. Thing
    b. Minima0
    c. Undefined
    d. Undefined

36. _____ is a free computer algebra system based on a 1982 version of Macsyma
    a. Maxima0
    b. Thing
    c. Undefined
    d. Undefined

37. In mathematics, a _____ in elementary terms is any of a variety of different functions from geometry, such as rotations, reflections and translations.
    a. Transformation0
    b. Thing
    c. Undefined
    d. Undefined

38. _____ are the basic objects of study in graph theory. Informally speaking, a graph is a set of objects called points, nodes, or vertices connected by links called lines or edges.

66   *Chapter 4. Applications of Differentiation*

    a. Thing   b. Graphs0
    c. Undefined   d. Undefined

39. The _____ of a solid object is the three-dimensional concept of how much space it occupies, often quantified numerically.
    a. Thing   b. Volume0
    c. Undefined   d. Undefined

40. In mathematics, a _____ is a constant multiplicative factor of a certain object. The object can be such things as a variable, a vector, a function, etc. For example, the _____ of $9x^2$ is 9.
    a. Coefficient0   b. Thing
    c. Undefined   d. Undefined

41. _____ is a physical property of a system that underlies the common notions of hot and cold; something that is hotter has the greater _____.
    a. Temperature0   b. Thing
    c. Undefined   d. Undefined

42. In mathematics and the mathematical sciences, a _____ is a fixed, but possibly unspecified, value. This is in contrast to a variable, which is not fixed.
    a. Constant0   b. Thing
    c. Undefined   d. Undefined

43. _____ is the force that opposes the relative motion or tendency toward such motion of two surfaces in contact.
    a. Friction0   b. Thing
    c. Undefined   d. Undefined

44. _____ is a set, with some particular properties and usually some additional structure, such as the operations of addition or multiplication, for instance.
    a. Space0   b. Thing
    c. Undefined   d. Undefined

45. _____ are procedures that allow people to exchange information by one of several methods.
    a. Thing   b. Communications0
    c. Undefined   d. Undefined

46. The word _____ is used in a variety of ways in mathematics.
    a. Index0   b. Thing
    c. Undefined   d. Undefined

47. _____ is the point at which an object in orbit around the Earth makes its closest approach to the Earth.
    a. Perigee0   b. Thing
    c. Undefined   d. Undefined

48. In business, particularly accounting, a _____ is the time intervals that the accounts, statement, payments, or other calculations cover.

Chapter 4. Applications of Differentiation

a. Period0
b. Thing
c. Undefined
d. Undefined

49. In mathematics, a _____ is an expression that is constructed from one or more variables and constants, using only the operations of addition, subtraction, multiplication, and constant positive whole number exponents. is a _____. Note in particular that division by an expression containing a variable is not in general allowed in polynomials. [1]
   a. Thing
   b. Polynomial0
   c. Undefined
   d. Undefined

50. In mathematics, a _____ is a two-dimensional manifold or surface that is perfectly flat.
   a. Thing
   b. Plane0
   c. Undefined
   d. Undefined

51. In physics, _____ is an influence that may cause an object to accelerate. It may be experienced as a lift, a push, or a pull. The actual acceleration of the body is determined by the vector sum of all forces acting on it, known as net _____ or resultant _____.
   a. Force0
   b. Thing
   c. Undefined
   d. Undefined

52. In classical geometry, a _____ of a circle or sphere is any line segment from its center to its boundary. By extension, the _____ of a circle or sphere is the length of any such segment. The _____ is half the diameter. In science and engineering the term _____ of curvature is commonly used as a synonym for _____.
   a. Radius0
   b. Thing
   c. Undefined
   d. Undefined

53. A _____ is an abstract model that uses mathematical language to describe the behavior of a system. Eykhoff defined a _____ as 'a representation of the essential aspects of an existing system which presents knowledge of that system in usable form'.
   a. Mathematical model0
   b. Thing
   c. Undefined
   d. Undefined

54. In mathematics, an inequality is a statement about the relative size or order of two objects. For example 14 > 10, or 14 is _____ 10.
   a. Greater than0
   b. Thing
   c. Undefined
   d. Undefined

55. In mathematics, a class _____ is a structure used to organize the various Galois groups and modules that appear in class field theory. They were invented by Emil Artin and John Tate.
   a. Formation0
   b. Thing
   c. Undefined
   d. Undefined

56. A _____ given two distinct points A and B on the _____, is the set of points C on the line containing points A and B such that A is not strictly between C and B.
   a. Ray0
   b. Thing
   c. Undefined
   d. Undefined

Chapter 4. Applications of Differentiation

57. _____ is electromagnetic radiation with a wavelength that is visible to the eye (visible _____) or, in a technical or scientific context, electromagnetic radiation of any wavelength.
    a. Thing
    b. Light0
    c. Undefined
    d. Undefined

58. In geometry, the relations of _____ are those such as 'lies on' between points and lines (as in 'point P lies on line L'), and 'intersects' (as in 'line L_1 intersects line L_2', in three-dimensional space). That is, they are the binary relations describing how subsets meet.
    a. Thing
    b. Incidence0
    c. Undefined
    d. Undefined

59. A _____ is a movement of an object in a circular motion. A two-dimensional object rotates around a center (or point) of _____. A three-dimensional object rotates around a line called an axis. If the axis of _____ is within the body, the body is said to rotate upon itself, or spin—which implies relative speed and perhaps free-movement with angular momentum. A circular motion about an external point, e.g. the Earth about the Sun, is called an orbit or more properly an orbital revolution.
    a. Thing
    b. Rotation0
    c. Undefined
    d. Undefined

60. _____ is a kind of property which exists as magnitude or multitude. It is among the basic classes of things along with quality, substance, change, and relation.
    a. Amount0
    b. Thing
    c. Undefined
    d. Undefined

61. _____ is a measure of difference for interval and ratio variables between the observed value and the mean.
    a. Deviation0
    b. Thing
    c. Undefined
    d. Undefined

62. In geometry and physics, _____ are half-lines that continue forever in one direction.
    a. Rays0
    b. Thing
    c. Undefined
    d. Undefined

63. In the scientific method, an _____ (Latin: ex-+-periri, "of (or from) trying"), is a set of actions and observations, performed in the context of solving a particular problem or question, in order to support or falsify a hypothesis or research concerning phenomena.
    a. Thing
    b. Experiment0
    c. Undefined
    d. Undefined

64. In botany, _____ are above-ground plant organs specialized for photosynthesis. Their characteristics are typically analyzed by using Fiobonacci's sequences.
    a. Thing
    b. Leaves0
    c. Undefined
    d. Undefined

65. In mathematics, the additive inverse, or _____ of a number n is the number that, when added to n, yields zero. The additive inverse of n is denoted −n. For example, 7 is −7, because 7 + (−7) = 0, and the additive inverse of −0.3 is 0.3, because −0.3 + 0.3 = 0.

Chapter 4. Applications of Differentiation 69

    a. Opposite0
    b. Thing
    c. Undefined
    d. Undefined

66. In mathematics, the _____ of a number n is the number that, when added to n, yields zero. The _____ of n is denoted −n. For example, 7 is −7, because 7 + (−7) = 0, and the _____ of −0.3 is 0.3, because −0.3 + 0.3 = 0.
    a. Additive inverse0
    b. Thing
    c. Undefined
    d. Undefined

67. A _____ consists either of a suggested explanation for a phenomenon or of a reasoned proposal suggesting a possible correlation between multiple phenomena.
    a. Thing
    b. Hypothesis0
    c. Undefined
    d. Undefined

68. In mathematics, a _____ of a complex-valued function f is a member x of the domain of f such that f(x) vanishes at x, that is, x : f (x) = 0.
    a. Thing
    b. Root0
    c. Undefined
    d. Undefined

69. The _____ implies that on any great circle around the world, the temperature, pressure, elevation, carbon dioxide concentration, or anything else that varies continuously, there will always exist two antipodal points that share the same value for that variable.
    a. Thing
    b. Intermediate Value Theorem0
    c. Undefined
    d. Undefined

70. In mathematics, an _____ is a theorem with a statement beginning 'there exist ...'. That is, in more formal terms of symbolic logic, it is a theorem with a statement involving the existential quantifier.
    a. Existence theorem0
    b. Thing
    c. Undefined
    d. Undefined

71. A _____ is the result of the addition of a set of numbers. The numbers may be natural numbers, complex numbers, matrices, or still more complicated objects. An infinite _____ is a subtle procedure known as a series.
    a. Thing
    b. Sum0
    c. Undefined
    d. Undefined

72. _____ is the branch of pure mathematics concerned with the properties of numbers in general, and integers in particular, as well as the wider classes of problems that arise from their study.
    a. Number theory0
    b. Thing
    c. Undefined
    d. Undefined

73. Leonhard _____ was a pioneering Swiss mathematician and physicist, who spent most of his life in Russia and Germany.
    a. Euler0
    b. Person
    c. Undefined
    d. Undefined

74. A _____ is a special kind of ratio, indicating a relationship between two measurements with different units, such as miles to gallons or cents to pounds.

Chapter 4. Applications of Differentiation

    a. Rate0   b. Thing
    c. Undefined   d. Undefined

75. In mathematics, an _____, mean, or central tendency of a data set refers to a measure of the "middle" or "expected" value of the data set.
    a. Concept   b. Average0
    c. Undefined   d. Undefined

76. In mathematics, an _____ is a statement about the relative size or order of two objects.
    a. Inequality0   b. Thing
    c. Undefined   d. Undefined

77. An _____ is an equality that remains true regardless of the values of any variables that appear within it, to distinguish it from an equality which is true under more particular conditions.
    a. Identity0   b. Thing
    c. Undefined   d. Undefined

78. In a mathematical proof or a syllogism, a _____ is a statement that is the logical consequence of preceding statements.
    a. Conclusion0   b. Concept
    c. Undefined   d. Undefined

79. _____ is a trigonometric function that is the reciprocal of cosine.
    a. Secant0   b. Thing
    c. Undefined   d. Undefined

80. _____ of a curve is a line that intersects two or more points on the curve.
    a. Secant line0   b. Thing
    c. Undefined   d. Undefined

81. _____ has two distinct but etymologically-related meanings: one in geometry and one in trigonometry.
    a. Tangent line0   b. Thing
    c. Undefined   d. Undefined

82. _____ consists either of a suggested explanation for a phenomenon or of a reasoned proposal suggesting a possible correlation between multiple phenomena.
    a. Event   b. Hypotheses0
    c. Undefined   d. Undefined

83. In mathematics, there are several meanings of _____ depending on the subject.
    a. Thing   b. Degree0
    c. Undefined   d. Undefined

84. A _____ is a mathematical statement which follows easily from a previously proven statement, typically a mathematical theorem.

Chapter 4. Applications of Differentiation

a. Corollary0
b. Thing
c. Undefined
d. Undefined

85. _____ is often used to describe the measurement of the steepness, incline, gradient, or grade of a straight line. The _____ is defined as the ratio of the "rise" divided by the "run" between two points on a line, or in other words, the ratio of the altitude change to the horizontal distance between any two points on the line.
   a. Slope0
   b. Thing
   c. Undefined
   d. Undefined

86. Acid _____ ratio measures the ability of a company to use its near cash or quick assets to immediately extinguish its current liabilities.
   a. Test0
   b. Thing
   c. Undefined
   d. Undefined

87. In mathematics, factorization (British English: factorisation) or factoring is the decomposition of an object (for example, a number, a polynomial, or a matrix) into a product of other objects, or _____, which when multiplied together give the original.
   a. Thing
   b. Factors0
   c. Undefined
   d. Undefined

88. An _____ is a combination of numbers, operators, grouping symbols and/or free variables and bound variables arranged in a meaningful way which can be evaluated..
   a. Expression0
   b. Thing
   c. Undefined
   d. Undefined

89. The plus and _____ signs are mathematical symbols used to represent the notions of positive and negative as well as the operations of addition and subtraction.
   a. Thing
   b. Minus0
   c. Undefined
   d. Undefined

90. In mathematics, a matrix can be thought of as each row or _____ being a vector. Hence, a space formed by row vectors or _____ vectors are said to be a row space or a _____ space.
   a. Concept
   b. Column0
   c. Undefined
   d. Undefined

91. _____ determines whether a given critical point of a function is a maximum, a minimum, or neither.
   a. First Derivative Test0
   b. Thing
   c. Undefined
   d. Undefined

92. The word _____ means curving in or hollowed inward.
   a. Concavity0
   b. Thing
   c. Undefined
   d. Undefined

93. In sociology and biology a _____ is the collection of people or organisms of a particular species living in a given geographic area or space, usually measured by a census.

a. Population0
c. Undefined
b. Thing
d. Undefined

94. _____ is a a point on a curve at which the tangent crosses the curve itself.
   a. Inflection point0
   b. Thing
   c. Undefined
   d. Undefined

95. _____ is the ability to hold, receive or absorb, or a measure thereof, similar to the concept of volume.
   a. Capacity0
   b. Concept
   c. Undefined
   d. Undefined

96. _____ usually refers to the biological _____ of a population level that can be supported for an organism, given the quantity of food, habitat, water and other life infrastructure present.
   a. Carrying capacity0
   b. Thing
   c. Undefined
   d. Undefined

97. _____ are points in the domain of a function at which the function takes a largest value or smallest value, either within a given neighborhood or on the function domain in its entirety.
   a. Thing
   b. Maxima and minima0
   c. Undefined
   d. Undefined

98. _____ determines whether a given stationary point of a function is a maximum or a minimum.
   a. Thing
   b. Second derivative test0
   c. Undefined
   d. Undefined

99. An _____ is a straight line or curve A to which another curve B approaches closer and closer as one moves along it. As one moves along B, the space between it and the _____ A becomes smaller and smaller, and can in fact be made as small as one could wish by going far enough along. A curve may or may not touch or cross its _____. In fact, the curve may intersect the _____ an infinite number of times.
   a. Thing
   b. Asymptote0
   c. Undefined
   d. Undefined

100. In calculus, the _____ is a formula for the derivative of the composite of two functions.
   a. Chain rule0
   b. Concept
   c. Undefined
   d. Undefined

101. A _____ is a set of numbers that designate location in a given reference system, such as x,y in a planar _____ system or an x,y,z in a three-dimensional _____ system.
   a. Thing
   b. Coordinate0
   c. Undefined
   d. Undefined

102. _____ is a straight line or curve A to which another curve B the one being studied approaches closer and closer as one moves along it.
   a. Thing
   b. Vertical asymptote0
   c. Undefined
   d. Undefined

Chapter 4. Applications of Differentiation

103. A _____ is a function that assigns a number to subsets of a given set.
   a. Thing
   b. Measure0
   c. Undefined
   d. Undefined

104. _____ is a branch of mathematics concerning the study of structure, relation and quantity.
   a. Concept
   b. Algebra0
   c. Undefined
   d. Undefined

105. _____ is the chance that something is likely to happen or be the case.
   a. Thing
   b. Probability0
   c. Undefined
   d. Undefined

106. _____ is a mathematical science pertaining to the collection, analysis, interpretation or explanation, and presentation of data. It is applicable to a wide variety of academic disciplines, from the physical and social sciences to the humanities.
   a. Thing
   b. Statistics0
   c. Undefined
   d. Undefined

107. _____ is mass m per unit volume V.
   a. Thing
   b. Density0
   c. Undefined
   d. Undefined

108. _____ of a probability distribution, random variable, or population or multiset of values is a measure of the spread of its values.
   a. Standard deviation0
   b. Thing
   c. Undefined
   d. Undefined

109. In mathematics, a _____ is the result of multiplying, or an expression that identifies factors to be multiplied.
   a. Product0
   b. Thing
   c. Undefined
   d. Undefined

110. _____ is a function of the form
   a. Cubic function0
   b. Thing
   c. Undefined
   d. Undefined

111. In calculus and other branches of mathematical analysis, an _____ is an algebraic expression obtained in the context of limits.
   a. Indeterminate form0
   b. Thing
   c. Undefined
   d. Undefined

112. A _____ is a numeral used to indicate a count. The most common use of the word today is to name the part of a fraction that tells the number or count of equal parts.
   a. Numerator0
   b. Thing
   c. Undefined
   d. Undefined

Chapter 4. Applications of Differentiation

113. A _____ is the part of a fraction that tells how many equal parts make up a whole, and which is used in the name of the fraction: "halves", "thirds", "fourths" or "quarters", "fifths" and so on.
    a. Concept
    b. Denominator0
    c. Undefined
    d. Undefined

114. In mathematics, a set is called _____ if there is a bijection between the set and some set of the form {1, 2, ..., n} where n is a natural number.
    a. Finite0
    b. Thing
    c. Undefined
    d. Undefined

115. In mathematics, a _____ number is a number which can be expressed as a ratio of two integers. Non-integer _____ numbers (commonly called fractions) are usually written as the vulgar fraction a / b, where b is not zero.
    a. Thing
    b. Rational0
    c. Undefined
    d. Undefined

116. In mathematics, a _____ is any function which can be written as the ratio of two polynomial functions.
    a. Rational function0
    b. Thing
    c. Undefined
    d. Undefined

117. _____ has many meanings, most of which simply .
    a. Power0
    b. Thing
    c. Undefined
    d. Undefined

118. In mathematics, a _____ is the end result of a division problem. It can also be expressed as the number of times the divisor divides into the dividend.
    a. Thing
    b. Quotient0
    c. Undefined
    d. Undefined

119. The word _____ comes from the Latin word linearis, which means created by lines.
    a. Linear0
    b. Thing
    c. Undefined
    d. Undefined

120. In mathematics, the _____ functions are functions of an angle; they are important when studying triangles and modeling periodic phenomena, among many other applications.
    a. Trigonometric0
    b. Thing
    c. Undefined
    d. Undefined

121. A _____ is a deliberate process for transforming one or more inputs into one or more results.
    a. Calculation0
    b. Thing
    c. Undefined
    d. Undefined

122. A _____ is a quantity that denotes the proportional amount or magnitude of one quantity relative to another.
    a. Thing
    b. Ratio0
    c. Undefined
    d. Undefined

123. Initial objects are also called _____, and terminal objects are also called final.

Chapter 4. Applications of Differentiation

   a. Thing
   c. Undefined
   b. Coterminal0
   d. Undefined

124. _____ is the fee paid on borrowed money.
   a. Thing
   c. Undefined
   b. Interest0
   d. Undefined

125. An _____ is the fee paid on borrow money.
   a. Interest rate0
   c. Undefined
   b. Concept
   d. Undefined

126. _____ or investing is a term with several closely-related meanings in business management, finance and economics, related to saving or deferring consumption.
   a. Thing
   c. Undefined
   b. Investment0
   d. Undefined

127. The deductive-nomological model is a formalized view of scientific _____ in natural language.
   a. Thing
   c. Undefined
   b. Explanation0
   d. Undefined

128. In Euclidean geometry, a _____ is moving every point a constant distance in a specified direction.
   a. Translation0
   c. Undefined
   b. Concept
   d. Undefined

129. In common philosophical language, a proposition or _____, is the content of an assertion, that is, it is true-or-false and defined by the meaning of a particular piece of language.
   a. Statement0
   c. Undefined
   b. Concept
   d. Undefined

130. A _____ consists of one quarter of the coordinate plane.
   a. Quadrant0
   c. Undefined
   b. Thing
   d. Undefined

131. In Euclidean geometry, a _____ is the set of all points in a plane at a fixed distance, called the radius, from a given point, the center.
   a. Thing
   c. Undefined
   b. Circle0
   d. Undefined

132. _____ was an American mathematician, known for his work in geometry and the history of mathematics.
   a. Howard Eves0
   c. Undefined
   b. Person
   d. Undefined

133. _____ (Basel, July 27, 1667 - January 1, 1748) was a Swiss mathematician.
   a. Person
   c. Undefined
   b. Johann Bernoulli0
   d. Undefined

Chapter 4. Applications of Differentiation

134. In geographic information systems, a _____ comprises an entity with a geographic location, typically determined by points, arcs, or polygons. Carriageways and cadastres exemplify _____ data.
   a. Thing
   b. Feature0
   c. Undefined
   d. Undefined

135. _____ the expected value of a random variable displays the average or central value of the variable. It is a summary value of the distribution of the variable.
   a. Determining0
   b. Thing
   c. Undefined
   d. Undefined

136. In mathematics, the _____ of a coordinate system is the point where the axes of the system intersect.
   a. Thing
   b. Origin0
   c. Undefined
   d. Undefined

137. A _____ is a function that repeats its values after some definite period has been added to its independent variable.
   a. Thing
   b. Periodic function0
   c. Undefined
   d. Undefined

138. _____ is the state of being greater than any finite real or natural number, however large.
   a. Thing
   b. Infinite0
   c. Undefined
   d. Undefined

139. Any point where a graph makes contact with an coordinate axis is called an _____ of the graph
   a. Intercept0
   b. Thing
   c. Undefined
   d. Undefined

140. _____ are any documents that aim to streamline particular processes according to a set routine.
   a. Guidelines0
   b. Thing
   c. Undefined
   d. Undefined

141. _____ of a polynomial with real or complex coefficients is a certain expression in the coefficients of the polynomial which is equal to zero if and only if the polynomial has a multiple root i.e. a root with multiplicity greater than one in the complex numbers.
   a. Thing
   b. Discriminant0
   c. Undefined
   d. Undefined

142. _____ means "constancy", i.e. if something retains a certain feature even after we change a way of looking at it, then it is symmetric.
   a. Symmetry0
   b. Thing
   c. Undefined
   d. Undefined

143. In mathematics, two quantities are called _____ if they vary in such a way that one of the quantities is a constant multiple of the other, or equivalently if they have a constant ratio.

Chapter 4. Applications of Differentiation

a. Thing
b. Proportional0
c. Undefined
d. Undefined

144. In plane geometry, a _____ is a polygon with four equal sides, four right angles, and parallel opposite sides. In algebra, the _____ of a number is that number multiplied by itself.
 a. Square0
 b. Thing
 c. Undefined
 d. Undefined

145. In topology and related areas of mathematics a _____ or Moore-Smith sequence is a generalization of a sequence, intended to unify the various notions of limit and generalize them to arbitrary topological spaces.
 a. Thing
 b. Net0
 c. Undefined
 d. Undefined

146. _____ is a vector produced when two or more forces act upon a single object.
 a. Thing
 b. Resultant force0
 c. Undefined
 d. Undefined

147. In mathematics, a _____ is a type of conic section defined as the intersection between a right circular conical surface and a plane which cuts through both halves of the cone.
 a. Hyperbola0
 b. Thing
 c. Undefined
 d. Undefined

148. _____ is a method of describing limiting behavior.
 a. Asymptotic0
 b. Thing
 c. Undefined
 d. Undefined

149. In mathematics, the _____ is a conic section generated by the intersection of a right circular conical surface and a plane parallel to a generating straight line of that surface. It can also be defined as locus of points in a plane which are equidistant from a given point.
 a. Parabola0
 b. Thing
 c. Undefined
 d. Undefined

150. A quadratic equation with real solutions, called roots, which may be real or complex, is given by the _____: $x = \frac{-b \pm \sqrt{b^2 - 4ac}}{2a}$.
 a. Thing
 b. Quadratic formula0
 c. Undefined
 d. Undefined

151. In statistics the _____ of an event i is the number n_i of times the event occurred in the experiment or the study. These frequencies are often graphically represented in histograms.
 a. Frequency0
 b. Concept
 c. Undefined
 d. Undefined

152. _____ is a trigonemtric function that is important when studying triangles and modeling periodic phenomena, among other applications.

Chapter 4. Applications of Differentiation

   a. Thing
   c. Undefined

   b. Sine0
   d. Undefined

153. In mathematics, a _____ is a polynomial equation of the second degree. The general form is $ax^2 + bx + c = 0$.
   a. Quadratic equation0
   c. Undefined

   b. Thing
   d. Undefined

154. In mathematics, a _____ may be described informally as a number that can be given by an infinite decimal representation.
   a. Real number0
   c. Undefined

   b. Thing
   d. Undefined

155. _____, from Latin meaning "to make progress", is defined in two different ways. Pure economic _____ is the increase in wealth that an investor has from making an investment, taking into consideration all costs associated with that investment including the opportunity cost of capital.
   a. Profit0
   c. Undefined

   b. Thing
   d. Undefined

156. Transport or _____ is the movement of people and goods from one place to another.
   a. Thing
   c. Undefined

   b. Transportation0
   d. Undefined

157. A _____ signifies a point or points of probability on a subject e.g., the _____ of creativity, which allows for the formation of rule or norm or law by interpretation of the phenomena events that can be created.
   a. Thing
   c. Undefined

   b. Principle0
   d. Undefined

158. _____ are objects, characters, or other concrete representations of ideas, concepts, or other abstractions.
   a. Thing
   c. Undefined

   b. Symbols0
   d. Undefined

159. _____ is bother the congnitive process of transferring information from a particular subject , and a linguistic expression corresponding to such a process.
   a. Thing
   c. Undefined

   b. Analogy0
   d. Undefined

160. A _____ is a symbolic representation denoting a quantity or expression. It often represents an "unknown" quantity that has the potential to change.
   a. Thing
   c. Undefined

   b. Variable0
   d. Undefined

161. In mathematics, science including computer science, linguistics and engineering, an _____ is, generally speaking, an independent variable or input to a function.
   a. Argument0
   c. Undefined

   b. Thing
   d. Undefined

Chapter 4. Applications of Differentiation

162. In geometry, a _____ (Greek words diairo = divide and metro = measure) of a circle is any straight line segment that passes through the centre and whose endpoints are on the circular boundary, or, in more modern usage, the length of such a line segment. When using the word in the more modern sense, one speaks of the _____ rather than a _____, because all diameters of a circle have the same length. This length is twice the radius. The _____ of a circle is also the longest chord that the circle has.
- a. Diameter0
- b. Thing
- c. Undefined
- d. Undefined

163. A frame of _____ is a particular perspective from which the universe is observed.
- a. Thing
- b. Reference0
- c. Undefined
- d. Undefined

164. _____ is to give an equation R(x,y) = S(x,y) that at least in part has the same graph as y = f(x).
- a. Thing
- b. Implicit differentiation0
- c. Undefined
- d. Undefined

165. _____ is a relation in Euclidean geometry among the three sides of a right triangle.
- a. Pythagorean Theorem0
- b. Thing
- c. Undefined
- d. Undefined

166. In geometry, the _____ of an object is a point in some sense in the middle of the object.
- a. Thing
- b. Center0
- c. Undefined
- d. Undefined

167. In mathematics, the multiplicative inverse of a number x, denoted 1/x or x^{-1}, is the number which, when multiplied by x, yields 1. The multiplicative inverse of x is also called the _____ of x.
- a. Thing
- b. Reciprocal0
- c. Undefined
- d. Undefined

168. _____ is the distance around a given two-dimensional object. As a general rule, the _____ of a polygon can always be calculated by adding all the length of the sides together. So, the formula for triangles is P = a + b + c, where a, b and c stand for each side of it. For quadrilaterals the equation is P = a + b + c + d. For equilateral polygons, P = na, where n is the number of sides and a is the side length.
- a. Thing
- b. Perimeter0
- c. Undefined
- d. Undefined

169. A _____ is a simplified and structured visual representation of concepts, ideas, constructions, relations, statistical data, anatomy etc used in all aspects of human activities to visualize and clarify the topic.
- a. Diagram0
- b. Thing
- c. Undefined
- d. Undefined

170. The metre (or _____, see spelling differences) is a measure of length. It is the basic unit of length in the metric system and in the International System of Units (SI), used around the world for general and scientific purposes.
- a. Meter0
- b. Concept
- c. Undefined
- d. Undefined

Chapter 4. Applications of Differentiation

171. In mathematics, an _____ .
   a. Thing
   b. Ellipse0
   c. Undefined
   d. Undefined

172. A _____ is one of the basic shapes of geometry: a polygon with three vertices and three sides which are straight line segments.
   a. Triangle0
   b. Thing
   c. Undefined
   d. Undefined

173. In geometry, an _____ polygon is a polygon which has all sides of the same length.
   a. Equilateral0
   b. Thing
   c. Undefined
   d. Undefined

174. An _____ is a triangle in which all sides are of equal length.
   a. Equilateral triangle0
   b. Thing
   c. Undefined
   d. Undefined

175. In geometry, a _____ is a special kind of point, usually a corner of a polygon, polyhedron, or higher dimensional polytope. In the geometry of curves a _____ is a point of where the first derivative of curvature is zero. In graph theory, a _____ is the fundamental unit out of which graphs are formed
   a. Vertex0
   b. Thing
   c. Undefined
   d. Undefined

176. An _____ triange is a triangle with at least two sides of equal length.
   a. Isosceles0
   b. Thing
   c. Undefined
   d. Undefined

177. In a right triangle, the _____ of the triangle are the two sides that are perpendicular to each other, as opposed to the hypotenuse.
   a. Legs0
   b. Thing
   c. Undefined
   d. Undefined

178. _____ has one 90° internal angle a right angle.
   a. Thing
   b. Right triangle0
   c. Undefined
   d. Undefined

179. In mathematics, a _____ is the set of all points in three-dimensional space (R^3) which are at distance r from a fixed point of that space, where r is a positive real number called the radius of the _____. The fixed point is called the center or centre, and is not part of the _____ itself.
   a. Sphere0
   b. Thing
   c. Undefined
   d. Undefined

180. In mathematics, a _____ is a quadric surface, with the following equation in Cartesian coordinates: $(x/_a)^2 + (y/_b)^2 = 1$.

Chapter 4. Applications of Differentiation

    a. Thing
    c. Undefined
    b. Cylinder0
    d. Undefined

181. A _____ is a three-dimensional geometric shape formed by straight lines through a fixed point (vertex) to the points of a fixed curve (directrix)
    a. Cone0
    c. Undefined
    b. Concept
    d. Undefined

182. In finance, a _____ is collateral that the holder of a position in securities, options, or futures contracts has to deposit to cover the credit risk of his counterparty.
    a. Margin0
    c. Undefined
    b. Thing
    d. Undefined

183. In geometry, a _____ planar shape or solid is one that encloses and "fits snugly" around another geometric shape or solid.
    a. Thing
    c. Undefined
    b. Circumscribed0
    d. Undefined

184. In geometry, a _____ planar shape or solid is one that encloses and "fits snugly" around another geometric shape or solid.
    a. Circumscribed about0
    c. Undefined
    b. Thing
    d. Undefined

185. _____ is the SI unit of energy.
    a. Thing
    c. Undefined
    b. Joule0
    d. Undefined

186. A _____ is a unit of length in the metric system, equal to one thousand metres, the current SI base unit of length
    a. Kilometer0
    c. Undefined
    b. Thing
    d. Undefined

187. _____ is the middle point of a line segment.
    a. Midpoint0
    c. Undefined
    b. Thing
    d. Undefined

188. A _____ is a polygon with six edges and six vertices.
    a. Thing
    c. Undefined
    b. Hexagon0
    d. Undefined

189. _____ is the application of tools and a processing medium to the transformation of raw materials into finished goods for sale.
    a. Thing
    c. Undefined
    b. Manufacturing0
    d. Undefined

190. _____ is the change in total cost that arises when the quantity produced changes by one unit.

Chapter 4. Applications of Differentiation

    a. Thing
    c. Undefined
    b. Marginal cost0
    d. Undefined

191. The _____ of measurement are a globally standardized and modernized form of the metric system.
    a. Units0
    c. Undefined
    b. Thing
    d. Undefined

192. In Euclidean geometry, a uniform _____ is a linear transformation that enlargers or diminishes objects, and whose _____ factor is the same in all directions. This is also called homothethy.
    a. Thing
    c. Undefined
    b. Scale0
    d. Undefined

193. _____ is the amount of time someone works beyond normal working hours.
    a. Thing
    c. Undefined
    b. Compensatory time0
    d. Undefined

194. Fixed costs are expenses whose total does not change in proportion to the activity of a business.Unit fixed costs decline with volume following a retangular hyperbola as the volume of production.Variable costs by contrast change in relation to the activity of a business such as sales or production volume.Along with variable costs,fixed costs make up one of the two components of total cost. In the most simple production function total cost is equal to fixed costs plus variable costs.In accounting terminology, fixed costs will broadly include all costs which are not included in cost of goods sold, and variable costs are those captured in costs of goods sold. The implicit assumption required to make the equivalence between the accounting and economics terminology is that the accounting period is equal to the period in which fixed costs do not vary in relation to production. In practice, this equivalence does not always hold and depending on the period under consideration by management, some overhead expenses can be adjusted by management, and the specific allocation of each expense to each category will be decided under cost accounting.In business planning and management accounting, usage of the terms fixed costs, variable costs and others will often differ from usage in economics, and may depend on the intended use. For example, costs may be segregated into per unit costs fixed costs per period, and variable costs as a proportion of revenue. Capital expenditures will usually be allocated separately, and depending on the purpose, a portion may be regularly allocated to expenses as depreciation and amortization and seen as a _____ per period, or the entire amount may be considered upfront fixed costs.
    a. Thing
    c. Undefined
    b. Fixed cost0
    d. Undefined

195. _____ are expenses whose total does not change in proportion to the activity of a business, within the relevant time period or scale of production
    a. Thing
    c. Undefined
    b. Fixed costs0
    d. Undefined

196. The _____ is a method of finding the derivative of a function that is the quotient of two other functions for which derivatives exist.
    a. Thing
    c. Undefined
    b. Quotient rule0
    d. Undefined

197. _____ is the extra revenue that an additional unit of product will bring a firm. It can also be described as the change in total revenue/change in number of units sold.

Chapter 4. Applications of Differentiation

a. Marginal revenue0
b. Thing
c. Undefined
d. Undefined

198. _____ is a business term for the amount of money that a company receives from its activities in a given period, mostly from sales of products and/or services to customers
a. Revenue0
b. Thing
c. Undefined
d. Undefined

199. In economics, supply and _____ describe market relations between prospective sellers and buyers of a good.
a. Demand0
b. Thing
c. Undefined
d. Undefined

200. In mathematics, _____ are two-dimensional manifolds or surfaces that are perfectly flat.
a. Planes0
b. Thing
c. Undefined
d. Undefined

201. In mathematics, a _____ or rhodonea curve is a sinusoid plotted in polar coordinates.
a. Rose0
b. Thing
c. Undefined
d. Undefined

202. A _____ is a plan of action to guide decisions and actions.
a. Thing
b. Policy0
c. Undefined
d. Undefined

203. _____ is a list of goods and materials, or those goods and materials themselves, held available in stock by a business
a. Inventory0
b. Thing
c. Undefined
d. Undefined

204. In combinatorial mathematics, a _____ is an un-ordered collection of unique elements.
a. Concept
b. Combination0
c. Undefined
d. Undefined

205. _____ usually refers to money in the form of liquid currency, such as banknotes or coins.
a. Thing
b. Cash0
c. Undefined
d. Undefined

206. A _____ is 360° or 2δ radians.
a. Turn0
b. Thing
c. Undefined
d. Undefined

207. Equivalence is the condition of being _____ or essentially equal.
a. Thing
b. Equivalent0
c. Undefined
d. Undefined

Chapter 4. Applications of Differentiation

208. _____ is a notation for writing numbers that is often used by scientists and mathematicians to make it easier to write large and small numbers.
   a. Scientific notation0
   b. Thing
   c. Undefined
   d. Undefined

209. In Euclidean geometry, an _____ is a closed segment of a differentiable curve in the two-dimensional plane; for example, a circular _____ is a segment of a circle.
   a. Arc0
   b. Concept
   c. Undefined
   d. Undefined

210. _____ is the income from capital investment paid in a series of regular payments.
   a. Annuity0
   b. Thing
   c. Undefined
   d. Undefined

211. _____ of a single or multiple future payments is the nominal amounts of money to change hands at some future date, discounted to account for the time value of money, and other factors such as investment risk.
   a. Present value0
   b. Thing
   c. Undefined
   d. Undefined

212. In banking and accountancy, the outstanding _____ is the amount of money owned, or due, that remains in a deposit account or a loan account at a given date, after all past remittances, payments and withdrawal have been accounted for.
   a. Balance0
   b. Thing
   c. Undefined
   d. Undefined

213. _____ is the property of a physical object that quantifies the amount of matter and energy it is equivalent to.
   a. Thing
   b. Mass0
   c. Undefined
   d. Undefined

214. An _____ of a function f is a function F whose derivative is equal to f, i.e., F' = f.
   a. Thing
   b. Antiderivative0
   c. Undefined
   d. Undefined

215. _____ is a method for differentiating expressions involving exponentiation the power operation.
   a. Power rule0
   b. Thing
   c. Undefined
   d. Undefined

216. In statistics, a _____ measure is one which is measuring what is supposed to measure.
   a. Valid0
   b. Thing
   c. Undefined
   d. Undefined

217. _____ in calculus is primitive or indefinite integral of a function f is a function F whose derivative is equal to f, i.e., F Œ = f. The process of solving for antiderivatives is _____
   a. Antidifferentiation0
   b. Thing
   c. Undefined
   d. Undefined

Chapter 4. Applications of Differentiation

218. A _____ is a mathematical equation for an unknown function of one or several variables which relates the values of the function itself and of its derivatives of various orders.
   a. Differential equation0
   b. Thing
   c. Undefined
   d. Undefined

219. In geometry, a line _____ is a part of a line that is bounded by two end points, and contains every point on the line between its end points.
   a. Segment0
   b. Concept
   c. Undefined
   d. Undefined

220. A _____ is a graphical tool to qualitatively visualize, or aid in numerical approximation of, solutions to differential equations.
   a. Thing
   b. Slope field0
   c. Undefined
   d. Undefined

221. A _____ is a part of a line that is bounded by two end points, and contains every point on the line between its end points.
   a. Thing
   b. Line segment0
   c. Undefined
   d. Undefined

222. In mathematics, in the field of differential equations, an initial value problem is a differential equation together with specified value, called the _____, of the unknown function at a given point in the domain of the solution.
   a. Initial condition0
   b. Thing
   c. Undefined
   d. Undefined

223. _____ is a synonym for information.
   a. Data0
   b. Thing
   c. Undefined
   d. Undefined

224. _____ is the transport of people on a trip/journey or the process or time involved in a person or object moving from one location to another.
   a. Thing
   b. Travel0
   c. Undefined
   d. Undefined

225. _____ means in succession or back-to-back
   a. Consecutive0
   b. Thing
   c. Undefined
   d. Undefined

226. A _____ is a unit of length, usually used to measure distance, in a number of different systems, including Imperial units, United States customary units and Norwegian/Swedish mil. Its size can vary from system to system, but in each is between 1 and 10 kilometers. In contemporary English contexts _____ refers to either:
   a. Thing
   b. Mile0
   c. Undefined
   d. Undefined

227. _____ are a measure of time.

Chapter 4. Applications of Differentiation

    a. Thing
    b. Minutes0
    c. Undefined
    d. Undefined

228. The _____ are the only integral domain whose positive elements are well-ordered, and in which order is preserved by addition. Like the natural numbers, the _____ form a countably infinite set. The set of all _____ is usually denoted in mathematics by a boldface Z .
    a. Thing
    b. Integers0
    c. Undefined
    d. Undefined

229. _____ are external two-dimensional outlines, with the appearance or configuration of some thing - in contrast to the matter or content or substance of which it is composed.
    a. Shapes0
    b. Thing
    c. Undefined
    d. Undefined

230. A _____ is any object propelled through space by the applicationp of a force.
    a. Projectile0
    b. Thing
    c. Undefined
    d. Undefined

231. The _____ of an angle is the ratio of the length of the adjacent side to the length of the hypotenuse.
    a. Cosine0
    b. Concept
    c. Undefined
    d. Undefined

232. In mathematics, _____ is an elementary arithmetic operation. When one of the numbers is a whole number, _____ is the repeated sum of the other number.
    a. Multiplication0
    b. Thing
    c. Undefined
    d. Undefined

233. In geometry, an _____ divides an angle into two equal angles. Each point of an _____ is equidistant from the sides of the angle.
    a. Thing
    b. Angle bisector0
    c. Undefined
    d. Undefined

234. _____ is an adjective usually refering to being in the centre.
    a. Central0
    b. Thing
    c. Undefined
    d. Undefined

235. In economics, economic _____ is simply a state of the world where economic forces are balanced and in the absence of external influences the values of economic variables will not change.
    a. Thing
    b. Equilibrium0
    c. Undefined
    d. Undefined

236. An n-sided _____ is a polyhedron formed by connecting an n-sided polygonal base and a point, called the apex, by n triangular faces. In other words, it is a conic solid with polygonal base.
    a. Pyramid0
    b. Thing
    c. Undefined
    d. Undefined

237. _____ is a method of mathematical proof typically used to establish that a given statement is true of all natural numbers
   a. Mathematical induction0
   b. Thing
   c. Undefined
   d. Undefined

1. _____ is an extension of the concept of a sum.
   a. Thing
   b. Definite integral0
   c. Undefined
   d. Undefined

2. The _____ of a function is an extension of the concept of a sum, and are identified or found through the use of integration.
   a. Thing
   b. Integral0
   c. Undefined
   d. Undefined

3. _____ is a mathematical subject that includes the study of limits, derivatives, integrals, and power series and constitutes a major part of modern university curriculum.
   a. Thing
   b. Calculus0
   c. Undefined
   d. Undefined

4. A _____ is traditionally an infinitesimally small change in a variable.
   a. Thing
   b. Differential0
   c. Undefined
   d. Undefined

5. _____, a field in mathematics, is the study of how functions change when their inputs change. The primary object of study in _____ is the derivative.
   a. Differential calculus0
   b. Thing
   c. Undefined
   d. Undefined

6. In mathematics, the concept of a _____ tries to capture the intuitive idea of a geometrical one-dimensional and continuous object. A simple example is the circle.
   a. Thing
   b. Curve0
   c. Undefined
   d. Undefined

7. A _____ is one of the basic shapes of geometry: a polygon with three vertices and three sides which are straight line segments.
   a. Triangle0
   b. Thing
   c. Undefined
   d. Undefined

8. In geometry a _____ is a plane figure that is bounded by a closed path or circuit, composed of a finite number of sequential line segments.
   a. Polygon0
   b. Thing
   c. Undefined
   d. Undefined

9. The act of _____ is the calculated approximation of a result which is usable even if input data may be incomplete, uncertain, or noisy.
   a. Estimating0
   b. Thing
   c. Undefined
   d. Undefined

10. In mathematics, the _____ is a conic section generated by the intersection of a right circular conical surface and a plane parallel to a generating straight line of that surface. It can also be defined as locus of points in a plane which are equidistant from a given point.

Chapter 5. Integrals

a. Parabola0
b. Thing
c. Undefined
d. Undefined

11. _____ is often used to describe the measurement of the steepness, incline, gradient, or grade of a straight line. The _____ is defined as the ratio of the "rise" divided by the "run" between two points on a line, or in other words, the ratio of the altitude change to the horizontal distance between any two points on the line.
a. Thing
b. Slope0
c. Undefined
d. Undefined

12. In trigonometry, the _____ is a function defined as $\tan x = \sin x / \cos x$. The function is so-named because it can be defined as the length of a certain segment of a _____ (in the geometric sense) to the unit circle. In plane geometry, a line is _____ to a curve, at some point, if both line and curve pass through the point with the same direction.
a. Thing
b. Tangent0
c. Undefined
d. Undefined

13. _____ has two distinct but etymologically-related meanings: one in geometry and one in trigonometry.
a. Tangent line0
b. Thing
c. Undefined
d. Undefined

14. _____ is a trigonometric function that is the reciprocal of cosine.
a. Secant0
b. Thing
c. Undefined
d. Undefined

15. _____ of a curve is a line that intersects two or more points on the curve.
a. Secant line0
b. Thing
c. Undefined
d. Undefined

16. In geometry, a _____ is defined as a quadrilateral where all four of its angles are right angles.
a. Thing
b. Rectangle0
c. Undefined
d. Undefined

17. In plane geometry, a _____ is a polygon with four equal sides, four right angles, and parallel opposite sides. In algebra, the _____ of a number is that number multiplied by itself.
a. Thing
b. Square0
c. Undefined
d. Undefined

18. A _____ is the result of the addition of a set of numbers. The numbers may be natural numbers, complex numbers, matrices, or still more complicated objects. An infinite _____ is a subtle procedure known as a series.
a. Thing
b. Sum0
c. Undefined
d. Undefined

19. The _____ are the only integral domain whose positive elements are well-ordered, and in which order is preserved by addition. Like the natural numbers, the _____ form a countably infinite set. The set of all _____ is usually denoted in mathematics by a boldface Z.

a. Integers0   b. Thing
c. Undefined   d. Undefined

20. A _____ function is a function for which, intuitively, small changes in the input result in small changes in the output.
    a. Event   b. Continuous0
    c. Undefined   d. Undefined

21. The mathematical concept of a _____ expresses the intuitive idea of deterministic dependence between two quantities, one of which is viewed as primary and the other as secondary. A _____ then is a way to associate a unique output for each input of a specified type, for example, a real number or an element of a given set.
    a. Thing   b. Function0
    c. Undefined   d. Undefined

22. In geometry, an _____ is a point at which a line segment or ray terminates.
    a. Thing   b. Endpoint0
    c. Undefined   d. Undefined

23. _____ is a subset of a population.
    a. Sample0   b. Thing
    c. Undefined   d. Undefined

24. _____ is the middle point of a line segment.
    a. Midpoint0   b. Thing
    c. Undefined   d. Undefined

25. _____ is the eighteenth letter of the Greek alphabet.
    a. Thing   b. Sigma0
    c. Undefined   d. Undefined

26. _____ is used as the symbol for summation. Summation is the addition of a set of numbers; the result is their sum. The "numbers" to be summed may be natural numbers, complex numbers, matrices, or still more complicated objects. An infinite sum is a subtle procedure known as a series.
    a. Thing   b. Sigma notation0
    c. Undefined   d. Undefined

27. Mathematical _____ is used to represent ideas.
    a. Notation0   b. Thing
    c. Undefined   d. Undefined

28. _____ is a branch of mathematics concerning the study of structure, relation and quantity.
    a. Concept   b. Algebra0
    c. Undefined   d. Undefined

29. _____ of an object is its speed in a particular direction.

Chapter 5. Integrals

a. Thing
b. Velocity0
c. Undefined
d. Undefined

30. Initial objects are also called _____, and terminal objects are also called final.
   a. Coterminal0
   b. Thing
   c. Undefined
   d. Undefined

31. In mathematics and the mathematical sciences, a _____ is a fixed, but possibly unspecified, value. This is in contrast to a variable, which is not fixed.
   a. Constant0
   b. Thing
   c. Undefined
   d. Undefined

32. In elementary algebra, an _____ is a set that contains every real number between two indicated numbers and may contain the two numbers themselves.
   a. Interval0
   b. Thing
   c. Undefined
   d. Undefined

33. A _____ is a deliberate process for transforming one or more inputs into one or more results.
   a. Calculation0
   b. Thing
   c. Undefined
   d. Undefined

34. _____ means in succession or back-to-back
   a. Consecutive0
   b. Thing
   c. Undefined
   d. Undefined

35. An _____ is a combination of numbers, operators, grouping symbols and/or free variables and bound variables arranged in a meaningful way which can be evaluated..
   a. Thing
   b. Expression0
   c. Undefined
   d. Undefined

36. In business, particularly accounting, a _____ is the time intervals that the accounts, statement, payments, or other calculations cover.
   a. Thing
   b. Period0
   c. Undefined
   d. Undefined

37. In mathematics, _____ geometry was the traditional name for the geometry of three-dimensional Euclidean space — for practical purposes the kind of space we live in.
   a. Thing
   b. Solid0
   c. Undefined
   d. Undefined

38. _____ is a set, with some particular properties and usually some additional structure, such as the operations of addition or multiplication, for instance.
   a. Thing
   b. Space0
   c. Undefined
   d. Undefined

39. _____ is a synonym for information.

a. Data0
b. Thing
c. Undefined
d. Undefined

40. A _____ is a vehicle, missile or aircraft which obtains thrust by the reaction to the ejection of fast moving fluid from within a _____ engine.
   a. Thing
   b. Rocket0
   c. Undefined
   d. Undefined

41. In Euclidean geometry, a _____ is the set of all points in a plane at a fixed distance, called the radius, from a given point, the center.
   a. Circle0
   b. Thing
   c. Undefined
   d. Undefined

42. In classical geometry, a _____ of a circle or sphere is any line segment from its center to its boundary. By extension, the _____ of a circle or sphere is the length of any such segment. The _____ is half the diameter. In science and engineering the term _____ of curvature is commonly used as a synonym for _____.
   a. Thing
   b. Radius0
   c. Undefined
   d. Undefined

43. _____ is an adjective usually refering to being in the centre.
   a. Central0
   b. Thing
   c. Undefined
   d. Undefined

44. In geometry, two sets are called _____ if one can be transformed into the other by an isometry, i.e., a combination of translations, rotations and reflections.
   a. Congruent0
   b. Thing
   c. Undefined
   d. Undefined

45. A _____ is 360° or 2δ radians.
   a. Turn0
   b. Thing
   c. Undefined
   d. Undefined

46. A _____ is a function for which, intuitively, small changes in the input result in small changes in the output.
   a. Event
   b. Continuous function0
   c. Undefined
   d. Undefined

47. _____ is the state of being greater than any finite real or natural number, however large.
   a. Thing
   b. Infinite0
   c. Undefined
   d. Undefined

48. In mathematics, a set is called _____ if there is a bijection between the set and some set of the form {1, 2, ..., n} where n is a natural number.
   a. Thing
   b. Finite0
   c. Undefined
   d. Undefined

Chapter 5. Integrals

49. Continuous functions are of utmost importance in mathematics and applications. However, not all functions are continuous. If a function is not continuous at a point in its domain, one says that it has a _____ there. The set of all points of _____ of a function may be a discrete set, a dense set, or even the entire domain of the function.
   a. Thing
   b. Discontinuity0
   c. Undefined
   d. Undefined

50. _____ is a function that extends the concept of an ordinary sum
   a. Thing
   b. Integrand0
   c. Undefined
   d. Undefined

51. _____ is a process of combining or accumulating. It may also refer to:
   a. Integration0
   b. Thing
   c. Undefined
   d. Undefined

52. _____ is the level of functional and/or metabolic efficiency of an organism at both the micro level.
   a. Thing
   b. Health0
   c. Undefined
   d. Undefined

53. _____ is a method for approximating the values of integrals.
   a. Riemann sum0
   b. Thing
   c. Undefined
   d. Undefined

54. In topology and related areas of mathematics a _____ or Moore-Smith sequence is a generalization of a sequence, intended to unify the various notions of limit and generalize them to arbitrary topological spaces.
   a. Thing
   b. Net0
   c. Undefined
   d. Undefined

55. The _____ is a fundamental concept in analysis. Informally, a function f can be made as close to L as desired, by making x close enough to p.
   a. Thing
   b. Limit of a function0
   c. Undefined
   d. Undefined

56. The plus and _____ signs are mathematical symbols used to represent the notions of positive and negative as well as the operations of addition and subtraction.
   a. Minus0
   b. Thing
   c. Undefined
   d. Undefined

57. _____ Any process by which a specified characteristic usually amplitude of the output of a device is prevented from exceeding a predetermined value.
   a. Limiting0
   b. Thing
   c. Undefined
   d. Undefined

58. _____ was a German mathematician and philosopher. He invented calculus independently of Newton, and his notation is the one in general use since.

a. Person
b. Leibniz0
c. Undefined
d. Undefined

59. A _____ is the sum of the elements of a sequence.
   a. Thing
   b. Series0
   c. Undefined
   d. Undefined

60. In geometry, _____ angles are angles that have a common ray coming out of the vertex going between two other rays.
   a. Adjacent0
   b. Concept
   c. Undefined
   d. Undefined

61. In mathematics, an inequality is a statement about the relative size or order of two objects. For example 14 > 10, or 14 is _____ 10.
   a. Greater than0
   b. Thing
   c. Undefined
   d. Undefined

62. A _____ is a negotiable instrument instructing a financial institution to pay a specific amount of a specific currency from a specific demand account held in the maker/depositor's name with that institution. Both the maker and payee may be natural persons or legal entities.
   a. Check0
   b. Thing
   c. Undefined
   d. Undefined

63. _____ are the basic objects of study in graph theory. Informally speaking, a graph is a set of objects called points, nodes, or vertices connected by links called lines or edges.
   a. Graphs0
   b. Thing
   c. Undefined
   d. Undefined

64. A _____ is a simplified and structured visual representation of concepts, ideas, constructions, relations, statistical data, anatomy etc used in all aspects of human activities to visualize and clarify the topic.
   a. Thing
   b. Diagram0
   c. Undefined
   d. Undefined

65. In mathematics, an _____ is a statement about the relative size or order of two objects.
   a. Inequality0
   b. Thing
   c. Undefined
   d. Undefined

66. An _____ is an equality that remains true regardless of the values of any variables that appear within it, to distinguish it from an equality which is true under more particular conditions.
   a. Thing
   b. Identity0
   c. Undefined
   d. Undefined

67. The _____, the average in everyday English, which is also called the arithmetic _____ (and is distinguished from the geometric _____ or harmonic _____). The average is also called the sample _____. The expected value of a random variable, which is also called the population _____.

Chapter 5. Integrals

a. Mean0
b. Thing
c. Undefined
d. Undefined

68. The deductive-nomological model is a formalized view of scientific _____ in natural language.
   a. Thing
   b. Explanation0
   c. Undefined
   d. Undefined

69. Sir Isaac _____, was an English physicist, mathematician, astronomer, natural philosopher, and alchemist, regarded by many as the greatest figure in the history of science
   a. Newton0
   b. Person
   c. Undefined
   d. Undefined

70. _____ was an English divine, scholar and mathematician who is generally given minor credit for his role in the development of modern calculus; in particular, for his work regarding the tangent; for example, Barrow is given credit for being the first to calculate the tangents of the kappa curve. Isaac Newton was a student of Barrow's. Lunar crater Barrow is named after him.
   a. Isaac Barrow0
   b. Thing
   c. Undefined
   d. Undefined

71. In mathematics, a _____ is a statement that can be proved on the basis of explicitly stated or previously agreed assumptions.
   a. Thing
   b. Theorem0
   c. Undefined
   d. Undefined

72. The _____ is a measurement of how a function changes when the values of its inputs change.
   a. Derivative0
   b. Thing
   c. Undefined
   d. Undefined

73. _____ element of an element x with respect to a binary operation * with identity element e is an element y such that $x * y = y * x = e$. In particular,
   a. Inverse0
   b. Thing
   c. Undefined
   d. Undefined

74. In number theory, the _____ of arithmetic (or unique factorization theorem) states that every natural number greater than 1 can be written as a unique product of prime numbers.
   a. Concept
   b. Fundamental theorem0
   c. Undefined
   d. Undefined

75. _____ of calculus is the statement that the two central operations of calculus, differentiation and integration, are inverse operations: if a continuous function is first integrated and then differentiated, the original function is retrieved.
   a. Thing
   b. Fundamental Theorem of Calculus0
   c. Undefined
   d. Undefined

76. A _____ is a symbolic representation denoting a quantity or expression. It often represents an "unknown" quantity that has the potential to change.

Chapter 5. Integrals

    a. Thing
    b. Variable0
    c. Undefined
    d. Undefined

77. _____ named in honor of the 17th century German philosopher and mathematician Gottfried Wilhelm Leibniz, was originally the use of expressions such as dx and dy and to represent "infinitely small" or infinitesimal increments of quantities x and y, just as Äx and Äy represent finite increments of x and y respectively.
    a. Thing
    b. Leibniz notation0
    c. Undefined
    d. Undefined

78. _____ is a mathematical science pertaining to the collection, analysis, interpretation or explanation, and presentation of data. It is applicable to a wide variety of academic disciplines, from the physical and social sciences to the humanities.
    a. Thing
    b. Statistics0
    c. Undefined
    d. Undefined

79. _____, Greek for "knowledge of nature," is the branch of science concerned with the discovery and characterization of universal laws which govern matter, energy, space, and time.
    a. Physics0
    b. Thing
    c. Undefined
    d. Undefined

80. In calculus, the _____ is a formula for the derivative of the composite of two functions.
    a. Chain rule0
    b. Concept
    c. Undefined
    d. Undefined

81. In logic and mathematics, logical _____ (usual symbol and) is a two-place logical operation that results in a value of true if both of its operands are true, otherwise a value of false.
    a. Conjunction0
    b. Concept
    c. Undefined
    d. Undefined

82. An _____ of a function f is a function F whose derivative is equal to f, i.e., F' = f.
    a. Antiderivative0
    b. Thing
    c. Undefined
    d. Undefined

83. In mathematics, a _____ is a demonstration that, assuming certain axioms, some statement is necessarily true.
    a. Proof0
    b. Thing
    c. Undefined
    d. Undefined

84. A _____ is a mathematical statement which follows easily from a previously proven statement, typically a mathematical theorem.
    a. Corollary0
    b. Thing
    c. Undefined
    d. Undefined

85. _____ are objects, characters, or other concrete representations of ideas, concepts, or other abstractions.
    a. Symbols0
    b. Thing
    c. Undefined
    d. Undefined

Chapter 5. Integrals

86. The _____ of a solid object is the three-dimensional concept of how much space it occupies, often quantified numerically.
    a. Volume0
    b. Thing
    c. Undefined
    d. Undefined

87. In mathematics, _____ are the intuitive idea of a geometrical one-dimensional and continuous object.
    a. Curves0
    b. Thing
    c. Undefined
    d. Undefined

88. _____ of Syracuse was an ancient Greek mathematician, physicist and engineer. In addition to making important discoveries in the field of mathematics and geometry, he is credited with producing machines that were well ahead of their time.
    a. Person
    b. Archimedes0
    c. Undefined
    d. Undefined

89. _____ was an Italian physicist, mathematician, astronomer, and philosopher who is closely associated with the scientific revolution.
    a. Galileo Galilei0
    b. Person
    c. Undefined
    d. Undefined

90. In mathematics, the _____ also called the Gauss _____ is a non-elementary function which occurs in probability, statistics and partial differential equations.
    a. Error function0
    b. Thing
    c. Undefined
    d. Undefined

91. _____ is the chance that something is likely to happen or be the case.
    a. Thing
    b. Probability0
    c. Undefined
    d. Undefined

92. _____ is the design, analysis, and/or construction of works for practical purposes.
    a. Thing
    b. Engineering0
    c. Undefined
    d. Undefined

93. A _____ is a set of numbers that designate location in a given reference system, such as x,y in a planar _____ system or an x,y,z in a three-dimensional _____ system.
    a. Thing
    b. Coordinate0
    c. Undefined
    d. Undefined

94. In mathematics, the _____ of a coordinate system is the point where the axes of the system intersect.
    a. Origin0
    b. Thing
    c. Undefined
    d. Undefined

95. _____ is a a point on a curve at which the tangent crosses the curve itself.
    a. Thing
    b. Inflection point0
    c. Undefined
    d. Undefined

Chapter 5. Integrals

96. A _____ is a special kind of ratio, indicating a relationship between two measurements with different units, such as miles to gallons or cents to pounds.
   a. Rate0
   b. Thing
   c. Undefined
   d. Undefined

97. _____ is the application of tools and a processing medium to the transformation of raw materials into finished goods for sale.
   a. Manufacturing0
   b. Thing
   c. Undefined
   d. Undefined

98. Fixed costs are expenses whose total does not change in proportion to the activity of a business.Unit fixed costs decline with volume following a retangular hyperbola as the volume of production.Variable costs by contrast change in relation to the activity of a business such as sales or production volume.Along with variable costs,fixed costs make up one of the two components of total cost. In the most simple production function total cost is equal to fixed costs plus variable costs.In accounting terminology, fixed costs will broadly include all costs which are not included in cost of goods sold, and variable costs are those captured in costs of goods sold. The implicit assumption required to make the equivalence between the accounting and economics terminology is that the accounting period is equal to the period in which fixed costs do not vary in relation to production. In practice, this equivalence does not always hold and depending on the period under consideration by management, some overhead expenses can be adjusted by management, and the specific allocation of each expense to each category will be decided under cost accounting.In business planning and management accounting, usage of the terms fixed costs, variable costs and others will often differ from usage in economics, and may depend on the intended use. For example, costs may be segregated into per unit costs fixed costs per period, and variable costs as a proportion of revenue. Capital expenditures will usually be allocated separately, and depending on the purpose, a portion may be regularly allocated to expenses as depreciation and amortization and seen as a _____ per period, or the entire amount may be considered upfront fixed costs.
   a. Thing
   b. Fixed cost0
   c. Undefined
   d. Undefined

99. In mathematics and its applications, a _____ is a system for assigning an n-tuple of numbers or scalars to each point in an n-dimensional space.
   a. Concept
   b. Coordinate system0
   c. Undefined
   d. Undefined

100. In sociology and biology a _____ is the collection of people or organisms of a particular species living in a given geographic area or space, usually measured by a census.
   a. Population0
   b. Thing
   c. Undefined
   d. Undefined

101. The _____ of measurement are a globally standardized and modernized form of the metric system.
   a. Thing
   b. Units0
   c. Undefined
   d. Undefined

102. _____ is the change in total cost that arises when the quantity produced changes by one unit.
   a. Thing
   b. Marginal cost0
   c. Undefined
   d. Undefined

Chapter 5. Integrals

103. The metre (or _____, see spelling differences) is a measure of length. It is the basic unit of length in the metric system and in the International System of Units (SI), used around the world for general and scientific purposes.
   a. Meter0
   b. Concept
   c. Undefined
   d. Undefined

104. In mathematics, a _____ is the result of multiplying, or an expression that identifies factors to be multiplied.
   a. Thing
   b. Product0
   c. Undefined
   d. Undefined

105. _____ is the estimation of a physical quantity such as distance, energy, temperature, or time.
   a. Thing
   b. Measurement0
   c. Undefined
   d. Undefined

106. In mathematics, the _____ (or modulus) of a real number is its numerical value without regard to its sign.
   a. Thing
   b. Absolute value0
   c. Undefined
   d. Undefined

107. In topology, the _____ are subsets S of a topological space X is the set of points which can be approached both from S and from the outside of S.
   a. Boundaries0
   b. Thing
   c. Undefined
   d. Undefined

108. _____ is the extra revenue that an additional unit of product will bring a firm. It can also be described as the change in total revenue/change in number of units sold.
   a. Thing
   b. Marginal revenue0
   c. Undefined
   d. Undefined

109. _____ is a business term for the amount of money that a company receives from its activities in a given period, mostly from sales of products and/or services to customers
   a. Thing
   b. Revenue0
   c. Undefined
   d. Undefined

110. _____ is defined as the rate of change or derivative with respect to time of velocity.
   a. Acceleration0
   b. Thing
   c. Undefined
   d. Undefined

111. The _____ or kilogramme is the SI base unit of mass. It is defined as being equal to the mass of the international prototype of the _____.
   a. Kilogram0
   b. Thing
   c. Undefined
   d. Undefined

112. The word _____ comes from the Latin word linearis, which means created by lines.
   a. Linear0
   b. Thing
   c. Undefined
   d. Undefined

113. _____ is mass m per unit volume V.

Chapter 5. Integrals

   a. Density0
   c. Undefined
   b. Thing
   d. Undefined

114. _____ is a kind of property which exists as magnitude or multitude. It is among the basic classes of things along with quality, substance, change, and relation.
   a. Thing
   c. Undefined
   b. Amount0
   d. Undefined

115. _____ are a measure of time.
   a. Thing
   c. Undefined
   b. Minutes0
   d. Undefined

116. In mathematics a _____ is a function which defines a distance between elements of a set.
   a. Metric0
   c. Undefined
   b. Thing
   d. Undefined

117. In mathematical analysis, _____ are objects which generalize functions and probability distributions.
   a. Thing
   c. Undefined
   b. Distribution0
   d. Undefined

118. Two mathematical objects are equal if and only if they are precisely the same in every way. This defines a binary relation, _____, denoted by the sign of _____ "=" in such a way that the statement "x = y" means that x and y are equal.
   a. Thing
   c. Undefined
   b. Equality0
   d. Undefined

119. A _____ is a function that assigns a number to subsets of a given set.
   a. Thing
   c. Undefined
   b. Measure0
   d. Undefined

120. A _____ is a quantity that denotes the proportional amount or magnitude of one quantity relative to another.
   a. Ratio0
   c. Undefined
   b. Thing
   d. Undefined

121. In mathematics, a _____ is a constant multiplicative factor of a certain object. The object can be such things as a variable, a vector, a function, etc. For example, the _____ of $9x^2$ is 9.
   a. Coefficient0
   c. Undefined
   b. Thing
   d. Undefined

122. _____ are procedures that allow people to exchange information by one of several methods.
   a. Communications0
   c. Undefined
   b. Thing
   d. Undefined

123. _____ is the point at which an object in orbit around the Earth makes its closest approach to the Earth.

Chapter 5. Integrals

a. Perigee0
b. Thing
c. Undefined
d. Undefined

124. In mathematics, a _____ is an expression that is constructed from one or more variables and constants, using only the operations of addition, subtraction, multiplication, and constant positive whole number exponents. is a _____. Note in particular that division by an expression containing a variable is not in general allowed in polynomials. [1]
   a. Polynomial0
   b. Thing
   c. Undefined
   d. Undefined

125. Sir _____ was an English physicist, mathematician, astronomer, natural philosopher, and alchemist, regarded by many as the greatest figure in the history of science.
   a. Isaac Newton0
   b. Person
   c. Undefined
   d. Undefined

126. There are two simple _____ the greatest common factor and least common multiple: standard factorization and prime factorization.
   a. Methods for finding0
   b. Thing
   c. Undefined
   d. Undefined

127. In mathematics, the _____ of a function is the set of all "output" values produced by that function. Given a function $f : A \to B$, the _____ of f, is defined to be the set $\{x \in B : x = f(a) \text{ for some } a \in A\}$.
   a. Thing
   b. Range0
   c. Undefined
   d. Undefined

128. The _____ is a tool for finding antiderivatives and integrals. It is the counterpart to the chain rule of differentiation.
   a. Substitution rule0
   b. Thing
   c. Undefined
   d. Undefined

129. _____ is a trigonemtric function that is important when studying triangles and modeling periodic phenomena, among other applications.
   a. Sine0
   b. Thing
   c. Undefined
   d. Undefined

130. The _____ of an angle is the ratio of the length of the adjacent side to the length of the hypotenuse.
   a. Cosine0
   b. Concept
   c. Undefined
   d. Undefined

131. _____ means "constancy", i.e. if something retains a certain feature even after we change a way of looking at it, then it is symmetric.
   a. Symmetry0
   b. Thing
   c. Undefined
   d. Undefined

132. An _____ is a straight line around which a geometric figure can be rotated.
   a. Thing
   b. Axis0
   c. Undefined
   d. Undefined

Chapter 5. Integrals

133. The _____ consists of an inhalation and an exhalation.
    a. Respiratory cycle0
    b. Thing
    c. Undefined
    d. Undefined

134. In mathematics, _____ growth occurs when the growth rate of a function is always proportional to the function's current size.
    a. Exponential0
    b. Thing
    c. Undefined
    d. Undefined

135. In mathematics, a _____ of a number x is the exponent y of the power by such that $x = b^y$. The value used for the base b must be neither 0 nor 1, nor a root of 1 in the case of the extension to complex numbers, and is typically 10, e, or 2.
    a. Logarithm0
    b. Thing
    c. Undefined
    d. Undefined

136. _____ is the logarithm to the base e, where e is an irrational constant approximately equal to 2.718281828459.
    a. Thing
    b. Natural logarithm0
    c. Undefined
    d. Undefined

137. In mathematics, a _____ is a type of conic section defined as the intersection between a right circular conical surface and a plane which cuts through both halves of the cone.
    a. Thing
    b. Hyperbola0
    c. Undefined
    d. Undefined

138. In mathematics, a _____ number is a number which can be expressed as a ratio of two integers. Non-integer _____ numbers (commonly called fractions) are usually written as the vulgar fraction a / b, where b is not zero.
    a. Rational0
    b. Thing
    c. Undefined
    d. Undefined

139. The _____ implies that on any great circle around the world, the temperature, pressure, elevation, carbon dioxide concentration, or anything else that varies continuously, there will always exist two antipodal points that share the same value for that variable.
    a. Intermediate Value Theorem0
    b. Thing
    c. Undefined
    d. Undefined

140. _____ is one of the most important functions in mathematics. A function commonly used to study growth and decay
    a. Thing
    b. Exponential function0
    c. Undefined
    d. Undefined

141. An _____ is a function which does the reverse of a given function.
    a. Inverse function0
    b. Thing
    c. Undefined
    d. Undefined

142. In mathematics, a _____ of a k-place relation $L \subseteq X_1 \times ... \times X_k$ is one of the sets X_j, $1 \leq j \leq k$. In the special case where k = 2 and $L \subseteq X_1 \times X_2$ is a function $L : X_1 \to X_2$, it is conventional to refer to X_1 as the _____ of the function and to refer to X_2 as the codomain of the function.

Chapter 5. Integrals

a. Domain0
b. Thing
c. Undefined
d. Undefined

143. In mathematics, a _____ may be described informally as a number that can be given by an infinite decimal representation.
   a. Real number0
   b. Thing
   c. Undefined
   d. Undefined

144. _____ is a mathematical operation, written a^n, involving two numbers, the base a and the exponent n.
   a. Thing
   b. Exponentiating0
   c. Undefined
   d. Undefined

145. _____ is a mathematical operation, written a^n, involving two numbers, the base a and the exponent n.
   a. Exponentiation0
   b. Thing
   c. Undefined
   d. Undefined

146. Mathematical _____ are demonstrations that, assuming certain axioms, some statement is necessarily true.
   a. Thing
   b. Proofs0
   c. Undefined
   d. Undefined

147. In common philosophical language, a proposition or _____, is the content of an assertion, that is, it is true-or-false and defined by the meaning of a particular piece of language.
   a. Concept
   b. Statement0
   c. Undefined
   d. Undefined

148. _____ is a physical property of a system that underlies the common notions of hot and cold; something that is hotter has the greater _____.
   a. Thing
   b. Temperature0
   c. Undefined
   d. Undefined

149. A _____ is a numeral used to indicate a count. The most common use of the word today is to name the part of a fraction that tells the number or count of equal parts.
   a. Numerator0
   b. Thing
   c. Undefined
   d. Undefined

150. A _____ is the part of a fraction that tells how many equal parts make up a whole, and which is used in the name of the fraction: "halves", "thirds", "fourths" or "quarters", "fifths" and so on.
   a. Denominator0
   b. Concept
   c. Undefined
   d. Undefined

151. A _____ signifies a point or points of probability on a subject e.g., the _____ of creativity, which allows for the formation of rule or norm or law by interpretation of the phenomena events that can be created.
   a. Principle0
   b. Thing
   c. Undefined
   d. Undefined

Chapter 5. Integrals

152. _____ forms part of thinking. Considered the most complex of all intellectual functions, _____ has been defined as higher-order cognitive process that requires the modulation and control of more routine or fundamental skills.
   a. Problem solving0
   b. Thing
   c. Undefined
   d. Undefined

153. In mathematics, a _____ is a mathematical statement which appears likely to be true, but has not been formally proven to be true under the rules of mathematical logic.
   a. Conjecture0
   b. Concept
   c. Undefined
   d. Undefined

154. In geometry, a _____ is a special kind of point, usually a corner of a polygon, polyhedron, or higher dimensional polytope. In the geometry of curves a _____ is a point of where the first derivative of curvature is zero. In graph theory, a _____ is the fundamental unit out of which graphs are formed
   a. Thing
   b. Vertex0
   c. Undefined
   d. Undefined

155. In mathematics, a _____ is a two-dimensional manifold or surface that is perfectly flat.
   a. Thing
   b. Plane0
   c. Undefined
   d. Undefined

156. In geometry, the _____ of an object is a point in some sense in the middle of the object.
   a. Center0
   b. Thing
   c. Undefined
   d. Undefined

Chapter 6. Applications of Integration

1. _____ are the basic objects of study in graph theory. Informally speaking, a graph is a set of objects called points, nodes, or vertices connected by links called lines or edges.
   a. Thing
   b. Graphs0
   c. Undefined
   d. Undefined

2. In mathematics, the concept of a _____ tries to capture the intuitive idea of a geometrical one-dimensional and continuous object. A simple example is the circle.
   a. Thing
   b. Curve0
   c. Undefined
   d. Undefined

3. In mathematics, _____ are the intuitive idea of a geometrical one-dimensional and continuous object.
   a. Thing
   b. Curves0
   c. Undefined
   d. Undefined

4. The mathematical concept of a _____ expresses the intuitive idea of deterministic dependence between two quantities, one of which is viewed as primary and the other as secondary. A _____ then is a way to associate a unique output for each input of a specified type, for example, a real number or an element of a given set.
   a. Function0
   b. Thing
   c. Undefined
   d. Undefined

5. The _____ of a function is an extension of the concept of a sum, and are identified or found through the use of integration.
   a. Thing
   b. Integral0
   c. Undefined
   d. Undefined

6. In geometry, an _____ is a point at which a line segment or ray terminates.
   a. Endpoint0
   b. Thing
   c. Undefined
   d. Undefined

7. In geometry, a _____ is defined as a quadrilateral where all four of its angles are right angles.
   a. Rectangle0
   b. Thing
   c. Undefined
   d. Undefined

8. A _____ is the result of the addition of a set of numbers. The numbers may be natural numbers, complex numbers, matrices, or still more complicated objects. An infinite _____ is a subtle procedure known as a series.
   a. Sum0
   b. Thing
   c. Undefined
   d. Undefined

9. _____ Any process by which a specified characteristic usually amplitude of the output of a device is prevented from exceeding a predetermined value.
   a. Thing
   b. Limiting0
   c. Undefined
   d. Undefined

10. _____ is a method for approximating the values of integrals.
    a. Thing
    b. Riemann sum0
    c. Undefined
    d. Undefined

11. _____ is a subset of a population.
   a. Thing
   b. Sample0
   c. Undefined
   d. Undefined

12. A _____ function is a function for which, intuitively, small changes in the input result in small changes in the output.
   a. Continuous0
   b. Event
   c. Undefined
   d. Undefined

13. In mathematical analysis and related areas of mathematics, a set is called _____, if it is, in a certain sense, of finite size.
   a. Thing
   b. Bounded0
   c. Undefined
   d. Undefined

14. In mathematics, the _____ is a conic section generated by the intersection of a right circular conical surface and a plane parallel to a generating straight line of that surface. It can also be defined as locus of points in a plane which are equidistant from a given point.
   a. Thing
   b. Parabola0
   c. Undefined
   d. Undefined

15. In mathematics, the _____ of two sets A and B is the set that contains all elements of A that also belong to B (or equivalently, all elements of B that also belong to A), but no other elements.
   a. Intersection0
   b. Thing
   c. Undefined
   d. Undefined

16. In mathematics, the _____ of a coordinate system is the point where the axes of the system intersect.
   a. Thing
   b. Origin0
   c. Undefined
   d. Undefined

17. _____ of an object is its speed in a particular direction.
   a. Velocity0
   b. Thing
   c. Undefined
   d. Undefined

18. A _____ is one of the basic shapes of geometry: a polygon with three vertices and three sides which are straight line segments.
   a. Thing
   b. Triangle0
   c. Undefined
   d. Undefined

19. In geometry, a _____ is a special kind of point, usually a corner of a polygon, polyhedron, or higher dimensional polytope. In the geometry of curves a _____ is a point of where the first derivative of curvature is zero. In graph theory, a _____ is the fundamental unit out of which graphs are formed
   a. Vertex0
   b. Thing
   c. Undefined
   d. Undefined

20. _____ is a mathematical subject that includes the study of limits, derivatives, integrals, and power series and constitutes a major part of modern university curriculum.

Chapter 6. Applications of Integration 107

    a. Calculus0
    c. Undefined
    b. Thing
    d. Undefined

21. _____ is the middle point of a line segment.
    a. Thing
    b. Midpoint0
    c. Undefined
    d. Undefined

22. _____ is a branch of mathematics concerning the study of structure, relation and quantity.
    a. Concept
    b. Algebra0
    c. Undefined
    d. Undefined

23. In mathematics, an _____ is a statement about the relative size or order of two objects.
    a. Inequality0
    b. Thing
    c. Undefined
    d. Undefined

24. _____ is the transport of people on a trip/journey or the process or time involved in a person or object moving from one location to another.
    a. Thing
    b. Travel0
    c. Undefined
    d. Undefined

25. The _____ of measurement are a globally standardized and modernized form of the metric system.
    a. Thing
    b. Units0
    c. Undefined
    d. Undefined

26. _____ is a business term for the amount of money that a company receives from its activities in a given period, mostly from sales of products and/or services to customers
    a. Revenue0
    b. Thing
    c. Undefined
    d. Undefined

27. In trigonometry, the _____ is a function defined as $\tan x = \sin x / \cos x$. The function is so-named because it can be defined as the length of a certain segment of a _____ (in the geometric sense) to the unit circle. In plane geometry, a line is _____ to a curve, at some point, if both line and curve pass through the point with the same direction.
    a. Tangent0
    b. Thing
    c. Undefined
    d. Undefined

28. _____ has two distinct but etymologically-related meanings: one in geometry and one in trigonometry.
    a. Thing
    b. Tangent line0
    c. Undefined
    d. Undefined

29. In geometry, a line _____ is a part of a line that is bounded by two end points, and contains every point on the line between its end points.
    a. Concept
    b. Segment0
    c. Undefined
    d. Undefined

30. The _____ of a solid object is the three-dimensional concept of how much space it occupies, often quantified numerically.

a. Volume0
b. Thing
c. Undefined
d. Undefined

31. In Euclidean geometry, a _____ is the set of all points in a plane at a fixed distance, called the radius, from a given point, the center.
    a. Circle0
    b. Thing
    c. Undefined
    d. Undefined

32. In classical geometry, a _____ of a circle or sphere is any line segment from its center to its boundary. By extension, the _____ of a circle or sphere is the length of any such segment. The _____ is half the diameter. In science and engineering the term _____ of curvature is commonly used as a synonym for _____.
    a. Radius0
    b. Thing
    c. Undefined
    d. Undefined

33. In mathematics, a _____ is a quadric surface, with the following equation in Cartesian coordinates: $(x/a)^2 + (y/b)^2 = 1$.
    a. Cylinder0
    b. Thing
    c. Undefined
    d. Undefined

34. In geometry, a _____ is a three-dimensional figure formed by six parallelograms.
    a. Thing
    b. Parallelepiped0
    c. Undefined
    d. Undefined

35. A _____ is a part of a line that is bounded by two end points, and contains every point on the line between its end points.
    a. Line segment0
    b. Thing
    c. Undefined
    d. Undefined

36. In geometry, two lines or planes if one falls on the other in such a way as to create congruent adjacent angles. The term may be used as a noun or adjective. Thus, referring to Figure 1, the line AB is the _____ to CD through the point B.
    a. Thing
    b. Perpendicular0
    c. Undefined
    d. Undefined

37. In mathematics, _____ geometry was the traditional name for the geometry of three-dimensional Euclidean space — for practical purposes the kind of space we live in.
    a. Solid0
    b. Thing
    c. Undefined
    d. Undefined

38. In mathematics, a _____ is a two-dimensional manifold or surface that is perfectly flat.
    a. Thing
    b. Plane0
    c. Undefined
    d. Undefined

39. In mathematics, _____ are two-dimensional manifolds or surfaces that are perfectly flat.
    a. Thing
    b. Planes0
    c. Undefined
    d. Undefined

Chapter 6. Applications of Integration

40. A _____ is a function for which, intuitively, small changes in the input result in small changes in the output.
    a. Continuous function0
    b. Event
    c. Undefined
    d. Undefined

41. In mathematics and the mathematical sciences, a _____ is a fixed, but possibly unspecified, value. This is in contrast to a variable, which is not fixed.
    a. Thing
    b. Constant0
    c. Undefined
    d. Undefined

42. In mathematics, a _____ is the set of all points in three-dimensional space (R^3) which are at distance r from a fixed point of that space, where r is a positive real number called the radius of the _____. The fixed point is called the center or centre, and is not part of the _____ itself.
    a. Sphere0
    b. Thing
    c. Undefined
    d. Undefined

43. A _____ is a negotiable instrument instructing a financial institution to pay a specific amount of a specific currency from a specific demand account held in the maker/depositor's name with that institution. Both the maker and payee may be natural persons or legal entities.
    a. Check0
    b. Thing
    c. Undefined
    d. Undefined

44. In plane geometry, a _____ is a polygon with four equal sides, four right angles, and parallel opposite sides. In algebra, the _____ of a number is that number multiplied by itself.
    a. Thing
    b. Square0
    c. Undefined
    d. Undefined

45. In mathematics, a _____ is an algebraic structure in which addition and multiplication are defined and have properties listed below.
    a. Thing
    b. Ring0
    c. Undefined
    d. Undefined

46. A _____ is a movement of an object in a circular motion. A two-dimensional object rotates around a center (or point) of _____. A three-dimensional object rotates around a line called an axis. If the axis of _____ is within the body, the body is said to rotate upon itself, or spinâ€"which implies relative speed and perhaps free-movement with angular momentum. A circular motion about an external point, e.g. the Earth about the Sun, is called an orbit or more properly an orbital revolution.
    a. Thing
    b. Rotation0
    c. Undefined
    d. Undefined

47. In mathematics, a class _____ is a structure used to organize the various Galois groups and modules that appear in class field theory. They were invented by Emil Artin and John Tate.
    a. Formation0
    b. Thing
    c. Undefined
    d. Undefined

48. In geometry, an _____ polygon is a polygon which has all sides of the same length.

Chapter 6. Applications of Integration

a. Thing
c. Undefined
b. Equilateral0
d. Undefined

49. An _____ is a triangle in which all sides are of equal length.
   a. Thing
   c. Undefined
   b. Equilateral triangle0
   d. Undefined

50. An n-sided _____ is a polyhedron formed by connecting an n-sided polygonal base and a point, called the apex, by n triangular faces. In other words, it is a conic solid with polygonal base.
   a. Thing
   c. Undefined
   b. Pyramid0
   d. Undefined

51. An _____ is a straight line around which a geometric figure can be rotated.
   a. Thing
   c. Undefined
   b. Axis0
   d. Undefined

52. _____ is often used to describe the measurement of the steepness, incline, gradient, or grade of a straight line. The _____ is defined as the ratio of the "rise" divided by the "run" between two points on a line, or in other words, the ratio of the altitude change to the horizontal distance between any two points on the line.
   a. Thing
   c. Undefined
   b. Slope0
   d. Undefined

53. In geometry, a _____ (Greek words diairo = divide and metro = measure) of a circle is any straight line segment that passes through the centre and whose endpoints are on the circular boundary, or, in more modern usage, the length of such a line segment. When using the word in the more modern sense, one speaks of the _____ rather than a _____, because all diameters of a circle have the same length. This length is twice the radius. The _____ of a circle is also the longest chord that the circle has.
   a. Diameter0
   c. Undefined
   b. Thing
   d. Undefined

54. The _____ of a right triangle is the triangle's longest side; the side opposite the right angle.
   a. Hypotenuse0
   c. Undefined
   b. Thing
   d. Undefined

55. _____ has one 90° internal angle a right angle.
   a. Thing
   c. Undefined
   b. Right triangle0
   d. Undefined

56. An _____ triange is a triangle with at least two sides of equal length.
   a. Isosceles0
   c. Undefined
   b. Thing
   d. Undefined

57. In geometry, a _____ is a surface of revolution generated by revolving a circle in three dimensional space about an axis coplanar with the circle, which does not touch the circle. Examples of tori include the surfaces of doughnuts and inner tubes. A circle rotated about a chord of the circle is called a _____ in some contexts, but this is not a common usage in mathematics. The shape produced when a circle is rotated about a chord resembles a round cushion. _____ was the Latin word for a cushion of this shape.
   a. Torus0
   b. Thing
   c. Undefined
   d. Undefined

58. A _____ signifies a point or points of probability on a subject e.g., the _____ of creativity, which allows for the formation of rule or norm or law by interpretation of the phenomena events that can be created.
   a. Principle0
   b. Thing
   c. Undefined
   d. Undefined

59. Bonaventura Francesco _____ was an Italian mathematician known for _____'s principle,
   a. Person
   b. Cavalieri0
   c. Undefined
   d. Undefined

60. In geometry, an _____ angle is an angle that is not a 90 degree angle, or an angle that is divisible by 90: 180, 270, 360/0
   a. Oblique0
   b. Thing
   c. Undefined
   d. Undefined

61. An _____ is when two lines intersect somewhere on a plane creating a right angle at intersection
   a. Axes0
   b. Thing
   c. Undefined
   d. Undefined

62. In geometry and trigonometry, a _____ is defined as an angle between two straight intersecting lines of ninety degrees, or one-quarter of a circle.
   a. Right angle0
   b. Thing
   c. Undefined
   d. Undefined

63. In geometry, the _____ of an object is a point in some sense in the middle of the object.
   a. Center0
   b. Thing
   c. Undefined
   d. Undefined

64. Sir Isaac _____, was an English physicist, mathematician, astronomer, natural philosopher, and alchemist, regarded by many as the greatest figure in the history of science
   a. Person
   b. Newton0
   c. Undefined
   d. Undefined

65. In elementary algebra, an _____ is a set that contains every real number between two indicated numbers and may contain the two numbers themselves.
   a. Thing
   b. Interval0
   c. Undefined
   d. Undefined

Chapter 6. Applications of Integration

66. _____ is a means of calculating the volume of a solid of revolution, when integrating along an axis perpendicular to the axis of revolution.
    a. Shell method0
    b. Thing
    c. Undefined
    d. Undefined

67. The _____ is the distance around a closed curve. _____ is a kind of perimeter.
    a. Thing
    b. Circumference0
    c. Undefined
    d. Undefined

68. A _____ is a simplified and structured visual representation of concepts, ideas, constructions, relations, statistical data, anatomy etc used in all aspects of human activities to visualize and clarify the topic.
    a. Thing
    b. Diagram0
    c. Undefined
    d. Undefined

69. _____, Greek for "knowledge of nature," is the branch of science concerned with the discovery and characterization of universal laws which govern matter, energy, space, and time.
    a. Physics0
    b. Thing
    c. Undefined
    d. Undefined

70. In physics, _____ is an influence that may cause an object to accelerate. It may be experienced as a lift, a push, or a pull. The actual acceleration of the body is determined by the vector sum of all forces acting on it, known as net _____ or resultant _____.
    a. Force0
    b. Thing
    c. Undefined
    d. Undefined

71. In mathematics, a _____ is the result of multiplying, or an expression that identifies factors to be multiplied.
    a. Product0
    b. Thing
    c. Undefined
    d. Undefined

72. The _____ or kilogramme is the SI base unit of mass. It is defined as being equal to the mass of the international prototype of the _____.
    a. Thing
    b. Kilogram0
    c. Undefined
    d. Undefined

73. _____ is the property of a physical object that quantifies the amount of matter and energy it is equivalent to.
    a. Thing
    b. Mass0
    c. Undefined
    d. Undefined

74. _____ is defined as the rate of change or derivative with respect to time of velocity.
    a. Thing
    b. Acceleration0
    c. Undefined
    d. Undefined

75. The metre (or _____, see spelling differences) is a measure of length. It is the basic unit of length in the metric system and in the International System of Units (SI), used around the world for general and scientific purposes.

Chapter 6. Applications of Integration

    a. Meter0
    c. Undefined
    b. Concept
    d. Undefined

76. In mathematics a _____ is a function which defines a distance between elements of a set.
    a. Thing
    b. Metric0
    c. Undefined
    d. Undefined

77. The _____ is a decimalized system of measurement based on the metre and the gram.
    a. Metric system0
    b. Concept
    c. Undefined
    d. Undefined

78. In mathematics, the additive inverse, or _____ of a number n is the number that, when added to n, yields zero. The additive inverse of n is denoted −n. For example, 7 is −7, because 7 + (−7) = 0, and the additive inverse of −0.3 is 0.3, because −0.3 + 0.3 = 0.
    a. Opposite0
    b. Thing
    c. Undefined
    d. Undefined

79. In mathematics, the _____ of a number n is the number that, when added to n, yields zero. The _____ of n is denoted −n. For example, 7 is −7, because 7 + (−7) = 0, and the _____ of −0.3 is 0.3, because −0.3 + 0.3 = 0.
    a. Additive inverse0
    b. Thing
    c. Undefined
    d. Undefined

80. _____ is a kind of property which exists as magnitude or multitude. It is among the basic classes of things along with quality, substance, change, and relation.
    a. Amount0
    b. Thing
    c. Undefined
    d. Undefined

81. In mathematics, science including computer science, linguistics and engineering, an _____ is, generally speaking, an independent variable or input to a function.
    a. Thing
    b. Argument0
    c. Undefined
    d. Undefined

82. A _____ is a three-dimensional geometric shape formed by straight lines through a fixed point (vertex) to the points of a fixed curve (directrix)
    a. Concept
    b. Cone0
    c. Undefined
    d. Undefined

83. A _____ is a set of numbers that designate location in a given reference system, such as x,y in a planar _____ system or an x,y,z in a three-dimensional _____ system.
    a. Coordinate0
    b. Thing
    c. Undefined
    d. Undefined

84. A _____ is a function that assigns a number to subsets of a given set.
    a. Measure0
    b. Thing
    c. Undefined
    d. Undefined

85. _____ is mass m per unit volume V.
   a. Density0
   b. Thing
   c. Undefined
   d. Undefined

86. A _____ is a special kind of ratio, indicating a relationship between two measurements with different units, such as miles to gallons or cents to pounds.
   a. Rate0
   b. Thing
   c. Undefined
   d. Undefined

87. Isaac Newton's _____ states the following: Every single point mass attracts every other point mass by a force pointing along the line combining the two.
   a. Thing
   b. Law of gravitation0
   c. Undefined
   d. Undefined

88. In physics, an _____ is the path that an object makes around another object while under the influence of a source of centripetal force, such as gravity.
   a. Orbit0
   b. Thing
   c. Undefined
   d. Undefined

89. In mathematics, an _____, mean, or central tendency of a data set refers to a measure of the "middle" or "expected" value of the data set.
   a. Concept
   b. Average0
   c. Undefined
   d. Undefined

90. _____ is an extension of the concept of a sum.
   a. Thing
   b. Definite integral0
   c. Undefined
   d. Undefined

91. The _____, the average in everyday English, which is also called the arithmetic _____ (and is distinguished from the geometric _____ or harmonic _____). The average is also called the sample _____. The expected value of a random variable, which is also called the population _____.
   a. Thing
   b. Mean0
   c. Undefined
   d. Undefined

92. In mathematics, a _____ is a statement that can be proved on the basis of explicitly stated or previously agreed assumptions.
   a. Thing
   b. Theorem0
   c. Undefined
   d. Undefined

93. The _____ is a measurement of how a function changes when the values of its inputs change.
   a. Derivative0
   b. Thing
   c. Undefined
   d. Undefined

94. In number theory, the _____ of arithmetic (or unique factorization theorem) states that every natural number greater than 1 can be written as a unique product of prime numbers.

Chapter 6. Applications of Integration

a. Concept
b. Fundamental theorem0
c. Undefined
d. Undefined

95. _____ of calculus is the statement that the two central operations of calculus, differentiation and integration, are inverse operations: if a continuous function is first integrated and then differentiated, the original function is retrieved.
a. Thing
b. Fundamental Theorem of Calculus0
c. Undefined
d. Undefined

96. In topology and related areas of mathematics a _____ or Moore-Smith sequence is a generalization of a sequence, intended to unify the various notions of limit and generalize them to arbitrary topological spaces.
a. Thing
b. Net0
c. Undefined
d. Undefined

97. The word _____ comes from the Latin word linearis, which means created by lines.
a. Thing
b. Linear0
c. Undefined
d. Undefined

98. The _____ consists of an inhalation and an exhalation.
a. Respiratory cycle0
b. Thing
c. Undefined
d. Undefined

99. In astronomy, geography, geometry and related sciences and contexts, a plane is said to be _____ at a given point if it is locally perpendicular to the gradient of the gravity field, i.e., with the direction of the gravitational force at that point.
a. Horizontal0
b. Thing
c. Undefined
d. Undefined

100. In geometry, _____ lines are two lines that share one or more common points.
a. Intersecting0
b. Thing
c. Undefined
d. Undefined

101. A _____ is a quadrilateral, which is defined as a shape with four sides, which has a pair of parallel sides.
a. Thing
b. Trapezoid0
c. Undefined
d. Undefined

102. _____ of Syracuse was an ancient Greek mathematician, physicist and engineer. In addition to making important discoveries in the field of mathematics and geometry, he is credited with producing machines that were well ahead of their time.
a. Archimedes0
b. Person
c. Undefined
d. Undefined

103. A _____ is a three-dimensional solid object bounded by six square faces, facets, or sides, with three meeting at each vertex.
a. Cube0
b. Thing
c. Undefined
d. Undefined

Chapter 6. Applications of Integration

104. In mathematics, two quantities are called _____ if they vary in such a way that one of the quantities is a constant multiple of the other, or equivalently if they have a constant ratio.
   a. Proportional0
   b. Thing
   c. Undefined
   d. Undefined

105. _____ means "constancy", i.e. if something retains a certain feature even after we change a way of looking at it, then it is symmetric.
   a. Symmetry0
   b. Thing
   c. Undefined
   d. Undefined

106. _____ of a two-dimensional figure is a line such that, if a perpendicular is constructed, any two points lying on the perpendicular at equal distances from the _____ are identical.
   a. Axis of symmetry0
   b. Thing
   c. Undefined
   d. Undefined

107. In linear algebra and geometry, a rotation (_____) is a type of transformation from one system of coordinates to another system of coordinates such that distance between any two points remains invariant under the transformation.
   a. Thing
   b. Rotational0
   c. Undefined
   d. Undefined

108. In physics, the _____ momentum of an object rotating about some reference point is the measure of the extent to which the object will continue to rotate about that point unless acted upon by an external torque.
   a. Thing
   b. Angular0
   c. Undefined
   d. Undefined

109. _____ is a scalar measure of rotation rate. It is the magnitude of the vector quantity angular velocity.
   a. Angular frequency0
   b. Thing
   c. Undefined
   d. Undefined

110. _____ is a scalar measure of rotation rate. It is the magnitude of the vector quantity angular velocity.
   a. Thing
   b. Angular speed0
   c. Undefined
   d. Undefined

111. A _____ function curves downwards. The graph of a _____ function of one variable remains above its tangents and below its cords.
   a. Convex0
   b. Thing
   c. Undefined
   d. Undefined

112. _____ is a quadric
   a. Paraboloid0
   b. Thing
   c. Undefined
   d. Undefined

113. _____ is an adjective usually refering to being in the centre.
   a. Central0
   b. Thing
   c. Undefined
   d. Undefined

Chapter 7. Techniques of Integration

1. The _____ of a function is an extension of the concept of a sum, and are identified or found through the use of integration.
   - a. Thing
   - b. Integral0
   - c. Undefined
   - d. Undefined

2. An _____ of a function f is a function F whose derivative is equal to f, i.e., F' = f.
   - a. Thing
   - b. Antiderivative0
   - c. Undefined
   - d. Undefined

3. In mathematics, a _____ is a statement that can be proved on the basis of explicitly stated or previously agreed assumptions.
   - a. Theorem0
   - b. Thing
   - c. Undefined
   - d. Undefined

4. _____ is a mathematical subject that includes the study of limits, derivatives, integrals, and power series and constitutes a major part of modern university curriculum.
   - a. Thing
   - b. Calculus0
   - c. Undefined
   - d. Undefined

5. The mathematical concept of a _____ expresses the intuitive idea of deterministic dependence between two quantities, one of which is viewed as primary and the other as secondary. A _____ then is a way to associate a unique output for each input of a specified type, for example, a real number or an element of a given set.
   - a. Thing
   - b. Function0
   - c. Undefined
   - d. Undefined

6. In number theory, the _____ of arithmetic (or unique factorization theorem) states that every natural number greater than 1 can be written as a unique product of prime numbers.
   - a. Concept
   - b. Fundamental theorem0
   - c. Undefined
   - d. Undefined

7. _____ of calculus is the statement that the two central operations of calculus, differentiation and integration, are inverse operations: if a continuous function is first integrated and then differentiated, the original function is retrieved.
   - a. Fundamental Theorem of Calculus0
   - b. Thing
   - c. Undefined
   - d. Undefined

8. _____ is a process of combining or accumulating. It may also refer to:
   - a. Thing
   - b. Integration0
   - c. Undefined
   - d. Undefined

9. _____, a field in mathematics, is the study of how functions change when their inputs change. The primary object of study in _____ is the derivative.
   - a. Differential calculus0
   - b. Thing
   - c. Undefined
   - d. Undefined

10. In mathematics, a _____ is the result of multiplying, or an expression that identifies factors to be multiplied.

Chapter 7. Techniques of Integration

    a. Product0   b. Thing
    c. Undefined   d. Undefined

11. The _____ governs the differentiation of products of differentiable functions.
    a. Product rule0   b. Thing
    c. Undefined   d. Undefined

12. A _____ is a negotiable instrument instructing a financial institution to pay a specific amount of a specific currency from a specific demand account held in the maker/depositor's name with that institution. Both the maker and payee may be natural persons or legal entities.
    a. Check0   b. Thing
    c. Undefined   d. Undefined

13. _____ is an extension of the concept of a sum.
    a. Definite integral0   b. Thing
    c. Undefined   d. Undefined

14. In mathematics and the mathematical sciences, a _____ is a fixed, but possibly unspecified, value. This is in contrast to a variable, which is not fixed.
    a. Thing   b. Constant0
    c. Undefined   d. Undefined

15. In calculus, the indefinite integral of a given function i.e. the set of all antiderivatives of the function is always written with a constant, the _____.
    a. Thing   b. Constant of integration0
    c. Undefined   d. Undefined

16. A _____ function is a function for which, intuitively, small changes in the input result in small changes in the output.
    a. Continuous0   b. Event
    c. Undefined   d. Undefined

17. In mathematics, _____ refers to the rewriting of an expression into a simpler form.
    a. Reduction0   b. Thing
    c. Undefined   d. Undefined

18. In mathematics, the concept of a _____ tries to capture the intuitive idea of a geometrical one-dimensional and continuous object. A simple example is the circle.
    a. Thing   b. Curve0
    c. Undefined   d. Undefined

19. In mathematics, _____ are the intuitive idea of a geometrical one-dimensional and continuous object.
    a. Thing   b. Curves0
    c. Undefined   d. Undefined

Chapter 7. Techniques of Integration

20. In mathematical analysis and related areas of mathematics, a set is called _____, if it is, in a certain sense, of finite size.
    a. Bounded0
    b. Thing
    c. Undefined
    d. Undefined

21. In mathematics, the _____ of two sets A and B is the set that contains all elements of A that also belong to B (or equivalently, all elements of B that also belong to A), but no other elements.
    a. Thing
    b. Intersection0
    c. Undefined
    d. Undefined

22. The _____ of a solid object is the three-dimensional concept of how much space it occupies, often quantified numerically.
    a. Thing
    b. Volume0
    c. Undefined
    d. Undefined

23. An _____ is a straight line around which a geometric figure can be rotated.
    a. Thing
    b. Axis0
    c. Undefined
    d. Undefined

24. In mathematics, an _____, mean, or central tendency of a data set refers to a measure of the "middle" or "expected" value of the data set.
    a. Concept
    b. Average0
    c. Undefined
    d. Undefined

25. In elementary algebra, an _____ is a set that contains every real number between two indicated numbers and may contain the two numbers themselves.
    a. Thing
    b. Interval0
    c. Undefined
    d. Undefined

26. _____ is the property of a physical object that quantifies the amount of matter and energy it is equivalent to.
    a. Thing
    b. Mass0
    c. Undefined
    d. Undefined

27. A _____ is a vehicle, missile or aircraft which obtains thrust by the reaction to the ejection of fast moving fluid from within a _____ engine.
    a. Rocket0
    b. Thing
    c. Undefined
    d. Undefined

28. _____ of an object is its speed in a particular direction.
    a. Velocity0
    b. Thing
    c. Undefined
    d. Undefined

29. The metre (or _____, see spelling differences) is a measure of length. It is the basic unit of length in the metric system and in the International System of Units (SI), used around the world for general and scientific purposes.

a. Concept   b. Meter0
c. Undefined   d. Undefined

30. A _____ is a simplified and structured visual representation of concepts, ideas, constructions, relations, statistical data, anatomy etc used in all aspects of human activities to visualize and clarify the topic.
a. Diagram0   b. Thing
c. Undefined   d. Undefined

31. _____ element of an element x with respect to a binary operation * with identity element e is an element y such that x * y = y * x = e. In particular,
a. Inverse0   b. Thing
c. Undefined   d. Undefined

32. An _____ is a function which does the reverse of a given function.
a. Inverse function0   b. Thing
c. Undefined   d. Undefined

33. John Brehaut _____ was born in Ashford, Kent, the third of five children.
a. Wallis0   b. Person
c. Undefined   d. Undefined

34. The _____ for π was written down in 1655 by John Wallis.
a. Wallis product0   b. Thing
c. Undefined   d. Undefined

35. _____ is the state of being greater than any finite real or natural number, however large.
a. Thing   b. Infinite0
c. Undefined   d. Undefined

36. In geometry, a _____ is defined as a quadrilateral where all four of its angles are right angles.
a. Thing   b. Rectangle0
c. Undefined   d. Undefined

37. A _____ is a quantity that denotes the proportional amount or magnitude of one quantity relative to another.
a. Thing   b. Ratio0
c. Undefined   d. Undefined

38. In plane geometry, a _____ is a polygon with four equal sides, four right angles, and parallel opposite sides. In algebra, the _____ of a number is that number multiplied by itself.
a. Square0   b. Thing
c. Undefined   d. Undefined

39. The _____ of an angle is the ratio of the length of the adjacent side to the length of the hypotenuse.
a. Cosine0   b. Concept
c. Undefined   d. Undefined

Chapter 7. Techniques of Integration

40. _____ has many meanings, most of which simply .
   a. Power0
   b. Thing
   c. Undefined
   d. Undefined

41. An _____ is a combination of numbers, operators, grouping symbols and/or free variables and bound variables arranged in a meaningful way which can be evaluated..
   a. Thing
   b. Expression0
   c. Undefined
   d. Undefined

42. _____ is a trigonemtric function that is important when studying triangles and modeling periodic phenomena, among other applications.
   a. Sine0
   b. Thing
   c. Undefined
   d. Undefined

43. _____ is a function that extends the concept of an ordinary sum
   a. Integrand0
   b. Thing
   c. Undefined
   d. Undefined

44. In mathematics, factorization (British English: factorisation) or factoring is the decomposition of an object (for example, a number, a polynomial, or a matrix) into a product of other objects, or _____, which when multiplied together give the original.
   a. Factors0
   b. Thing
   c. Undefined
   d. Undefined

45. In mathematics, the _____ functions are functions of an angle; they are important when studying triangles and modeling periodic phenomena, among many other applications.
   a. Trigonometric0
   b. Thing
   c. Undefined
   d. Undefined

46. An _____ is an equality that remains true regardless of the values of any variables that appear within it, to distinguish it from an equality which is true under more particular conditions.
   a. Thing
   b. Identity0
   c. Undefined
   d. Undefined

47. In trigonometry, the _____ is a function defined as $\tan x = \sin x / \cos x$. The function is so-named because it can be defined as the length of a certain segment of a _____ (in the geometric sense) to the unit circle. In plane geometry, a line is _____ to a curve, at some point, if both line and curve pass through the point with the same direction.
   a. Thing
   b. Tangent0
   c. Undefined
   d. Undefined

48. _____ is a trigonometric function that is the reciprocal of cosine.
   a. Secant0
   b. Thing
   c. Undefined
   d. Undefined

49. _____ is the difference of electrical potential between two points of an electrical or electronic circuit, expressed in volts

a. Thing
b. Voltage0
c. Undefined
d. Undefined

50. In mathematics, a _____ of a number x is a number r such that r^2 = x, or in words, a number r whose square (the result of multiplying the number by itself) is x.
    a. Thing
    b. Square root0
    c. Undefined
    d. Undefined

51. In mathematics, a _____ of a complex-valued function f is a member x of the domain of f such that f(x) vanishes at x, that is, x : f (x) = 0.
    a. Thing
    b. Root0
    c. Undefined
    d. Undefined

52. The _____ are the only integral domain whose positive elements are well-ordered, and in which order is preserved by addition. Like the natural numbers, the _____ form a countably infinite set. The set of all _____ is usually denoted in mathematics by a boldface Z .
    a. Integers0
    b. Thing
    c. Undefined
    d. Undefined

53. The _____ is a nonnegative scalar measure of a wave's magnitude of oscillation, that is, the magnitude of the maximum disturbance in the medium during one wave cycle.
    a. Amplitude0
    b. Thing
    c. Undefined
    d. Undefined

54. A _____ is the sum of the elements of a sequence.
    a. Series0
    b. Thing
    c. Undefined
    d. Undefined

55. A _____ is the result of the addition of a set of numbers. The numbers may be natural numbers, complex numbers, matrices, or still more complicated objects. An infinite _____ is a subtle procedure known as a series.
    a. Thing
    b. Sum0
    c. Undefined
    d. Undefined

56. In mathematics, a _____ is a constant multiplicative factor of a certain object. The object can be such things as a variable, a vector, a function, etc. For example, the _____ of $9x^2$ is 9.
    a. Coefficient0
    b. Thing
    c. Undefined
    d. Undefined

57. In mathematics, a set is called _____ if there is a bijection between the set and some set of the form {1, 2, ..., n} where n is a natural number.
    a. Thing
    b. Finite0
    c. Undefined
    d. Undefined

58. In mathematics,_____ is the substitution of trigonometric functions for other expressions.

Chapter 7. Techniques of Integration

a. Thing
b. Trigonometric substitution0
c. Undefined
d. Undefined

59. In Euclidean geometry, a _____ is the set of all points in a plane at a fixed distance, called the radius, from a given point, the center.
   a. Circle0
   b. Thing
   c. Undefined
   d. Undefined

60. In mathematics, an _____ .
   a. Thing
   b. Ellipse0
   c. Undefined
   d. Undefined

61. A _____ is a symbolic representation denoting a quantity or expression. It often represents an "unknown" quantity that has the potential to change.
   a. Thing
   b. Variable0
   c. Undefined
   d. Undefined

62. The _____ is a tool for finding antiderivatives and integrals. It is the counterpart to the chain rule of differentiation.
   a. Substitution rule0
   b. Thing
   c. Undefined
   d. Undefined

63. A _____ is a deliberate process for transforming one or more inputs into one or more results.
   a. Calculation0
   b. Thing
   c. Undefined
   d. Undefined

64. In mathematics and logic, a _____ proof is a way of showing the truth or falsehood of a given statement by a straightforward combination of established facts, usually existing lemmas and theorems, without making any further assumptions.
   a. Thing
   b. Direct0
   c. Undefined
   d. Undefined

65. A _____ is one of the basic shapes of geometry: a polygon with three vertices and three sides which are straight line segments.
   a. Thing
   b. Triangle0
   c. Undefined
   d. Undefined

66. Equivalence is the condition of being _____ or essentially equal.
   a. Thing
   b. Equivalent0
   c. Undefined
   d. Undefined

67. _____ is a technique used in algebra to solve quadratic equations, in analytic geometry for determining the shapes of graphs, and in calculus for computing integrals, including, but hardly limited to, the integrals that define Laplace transforms. The essential objective is to reduce a quadratic polynomial in a variable in an equation or expression to a squared polynomial of linear order. This can reduce an equation or integral to one that is more easily solved or evaluated.

Chapter 7. Techniques of Integration

a. Completing the square0
b. Thing
c. Undefined
d. Undefined

68. A circular _____ or circle _____ also known as a pie piece is the portion of a circle enclosed by two radii and an arc.
   a. Sector0
   b. Thing
   c. Undefined
   d. Undefined

69. In geometry, the _____ of an object is a point in some sense in the middle of the object.
   a. Center0
   b. Thing
   c. Undefined
   d. Undefined

70. _____ is an adjective usually refering to being in the centre.
   a. Central0
   b. Thing
   c. Undefined
   d. Undefined

71. In classical geometry, a _____ of a circle or sphere is any line segment from its center to its boundary. By extension, the _____ of a circle or sphere is the length of any such segment. The _____ is half the diameter. In science and engineering the term _____ of curvature is commonly used as a synonym for _____.
   a. Radius0
   b. Thing
   c. Undefined
   d. Undefined

72. In mathematics, the _____ of a coordinate system is the point where the axes of the system intersect.
   a. Thing
   b. Origin0
   c. Undefined
   d. Undefined

73. In mathematics, a _____ is a type of conic section defined as the intersection between a right circular conical surface and a plane which cuts through both halves of the cone.
   a. Hyperbola0
   b. Thing
   c. Undefined
   d. Undefined

74. In mathematics, a _____ is a quadric surface, with the following equation in Cartesian coordinates: $(x/_a)^2 + (y/_b)^2 = 1$.
   a. Cylinder0
   b. Thing
   c. Undefined
   d. Undefined

75. In geometry, a _____ (Greek words diairo = divide and metro = measure) of a circle is any straight line segment that passes through the centre and whose endpoints are on the circular boundary, or, in more modern usage, the length of such a line segment. When using the word in the more modern sense, one speaks of the _____ rather than a _____, because all diameters of a circle have the same length. This length is twice the radius. The _____ of a circle is also the longest chord that the circle has.
   a. Thing
   b. Diameter0
   c. Undefined
   d. Undefined

Chapter 7. Techniques of Integration

76. In geometry, a _____ is a surface of revolution generated by revolving a circle in three dimensional space about an axis coplanar with the circle, which does not touch the circle. Examples of tori include the surfaces of doughnuts and inner tubes. A circle rotated about a chord of the circle is called a _____ in some contexts, but this is not a common usage in mathematics. The shape produced when a circle is rotated about a chord resembles a round cushion. _____ was the Latin word for a cushion of this shape.
    a. Thing
    b. Torus0
    c. Undefined
    d. Undefined

77. A _____ fraction is a fraction in which the absolute value of the numerator is less than the denominator--hence, the absolute value of the fraction is less than 1.
    a. Thing
    b. Proper0
    c. Undefined
    d. Undefined

78. In mathematics, a _____ number is a number which can be expressed as a ratio of two integers. Non-integer _____ numbers (commonly called fractions) are usually written as the vulgar fraction a / b, where b is not zero.
    a. Thing
    b. Rational0
    c. Undefined
    d. Undefined

79. In mathematics, a _____ is any function which can be written as the ratio of two polynomial functions.
    a. Thing
    b. Rational function0
    c. Undefined
    d. Undefined

80. In mathematics, there are several meanings of _____ depending on the subject.
    a. Degree0
    b. Thing
    c. Undefined
    d. Undefined

81. In common philosophical language, a proposition or _____, is the content of an assertion, that is, it is true-or-false and defined by the meaning of a particular piece of language.
    a. Statement0
    b. Concept
    c. Undefined
    d. Undefined

82. In arithmetic, _____ is a procedure for calculating the division of one integer, called the dividend, by another integer called the divisor, to produce a result called the quotient.
    a. Long division0
    b. Thing
    c. Undefined
    d. Undefined

83. A _____ is the part of the dividend that is left over when the dividend is not evenly divisible by the divisor.
    a. Thing
    b. Remainder0
    c. Undefined
    d. Undefined

84. In mathematics, a _____ is an expression that is constructed from one or more variables and constants, using only the operations of addition, subtraction, multiplication, and constant positive whole number exponents. is a _____. Note in particular that division by an expression containing a variable is not in general allowed in polynomials. [1]
    a. Thing
    b. Polynomial0
    c. Undefined
    d. Undefined

Chapter 7. Techniques of Integration

85. The word _____ comes from the Latin word linearis, which means created by lines.
    a. Linear0
    b. Thing
    c. Undefined
    d. Undefined

86. In algebra, the _____ decomposition or _____ expansion is used to reduce the degree of either the numerator or the denominator of a rational function.
    a. Partial fraction0
    b. Thing
    c. Undefined
    d. Undefined

87. _____ is a branch of mathematics concerning the study of structure, relation and quantity.
    a. Concept
    b. Algebra0
    c. Undefined
    d. Undefined

88. A _____ is the part of a fraction that tells how many equal parts make up a whole, and which is used in the name of the fraction: "halves", "thirds", "fourths" or "quarters", "fifths" and so on.
    a. Denominator0
    b. Concept
    c. Undefined
    d. Undefined

89. A _____ is a numeral used to indicate a count. The most common use of the word today is to name the part of a fraction that tells the number or count of equal parts.
    a. Thing
    b. Numerator0
    c. Undefined
    d. Undefined

90. _____ is a fixed, but possibly unspecified, value. This is in contrast to a variable, which is not fixed.
    a. Constant term0
    b. Thing
    c. Undefined
    d. Undefined

91. The _____, the average in everyday English, which is also called the arithmetic _____ (and is distinguished from the geometric _____ or harmonic _____). The average is also called the sample _____. The expected value of a random variable, which is also called the population _____.
    a. Mean0
    b. Thing
    c. Undefined
    d. Undefined

92. _____ of a polynomial with real or complex coefficients is a certain expression in the coefficients of the polynomial which is equal to zero if and only if the polynomial has a multiple root i.e. a root with multiplicity greater than one in the complex numbers.
    a. Discriminant0
    b. Thing
    c. Undefined
    d. Undefined

93. _____ refers to the reduction of the body of a formerly living organism into simpler forms of matter.
    a. Decomposing0
    b. Thing
    c. Undefined
    d. Undefined

94. _____ has one 90° internal angle a right angle.

a. Right triangle0
b. Thing
c. Undefined
d. Undefined

95. In mathematics, _____ geometry was the traditional name for the geometry of three-dimensional Euclidean space — for practical purposes the kind of space we live in.
   a. Solid0
   b. Thing
   c. Undefined
   d. Undefined

96. In sociology and biology a _____ is the collection of people or organisms of a particular species living in a given geographic area or space, usually measured by a census.
   a. Population0
   b. Thing
   c. Undefined
   d. Undefined

97. In mathematics, _____ is the decomposition of an object into a product of other objects, or factors, which when multiplied together give the original.
   a. Thing
   b. Factoring0
   c. Undefined
   d. Undefined

98. In geographic information systems, a _____ comprises an entity with a geographic location, typically determined by points, arcs, or polygons. Carriageways and cadastres exemplify _____ data.
   a. Feature0
   b. Thing
   c. Undefined
   d. Undefined

99. A _____ is a polynomial function of the form $f(x) = ax^2 + bx + c$, where a, b, c are real numbers and a , 0.
   a. Event
   b. Quadratic function0
   c. Undefined
   d. Undefined

100. The _____ is a measurement of how a function changes when the values of its inputs change.
   a. Derivative0
   b. Thing
   c. Undefined
   d. Undefined

101. A _____ is traditionally an infinitesimally small change in a variable.
   a. Differential0
   b. Thing
   c. Undefined
   d. Undefined

102. The _____ are functions of an angle; they are important when studying triangles and modeling periodic phenomena, among many other applications.
   a. Thing
   b. Trigonometric functions0
   c. Undefined
   d. Undefined

103. In mathematics, a _____ number is a real or complex number which is not algebraic, that is, not a solution of a non-zero polynomial equation, with rational coefficients.
   a. Transcendental0
   b. Thing
   c. Undefined
   d. Undefined

Chapter 7. Techniques of Integration

104. In mathematics, _____ growth occurs when the growth rate of a function is always proportional to the function's current size.
   a. Thing
   b. Exponential0
   c. Undefined
   d. Undefined

105. _____ is the symbold used to indicate the nth root of a number
   a. Thing
   b. Radical0
   c. Undefined
   d. Undefined

106. In mathematics, _____ are used to indicate the square root of a number.
   a. Radicals0
   b. Thing
   c. Undefined
   d. Undefined

107. _____, or Rationalisation in mathematics is the process of removing a square root or imaginary number from the denominator of a fraction.
   a. Rationalizing0
   b. Thing
   c. Undefined
   d. Undefined

108. _____ is a method of solving problems of simultaneous congruences by using the definition of the congruence equation.
   a. Successive substitution0
   b. Thing
   c. Undefined
   d. Undefined

109. In mathematics, the _____ is an important formula giving the expansion of powers of sums.
   a. Binomial Theorem0
   b. Thing
   c. Undefined
   d. Undefined

110. In elementary algebra, a _____ is a polynomial with two terms: the sum of two monomials. It is the simplest kind of polynomial except for a monomial.
   a. Binomial0
   b. Thing
   c. Undefined
   d. Undefined

111. An _____ or an extremal point is a point that belongs to the extremity of something.
   a. Thing
   b. Extreme point0
   c. Undefined
   d. Undefined

112. _____ is a a point on a curve at which the tangent crosses the curve itself.
   a. Thing
   b. Inflection point0
   c. Undefined
   d. Undefined

113. In mathematics, a _____ is a mathematical statement which appears likely to be true, but has not been formally proven to be true under the rules of mathematical logic.
   a. Conjecture0
   b. Concept
   c. Undefined
   d. Undefined

114. _____ is a method for approximating the values of integrals.

Chapter 7. Techniques of Integration

a. Thing
b. Riemann sum0
c. Undefined
d. Undefined

115. In geometry, an _____ is a point at which a line segment or ray terminates.
   a. Endpoint0
   b. Thing
   c. Undefined
   d. Undefined

116. _____ is the middle point of a line segment.
   a. Midpoint0
   b. Thing
   c. Undefined
   d. Undefined

117. _____ the American term is a way to approximately calculate the definite integral
   a. Thing
   b. Trapezoidal Rule0
   c. Undefined
   d. Undefined

118. A _____ is a quadrilateral, which is defined as a shape with four sides, which has a pair of parallel sides.
   a. Thing
   b. Trapezoid0
   c. Undefined
   d. Undefined

119. _____ is a kind of property which exists as magnitude or multitude. It is among the basic classes of things along with quality, substance, change, and relation.
   a. Amount0
   b. Thing
   c. Undefined
   d. Undefined

120. In mathematics, the additive inverse, or _____ of a number n is the number that, when added to n, yields zero. The additive inverse of n is denoted −n. For example, 7 is −7, because 7 + (−7) = 0, and the additive inverse of −0.3 is 0.3, because −0.3 + 0.3 = 0.
   a. Opposite0
   b. Thing
   c. Undefined
   d. Undefined

121. In mathematics, the _____ of a number n is the number that, when added to n, yields zero. The _____ of n is denoted −n. For example, 7 is −7, because 7 + (−7) = 0, and the _____ of −0.3 is 0.3, because −0.3 + 0.3 = 0.
   a. Thing
   b. Additive inverse0
   c. Undefined
   d. Undefined

122. A _____ is 360° or 2δ radians.
   a. Thing
   b. Turn0
   c. Undefined
   d. Undefined

123. A _____ is a function that assigns a number to subsets of a given set.
   a. Thing
   b. Measure0
   c. Undefined
   d. Undefined

124. In mathematics, an _____ is a statement about the relative size or order of two objects.

Chapter 7. Techniques of Integration

a. Inequality0
b. Thing
c. Undefined
d. Undefined

125. In mathematics, especially in order theory, an _____ of a subset S of some partially ordered set is an element of P which is greater than or equal to every element of S.
   a. Upper bound0
   b. Thing
   c. Undefined
   d. Undefined

126. In geometry, a line _____ is a part of a line that is bounded by two end points, and contains every point on the line between its end points.
   a. Concept
   b. Segment0
   c. Undefined
   d. Undefined

127. In mathematics, the _____ is a conic section generated by the intersection of a right circular conical surface and a plane parallel to a generating straight line of that surface. It can also be defined as locus of points in a plane which are equidistant from a given point.
   a. Thing
   b. Parabola0
   c. Undefined
   d. Undefined

128. A _____ is a part of a line that is bounded by two end points, and contains every point on the line between its end points.
   a. Line segment0
   b. Thing
   c. Undefined
   d. Undefined

129. The _____ function (weight function) is a mathematical device used when performing a sum, integral, or average in order to give some elements more of a "weight" than others.
   a. Weighted0
   b. Thing
   c. Undefined
   d. Undefined

130. In mathematics, the _____(e) for L-functions are a class of summation formulae, expressing sums taken over the complex number zeroes of a given L-function, typically in terms of quantities studied by number theory by use of the theory of special functions.
   a. Thing
   b. Explicit formula0
   c. Undefined
   d. Undefined

131. In Graph theory, a _____ is a digraph with weighted edges.
   a. Concept
   b. Network0
   c. Undefined
   d. Undefined

132. _____ is a synonym for information.
   a. Data0
   b. Thing
   c. Undefined
   d. Undefined

133. _____ constitutes a broad family of algorithms for calculating the numerical value of a definite integral, and by extension, the term is also sometimes used to describe the numerical solution of differential equations.

Chapter 7. Techniques of Integration

a. Numerical integration0
c. Undefined
b. Thing
d. Undefined

134. In Euclidean geometry, an _____ is a closed segment of a differentiable curve in the two-dimensional plane; for example, a circular _____ is a segment of a circle.
   a. Concept
   b. Arc0
   c. Undefined
   d. Undefined

135. In physics, _____ is an influence that may cause an object to accelerate. It may be experienced as a lift, a push, or a pull. The actual acceleration of the body is determined by the vector sum of all forces acting on it, known as net _____ or resultant _____.
   a. Force0
   b. Thing
   c. Undefined
   d. Undefined

136. A _____ is an object that is attached to a pivot point so that it can swing freely.
   a. Thing
   b. Pendulum0
   c. Undefined
   d. Undefined

137. Sir Isaac _____, was an English physicist, mathematician, astronomer, natural philosopher, and alchemist, regarded by many as the greatest figure in the history of science
   a. Person
   b. Newton0
   c. Undefined
   d. Undefined

138. In business, particularly accounting, a _____ is the time intervals that the accounts, statement, payments, or other calculations cover.
   a. Thing
   b. Period0
   c. Undefined
   d. Undefined

139. _____ is defined as the rate of change or derivative with respect to time of velocity.
   a. Thing
   b. Acceleration0
   c. Undefined
   d. Undefined

140. _____ is electromagnetic radiation with a wavelength that is visible to the eye (visible _____) or, in a technical or scientific context, electromagnetic radiation of any wavelength.
   a. Thing
   b. Light0
   c. Undefined
   d. Undefined

141. A _____ is a function for which, intuitively, small changes in the input result in small changes in the output.
   a. Continuous function0
   b. Event
   c. Undefined
   d. Undefined

142. _____ is the chance that something is likely to happen or be the case.
   a. Probability0
   b. Thing
   c. Undefined
   d. Undefined

Chapter 7. Techniques of Integration

143. _____ that assigns a probability to every subset of its state space in such a way that the probability axioms are satisfied.
   a. Thing
   b. Probability distribution0
   c. Undefined
   d. Undefined

144. In mathematical analysis, _____ are objects which generalize functions and probability distributions.
   a. Thing
   b. Distribution0
   c. Undefined
   d. Undefined

145. In mathematics, _____ describes an entity with a limit.
   a. Convergent0
   b. Thing
   c. Undefined
   d. Undefined

146. In mathematics, a _____ series is an infinite series that is not convergent, meaning that the infinite sequence of the partial sums of the series does not have a limit.
   a. Thing
   b. Divergent0
   c. Undefined
   d. Undefined

147. An _____ is the limit of a definite integral, as an endpoint of the interval of integration approaches either a specified real number or ‡ or − ‡ or, in some cases, as both endpoints approach limits.
   a. Improper integral0
   b. Thing
   c. Undefined
   d. Undefined

148. Continuous functions are of utmost importance in mathematics and applications. However, not all functions are continuous. If a function is not continuous at a point in its domain, one says that it has a _____ there. The set of all points of _____ of a function may be a discrete set, a dense set, or even the entire domain of the function.
   a. Thing
   b. Discontinuity0
   c. Undefined
   d. Undefined

149. _____ is a straight line or curve A to which another curve B the one being studied approaches closer and closer as one moves along it.
   a. Thing
   b. Vertical asymptote0
   c. Undefined
   d. Undefined

150. An _____ is a straight line or curve A to which another curve B approaches closer and closer as one moves along it. As one moves along B, the space between it and the _____ A becomes smaller and smaller, and can in fact be made as small as one could wish by going far enough along. A curve may or may not touch or cross its _____. In fact, the curve may intersect the _____ an infinite number of times.
   a. Asymptote0
   b. Thing
   c. Undefined
   d. Undefined

151. Acid _____ ratio measures the ability of a company to use its near cash or quick assets to immediately extinguish its current liabilities.
   a. Test0
   b. Thing
   c. Undefined
   d. Undefined

Chapter 7. Techniques of Integration

152. _____ is a criterion for convergence or divergence of a series whose terms are real or complex numbers.
  a. Comparison test0
  b. Thing
  c. Undefined
  d. Undefined

153. _____ are the basic objects of study in graph theory. Informally speaking, a graph is a set of objects called points, nodes, or vertices connected by links called lines or edges.
  a. Graphs0
  b. Thing
  c. Undefined
  d. Undefined

154. _____ is a method of mathematical proof typically used to establish that a given statement is true of all natural numbers
  a. Mathematical induction0
  b. Thing
  c. Undefined
  d. Undefined

155. _____ is a physical property of a system that underlies the common notions of hot and cold; something that is hotter has the greater _____.
  a. Thing
  b. Temperature0
  c. Undefined
  d. Undefined

156. In _____ algebra, a *-ring is an associative ring with an antilinear, antiautomorphism * : A ¨ A which is an involution.
  a. Thing
  b. Star0
  c. Undefined
  d. Undefined

157. _____ is mass m per unit volume V.
  a. Thing
  b. Density0
  c. Undefined
  d. Undefined

158. Initial objects are also called _____, and terminal objects are also called final.
  a. Coterminal0
  b. Thing
  c. Undefined
  d. Undefined

159. _____ is a radiometric dating method that uses the naturally occurring isotope carbon-14 to determine the age of carbonaceous materials up to about 60,000 years.
  a. Radiocarbon dating0
  b. Thing
  c. Undefined
  d. Undefined

160. In mathematics, a _____ of a k-place relation $L \subseteq X_1 \times ... \times X_k$ is one of the sets X_j, $1 \leq j \leq k$. In the special case where k = 2 and $L \subseteq X_1 \times X_2$ is a function $L : X_1 \to X_2$, it is conventional to refer to X_1 as the _____ of the function and to refer to X_2 as the codomain of the function.
  a. Thing
  b. Domain0
  c. Undefined
  d. Undefined

161. The _____ of a mathematical object is its size: a property by which it can be larger or smaller than other objects of the same kind; in technical terms, an ordering of the class of objects to which it belongs.

a. Thing
b. Magnitude0
c. Undefined
d. Undefined

162. _____ is the state of being greater than any finite number, however large.
a. Infinity0
b. Thing
c. Undefined
d. Undefined

163. In physics, a _____ may refer to the scalar _____ or to the vector _____.
a. Thing
b. Potential0
c. Undefined
d. Undefined

164. The _____ or kilogramme is the SI base unit of mass. It is defined as being equal to the mass of the international prototype of the _____.
a. Thing
b. Kilogram0
c. Undefined
d. Undefined

165. A _____ is a special kind of ratio, indicating a relationship between two measurements with different units, such as miles to gallons or cents to pounds.
a. Thing
b. Rate0
c. Undefined
d. Undefined

166. In mathematics, in the field of differential equations, an initial value problem is a differential equation together with specified value, called the _____, of the unknown function at a given point in the domain of the solution.
a. Initial condition0
b. Thing
c. Undefined
d. Undefined

Chapter 8. Further Applications of Integration 135

1. The _____ of a solid object is the three-dimensional concept of how much space it occupies, often quantified numerically.
   a. Volume0
   b. Thing
   c. Undefined
   d. Undefined

2. In mathematics, an _____, mean, or central tendency of a data set refers to a measure of the "middle" or "expected" value of the data set.
   a. Average0
   b. Concept
   c. Undefined
   d. Undefined

3. The _____ of a function is an extension of the concept of a sum, and are identified or found through the use of integration.
   a. Integral0
   b. Thing
   c. Undefined
   d. Undefined

4. _____ is the design, analysis, and/or construction of works for practical purposes.
   a. Thing
   b. Engineering0
   c. Undefined
   d. Undefined

5. _____ is a mathematical science pertaining to the collection, analysis, interpretation or explanation, and presentation of data. It is applicable to a wide variety of academic disciplines, from the physical and social sciences to the humanities.
   a. Statistics0
   b. Thing
   c. Undefined
   d. Undefined

6. In mathematics, the concept of a _____ tries to capture the intuitive idea of a geometrical one-dimensional and continuous object. A simple example is the circle.
   a. Thing
   b. Curve0
   c. Undefined
   d. Undefined

7. _____ is a process of combining or accumulating. It may also refer to:
   a. Thing
   b. Integration0
   c. Undefined
   d. Undefined

8. _____, Greek for "knowledge of nature," is the branch of science concerned with the discovery and characterization of universal laws which govern matter, energy, space, and time.
   a. Physics0
   b. Thing
   c. Undefined
   d. Undefined

9. _____ is the fee paid on borrowed money.
   a. Interest0
   b. Thing
   c. Undefined
   d. Undefined

10. In geometry, a line _____ is a part of a line that is bounded by two end points, and contains every point on the line between its end points.

a. Concept
b. Segment0
c. Undefined
d. Undefined

11. A _____ is a part of a line that is bounded by two end points, and contains every point on the line between its end points.
   a. Thing
   b. Line segment0
   c. Undefined
   d. Undefined

12. In geometry a _____ is a plane figure that is bounded by a closed path or circuit, composed of a finite number of sequential line segments.
   a. Polygon0
   b. Thing
   c. Undefined
   d. Undefined

13. In geometry, a _____ is a special kind of point, usually a corner of a polygon, polyhedron, or higher dimensional polytope. In the geometry of curves a _____ is a point of where the first derivative of curvature is zero. In graph theory, a _____ is the fundamental unit out of which graphs are formed
   a. Thing
   b. Vertex0
   c. Undefined
   d. Undefined

14. _____ is an extension of the concept of a sum.
   a. Definite integral0
   b. Thing
   c. Undefined
   d. Undefined

15. An _____ is a combination of numbers, operators, grouping symbols and/or free variables and bound variables arranged in a meaningful way which can be evaluated..
   a. Thing
   b. Expression0
   c. Undefined
   d. Undefined

16. The _____, the average in everyday English, which is also called the arithmetic _____ (and is distinguished from the geometric _____ or harmonic _____). The average is also called the sample _____. The expected value of a random variable, which is also called the population _____.
   a. Mean0
   b. Thing
   c. Undefined
   d. Undefined

17. In mathematics, a _____ is a statement that can be proved on the basis of explicitly stated or previously agreed assumptions.
   a. Theorem0
   b. Thing
   c. Undefined
   d. Undefined

18. The mathematical concept of a _____ expresses the intuitive idea of deterministic dependence between two quantities, one of which is viewed as primary and the other as secondary. A _____ then is a way to associate a unique output for each input of a specified type, for example, a real number or an element of a given set.
   a. Thing
   b. Function0
   c. Undefined
   d. Undefined

Chapter 8. Further Applications of Integration

19. In elementary algebra, an _____ is a set that contains every real number between two indicated numbers and may contain the two numbers themselves.
    a. Thing
    b. Interval0
    c. Undefined
    d. Undefined

20. In Euclidean geometry, an _____ is a closed segment of a differentiable curve in the two-dimensional plane; for example, a circular _____ is a segment of a circle.
    a. Arc0
    b. Concept
    c. Undefined
    d. Undefined

21. In mathematics, the _____ is a conic section generated by the intersection of a right circular conical surface and a plane parallel to a generating straight line of that surface. It can also be defined as locus of points in a plane which are equidistant from a given point.
    a. Parabola0
    b. Thing
    c. Undefined
    d. Undefined

22. In plane geometry, a _____ is a polygon with four equal sides, four right angles, and parallel opposite sides. In algebra, the _____ of a number is that number multiplied by itself.
    a. Thing
    b. Square0
    c. Undefined
    d. Undefined

23. In mathematics, a _____ of a number x is a number r such that $r^2 = x$, or in words, a number r whose square (the result of multiplying the number by itself) is x.
    a. Square root0
    b. Thing
    c. Undefined
    d. Undefined

24. _____ also called rectification of a curve—was historically difficult.
    a. Arc length0
    b. Thing
    c. Undefined
    d. Undefined

25. In mathematics, a _____ of a complex-valued function f is a member x of the domain of f such that f(x) vanishes at x, that is, x : f (x) = 0.
    a. Root0
    b. Thing
    c. Undefined
    d. Undefined

26. A _____ is a deliberate process for transforming one or more inputs into one or more results.
    a. Calculation0
    b. Thing
    c. Undefined
    d. Undefined

27. In mathematics, a _____ is a type of conic section defined as the intersection between a right circular conical surface and a plane which cuts through both halves of the cone.
    a. Thing
    b. Hyperbola0
    c. Undefined
    d. Undefined

28. _____ is a branch of mathematics concerning the study of structure, relation and quantity.

a. Algebra0
b. Concept
c. Undefined
d. Undefined

29. A _____ is a function that assigns a number to subsets of a given set.
   a. Thing
   b. Measure0
   c. Undefined
   d. Undefined

30. A _____ is a negotiable instrument instructing a financial institution to pay a specific amount of a specific currency from a specific demand account held in the maker/depositor's name with that institution. Both the maker and payee may be natural persons or legal entities.
   a. Check0
   b. Thing
   c. Undefined
   d. Undefined

31. In geometry, _____ are plane figures that are bounded by a closed path or circuit, composed of a finite number of sequential line segments.
   a. Thing
   b. Polygons0
   c. Undefined
   d. Undefined

32. _____ means "constancy", i.e. if something retains a certain feature even after we change a way of looking at it, then it is symmetric.
   a. Thing
   b. Symmetry0
   c. Undefined
   d. Undefined

33. An _____ is the limit of a definite integral, as an endpoint of the interval of integration approaches either a specified real number or ‡ or − ‡ or, in some cases, as both endpoints approach limits.
   a. Thing
   b. Improper integral0
   c. Undefined
   d. Undefined

34. In geometry, an _____ of a triangle is a straight line through a vertex and perpendicular to (i.e. forming a right angle with) the opposite side or an extension of the opposite side.
   a. Altitude0
   b. Concept
   c. Undefined
   d. Undefined

35. _____ is the path a moving object follows through space.
   a. Projectile motion0
   b. Thing
   c. Undefined
   d. Undefined

36. In astronomy, geography, geometry and related sciences and contexts, a plane is said to be _____ at a given point if it is locally perpendicular to the gradient of the gravity field, i.e., with the direction of the gravitational force at that point.
   a. Thing
   b. Horizontal0
   c. Undefined
   d. Undefined

37. The metre (or _____, see spelling differences) is a measure of length. It is the basic unit of length in the metric system and in the International System of Units (SI), used around the world for general and scientific purposes.

a. Concept
b. Meter0
c. Undefined
d. Undefined

38. In geometry a _____, or deltoid, is a quadrilateral with two pairs of congruent adjacent sides.
   a. Kite0
   b. Thing
   c. Undefined
   d. Undefined

39. _____ is a trigonemtric function that is important when studying triangles and modeling periodic phenomena, among other applications.
   a. Sine0
   b. Thing
   c. Undefined
   d. Undefined

40. _____ is the shape of a hanging flexible chain or cable when supported at its ends and acted upon by a uniform gravitational force. The chain is steepest near the points of suspension because this part of the chain has the most weight pulling down on it. Toward the bottom, the slope of the chain decreases because the chain is supporting less weight.
   a. Catenary0
   b. Thing
   c. Undefined
   d. Undefined

41. In mathematics, _____ are the intuitive idea of a geometrical one-dimensional and continuous object.
   a. Thing
   b. Curves0
   c. Undefined
   d. Undefined

42. In Euclidean geometry, a _____ is the set of all points in a plane at a fixed distance, called the radius, from a given point, the center.
   a. Circle0
   b. Thing
   c. Undefined
   d. Undefined

43. _____ is a kind of property which exists as magnitude or multitude. It is among the basic classes of things along with quality, substance, change, and relation.
   a. Thing
   b. Amount0
   c. Undefined
   d. Undefined

44. In classical geometry, a _____ of a circle or sphere is any line segment from its center to its boundary. By extension, the _____ of a circle or sphere is the length of any such segment. The _____ is half the diameter. In science and engineering the term _____ of curvature is commonly used as a synonym for _____.
   a. Thing
   b. Radius0
   c. Undefined
   d. Undefined

45. In geometry, a _____ is defined as a quadrilateral where all four of its angles are right angles.
   a. Rectangle0
   b. Thing
   c. Undefined
   d. Undefined

46. In mathematics, a _____ is a quadric surface, with the following equation in Cartesian coordinates: $(x/a)^2 + (y/b)^2 = 1$.

a. Thing
b. Cylinder0
c. Undefined
d. Undefined

47. A _____ surface is the surface or face of a solid on its sides. It can also be defined as any face or surface that is not a base.
   a. Thing
   b. Lateral0
   c. Undefined
   d. Undefined

48. A circular _____ or circle _____ also known as a pie piece is the portion of a circle enclosed by two radii and an arc.
   a. Sector0
   b. Thing
   c. Undefined
   d. Undefined

49. The _____ of a right circular cone is the distance from any point on the circle to the apex of the cone.
   a. Thing
   b. Slant height0
   c. Undefined
   d. Undefined

50. A _____ is a three-dimensional geometric shape formed by straight lines through a fixed point (vertex) to the points of a fixed curve (directrix)
   a. Cone0
   b. Concept
   c. Undefined
   d. Undefined

51. An _____ is a straight line around which a geometric figure can be rotated.
   a. Thing
   b. Axis0
   c. Undefined
   d. Undefined

52. In geometry, an _____ is a point at which a line segment or ray terminates.
   a. Endpoint0
   b. Thing
   c. Undefined
   d. Undefined

53. _____ the expected value of a random variable displays the average or central value of the variable. It is a summary value of the distribution of the variable.
   a. Thing
   b. Determining0
   c. Undefined
   d. Undefined

54. A _____ function is a function for which, intuitively, small changes in the input result in small changes in the output.
   a. Continuous0
   b. Event
   c. Undefined
   d. Undefined

55. The _____ is the distance around a closed curve. _____ is a kind of perimeter.
   a. Circumference0
   b. Thing
   c. Undefined
   d. Undefined

Chapter 8. Further Applications of Integration 141

56. A _____ is a movement of an object in a circular motion. A two-dimensional object rotates around a center (or point) of _____. A three-dimensional object rotates around a line called an axis. If the axis of _____ is within the body, the body is said to rotate upon itself, or spin—which implies relative speed and perhaps free-movement with angular momentum. A circular motion about an external point, e.g. the Earth about the Sun, is called an orbit or more properly an orbital revolution.
   a. Rotation0
   b. Thing
   c. Undefined
   d. Undefined

57. _____ is the portion of a solid – normally a cone or pyramid – which lies between two parallel planes cutting the solid.
   a. Thing
   b. Truncated pyramid0
   c. Undefined
   d. Undefined

58. A _____ is a symbolic representation denoting a quantity or expression. It often represents an "unknown" quantity that has the potential to change.
   a. Thing
   b. Variable0
   c. Undefined
   d. Undefined

59. In mathematics, _____ geometry was the traditional name for the geometry of three-dimensional Euclidean space — for practical purposes the kind of space we live in.
   a. Solid0
   b. Thing
   c. Undefined
   d. Undefined

60. _____ is the state of being greater than any finite real or natural number, however large.
   a. Thing
   b. Infinite0
   c. Undefined
   d. Undefined

61. In mathematics, a set is called _____ if there is a bijection between the set and some set of the form {1, 2, ..., n} where n is a natural number.
   a. Thing
   b. Finite0
   c. Undefined
   d. Undefined

62. In geometry, a _____ (Greek words diairo = divide and metro = measure) of a circle is any straight line segment that passes through the centre and whose endpoints are on the circular boundary, or, in more modern usage, the length of such a line segment. When using the word in the more modern sense, one speaks of the _____ rather than a _____, because all diameters of a circle have the same length. This length is twice the radius. The _____ of a circle is also the longest chord that the circle has.
   a. Diameter0
   b. Thing
   c. Undefined
   d. Undefined

63. In mathematics, an _____ .
   a. Thing
   b. Ellipse0
   c. Undefined
   d. Undefined

64. An _____ is a type of quadric surface that is a higher dimensional analogue of an ellipse.

a. Thing
b. Ellipsoid0
c. Undefined
d. Undefined

65. In geometry, a _____ is a surface of revolution generated by revolving a circle in three dimensional space about an axis coplanar with the circle, which does not touch the circle. Examples of tori include the surfaces of doughnuts and inner tubes. A circle rotated about a chord of the circle is called a _____ in some contexts, but this is not a common usage in mathematics. The shape produced when a circle is rotated about a chord resembles a round cushion. _____ was the Latin word for a cushion of this shape.
   a. Thing
   b. Torus0
   c. Undefined
   d. Undefined

66. In mathematics, a _____ is the set of all points in three-dimensional space (R^3) which are at distance r from a fixed point of that space, where r is a positive real number called the radius of the _____. The fixed point is called the center or centre, and is not part of the _____ itself.
   a. Thing
   b. Sphere0
   c. Undefined
   d. Undefined

67. In mathematics, a _____ is a two-dimensional manifold or surface that is perfectly flat.
   a. Plane0
   b. Thing
   c. Undefined
   d. Undefined

68. In mathematics, _____ are two-dimensional manifolds or surfaces that are perfectly flat.
   a. Planes0
   b. Thing
   c. Undefined
   d. Undefined

69. In statistics, a _____ measure is one which is measuring what is supposed to measure.
   a. Thing
   b. Valid0
   c. Undefined
   d. Undefined

70. The _____ is a measurement of how a function changes when the values of its inputs change.
   a. Derivative0
   b. Thing
   c. Undefined
   d. Undefined

71. In mathematics and the mathematical sciences, a _____ is a fixed, but possibly unspecified, value. This is in contrast to a variable, which is not fixed.
   a. Thing
   b. Constant0
   c. Undefined
   d. Undefined

72. _____ is the pressure at some point withig the fluid
   a. Thing
   b. Water pressure0
   c. Undefined
   d. Undefined

73. In physics, _____ is an influence that may cause an object to accelerate. It may be experienced as a lift, a push, or a pull. The actual acceleration of the body is determined by the vector sum of all forces acting on it, known as net _____ or resultant _____.

Chapter 8. Further Applications of Integration

    a. Thing
    b. Force0
    c. Undefined
    d. Undefined

74. Sir Isaac _____, was an English physicist, mathematician, astronomer, natural philosopher, and alchemist, regarded by many as the greatest figure in the history of science
    a. Newton0
    b. Person
    c. Undefined
    d. Undefined

75. The _____ of measurement are a globally standardized and modernized form of the metric system.
    a. Thing
    b. Units0
    c. Undefined
    d. Undefined

76. Blaise _____ was a French mathematician, physicist, and religious philosopher.
    a. Person
    b. Pascal0
    c. Undefined
    d. Undefined

77. _____ is mass m per unit volume V.
    a. Thing
    b. Density0
    c. Undefined
    d. Undefined

78. A _____ is a quadrilateral, which is defined as a shape with four sides, which has a pair of parallel sides.
    a. Thing
    b. Trapezoid0
    c. Undefined
    d. Undefined

79. In mathematics, the _____ of a coordinate system is the point where the axes of the system intersect.
    a. Thing
    b. Origin0
    c. Undefined
    d. Undefined

80. A _____ is one of the basic shapes of geometry: a polygon with three vertices and three sides which are straight line segments.
    a. Triangle0
    b. Thing
    c. Undefined
    d. Undefined

81. In mathematics, a _____ is the result of multiplying, or an expression that identifies factors to be multiplied.
    a. Product0
    b. Thing
    c. Undefined
    d. Undefined

82. _____ of Syracuse was an ancient Greek mathematician, physicist and engineer. In addition to making important discoveries in the field of mathematics and geometry, he is credited with producing machines that were well ahead of their time.
    a. Archimedes0
    b. Person
    c. Undefined
    d. Undefined

83. In banking and accountancy, the outstanding _____ is the amount of money owned, or due, that remains in a deposit account or a loan account at a given date, after all past remittances, payments and withdrawal have been accounted for.

Chapter 8. Further Applications of Integration

    a. Thing
    b. Balance0
    c. Undefined
    d. Undefined

84. In geometry, the _____ of an object is a point in some sense in the middle of the object.
    a. Center0
    b. Thing
    c. Undefined
    d. Undefined

85. In physics, the _____ of a system of particles is a specific point at which, for many purposes, the system's mass behaves as if it were concentrated.
    a. Thing
    b. Center of mass0
    c. Undefined
    d. Undefined

86. A _____ is the result of the addition of a set of numbers. The numbers may be natural numbers, complex numbers, matrices, or still more complicated objects. An infinite _____ is a subtle procedure known as a series.
    a. Thing
    b. Sum0
    c. Undefined
    d. Undefined

87. _____ is the property of a physical object that quantifies the amount of matter and energy it is equivalent to.
    a. Thing
    b. Mass0
    c. Undefined
    d. Undefined

88. A _____ is a set of numbers that designate location in a given reference system, such as x,y in a planar _____ system or an x,y,z in a three-dimensional _____ system.
    a. Thing
    b. Coordinate0
    c. Undefined
    d. Undefined

89. A _____ signifies a point or points of probability on a subject e.g., the _____ of creativity, which allows for the formation of rule or norm or law by interpretation of the phenomena events that can be created.
    a. Principle0
    b. Thing
    c. Undefined
    d. Undefined

90. In mathematics, a _____ is a demonstration that, assuming certain axioms, some statement is necessarily true.
    a. Proof0
    b. Thing
    c. Undefined
    d. Undefined

91. In geometry, the _____ or barycenter of an object X in n-dimensional space is the intersection of all hyperplanes that divide X into two parts of equal moment about the hyperplane
    a. Thing
    b. Centroid0
    c. Undefined
    d. Undefined

92. In geometry, an _____ polygon is a polygon which has all sides of the same length.
    a. Equilateral0
    b. Thing
    c. Undefined
    d. Undefined

93. An _____ is a triangle in which all sides are of equal length.

Chapter 8. Further Applications of Integration

a. Equilateral triangle0
b. Thing
c. Undefined
d. Undefined

94. A _____ is a three-dimensional solid object bounded by six square faces, facets, or sides, with three meeting at each vertex.
   a. Thing
   b. Cube0
   c. Undefined
   d. Undefined

95. The _____ is one of the classical simple machines; as the name suggests, it is a flat surface whose endpoints are at different heights. By moving an object up an _____ rather than directly from one height to another, the amount of force required is reduced, at the expense of increasing the distance the object must travel. The mechanical advantage of an _____ is the ratio of the length of the sloped surface to the height it spans; this may also be expressed as the cosecant of the angle between the plane and the horizontal.
   a. Inclined plane0
   b. Thing
   c. Undefined
   d. Undefined

96. In mathematical analysis and related areas of mathematics, a set is called _____, if it is, in a certain sense, of finite size.
   a. Bounded0
   b. Thing
   c. Undefined
   d. Undefined

97. In mathematics, a planar _____ is a closed surface of mass
   a. Lamina0
   b. Thing
   c. Undefined
   d. Undefined

98. In mathematics, the _____ of two sets A and B is the set that contains all elements of A that also belong to B (or equivalently, all elements of B that also belong to A), but no other elements.
   a. Thing
   b. Intersection0
   c. Undefined
   d. Undefined

99. In probability theory and statistics, a _____ is a number dividing the higher half of a sample, a population, or a probability distribution from the lower half.
   a. Median0
   b. Concept
   c. Undefined
   d. Undefined

100. An _____ is when two lines intersect somewhere on a plane creating a right angle at intersection
   a. Thing
   b. Axes0
   c. Undefined
   d. Undefined

101. _____ is the middle point of a line segment.
   a. Midpoint0
   b. Thing
   c. Undefined
   d. Undefined

102. In mathematics, the additive inverse, or _____ of a number n is the number that, when added to n, yields zero. The additive inverse of n is denoted −n. For example, 7 is −7, because 7 + (−7) = 0, and the additive inverse of −0.3 is 0.3, because −0.3 + 0.3 = 0.

a. Opposite0
c. Undefined
b. Thing
d. Undefined

103. In mathematics, the _____ of a number n is the number that, when added to n, yields zero. The _____ of n is denoted −n. For example, 7 is −7, because 7 + (−7) = 0, and the _____ of −0.3 is 0.3, because −0.3 + 0.3 = 0.
   a. Thing
   b. Additive inverse0
   c. Undefined
   d. Undefined

104. The _____ are the only integral domain whose positive elements are well-ordered, and in which order is preserved by addition. Like the natural numbers, the _____ form a countably infinite set. The set of all _____ is usually denoted in mathematics by a boldface Z .
   a. Thing
   b. Integers0
   c. Undefined
   d. Undefined

105. A _____ is an individual or household that purchases and uses goods and services generated within the economy.
   a. Consumer0
   b. Thing
   c. Undefined
   d. Undefined

106. In economics, supply and _____ describe market relations between prospective sellers and buyers of a good.
   a. Thing
   b. Demand0
   c. Undefined
   d. Undefined

107. _____ can be defined as the graph depicting the relationship between the price of a certain commodity, and the amount of it that consumers are willing and able to purchase at that given price demand.
   a. Thing
   b. Demand curve0
   c. Undefined
   d. Undefined

108. _____, in economics and political economy, are the distributions or payments awarded to the various suppliers of the factors of production.
   a. Returns0
   b. Thing
   c. Undefined
   d. Undefined

109. A _____ is a special kind of ratio, indicating a relationship between two measurements with different units, such as miles to gallons or cents to pounds.
   a. Rate0
   b. Thing
   c. Undefined
   d. Undefined

110. _____ is the volume of blood being pumped by the heart, in particular a ventricle in a minute.
   a. Cardiac output0
   b. Thing
   c. Undefined
   d. Undefined

111. _____ is the change in total cost that arises when the quantity produced changes by one unit.
   a. Marginal cost0
   b. Thing
   c. Undefined
   d. Undefined

Chapter 8. Further Applications of Integration

112. In topology and related areas of mathematics a _____ or Moore-Smith sequence is a generalization of a sequence, intended to unify the various notions of limit and generalize them to arbitrary topological spaces.
   a. Net0
   b. Thing
   c. Undefined
   d. Undefined

113. _____ is the extra revenue that an additional unit of product will bring a firm. It can also be described as the change in total revenue/change in number of units sold.
   a. Marginal revenue0
   b. Thing
   c. Undefined
   d. Undefined

114. _____ is a business term for the amount of money that a company receives from its activities in a given period, mostly from sales of products and/or services to customers
   a. Thing
   b. Revenue0
   c. Undefined
   d. Undefined

115. _____ is used in economics for several related quantities
   a. Thing
   b. Producer surplus0
   c. Undefined
   d. Undefined

116. In mathematics, science including computer science, linguistics and engineering, an _____ is, generally speaking, an independent variable or input to a function.
   a. Thing
   b. Argument0
   c. Undefined
   d. Undefined

117. In economics, _____ describe market relations between prospective sellers and buyers of a good.
   a. Thing
   b. Supply and demand0
   c. Undefined
   d. Undefined

118. _____ is the technique and science of accurately determining the terrestrial or three-dimensional space position of points and the distances and angles between them.
   a. Thing
   b. Surveying0
   c. Undefined
   d. Undefined

119. In sociology and biology a _____ is the collection of people or organisms of a particular species living in a given geographic area or space, usually measured by a census.
   a. Thing
   b. Population0
   c. Undefined
   d. Undefined

120. In the field of electromagnetism, _____ is usually the integral of a vector quantity over a finite surface.
   a. Flux0
   b. Thing
   c. Undefined
   d. Undefined

121. _____ is a mathematical subject that includes the study of limits, derivatives, integrals, and power series and constitutes a major part of modern university curriculum.

Chapter 8. Further Applications of Integration

a. Calculus0
b. Thing
c. Undefined
d. Undefined

122. _____ is the chance that something is likely to happen or be the case.
   a. Probability0
   b. Thing
   c. Undefined
   d. Undefined

123. In statistics the _____ of an event i is the number n_i of times the event occurred in the experiment or the study. These frequencies are often graphically represented in histograms.
   a. Frequency0
   b. Concept
   c. Undefined
   d. Undefined

124. _____ is a function that represents a probability distribution in terms of integrals.
   a. Probability density function0
   b. Thing
   c. Undefined
   d. Undefined

125. In Euclidean geometry, a uniform _____ is a linear transformation that enlargers or diminishes objects, and whose _____ factor is the same in all directions. This is also called homothethy.
   a. Thing
   b. Scale0
   c. Undefined
   d. Undefined

126. _____ is a quantity whose values are random and to which a probability distribution is assigned.
   a. Random variable0
   b. Thing
   c. Undefined
   d. Undefined

127. _____ are a measure of time.
   a. Thing
   b. Minutes0
   c. Undefined
   d. Undefined

128. _____ is a subset of a population.
   a. Sample0
   b. Thing
   c. Undefined
   d. Undefined

129. In business, particularly accounting, a _____ is the time intervals that the accounts, statement, payments, or other calculations cover.
   a. Period0
   b. Thing
   c. Undefined
   d. Undefined

130. _____ is a special mathematical relationship between two quantities. Two quantities are called proportional if they vary in such a way that one of the quantities is a constant multiple of the other, or equivalently if they have a constant ratio.
   a. Thing
   b. Proportionality0
   c. Undefined
   d. Undefined

131. In mathematics, _____ growth occurs when the growth rate of a function is always proportional to the function's current size.

Chapter 8. Further Applications of Integration

    a. Thing
    c. Undefined
    b. Exponential0
    d. Undefined

132. In mathematical analysis, _____ are objects which generalize functions and probability distributions.
    a. Thing
    c. Undefined
    b. Distribution0
    d. Undefined

133. _____ of a probability distribution, random variable, or population or multiset of values is a measure of the spread of its values.
    a. Thing
    c. Undefined
    b. Standard deviation0
    d. Undefined

134. _____ is a measure of difference for interval and ratio variables between the observed value and the mean.
    a. Thing
    c. Undefined
    b. Deviation0
    d. Undefined

135. _____ is the eighteenth letter of the Greek alphabet.
    a. Sigma0
    c. Undefined
    b. Thing
    d. Undefined

136. The _____, also called Gaussian distribution by scientists , is a continuous probability distribution of great importance in many fields.
    a. Normal distribution0
    c. Undefined
    b. Thing
    d. Undefined

137. _____, also called Gaussian distribution by scientists, is a continuous probability distribution of great importance in many fields.
    a. Thing
    c. Undefined
    b. Normal distributions0
    d. Undefined

138. _____ is a synonym for information.
    a. Thing
    c. Undefined
    b. Data0
    d. Undefined

139. An _____ of a function f is a function F whose derivative is equal to f, i.e., F' = f.
    a. Thing
    c. Undefined
    b. Antiderivative0
    d. Undefined

140. _____ are determined by the level of intelligence performed by an individual.
    a. Thing
    c. Undefined
    b. IQ scores0
    d. Undefined

141. In mathematics, a _____ may be described informally as a number that can be given by an infinite decimal representation.

Chapter 8. Further Applications of Integration

a. Real number0
b. Thing
c. Undefined
d. Undefined

142. _____ is the level of functional and/or metabolic efficiency of an organism at both the micro level.
a. Thing
b. Health0
c. Undefined
d. Undefined

143. In physics, an _____ is the path that an object makes around another object while under the influence of a source of centripetal force, such as gravity.
a. Thing
b. Orbit0
c. Undefined
d. Undefined

144. _____, usually denoted symbolically by the Greek letter phi, Î¦, gives the location of a place on Earth north or south of the equator. _____ is an angular measurement in degrees (marked with Â°) ranging from 0Â° at the Equator (low _____) to 90Â° at the poles (90Â° N for the North Pole or 90Â° S for the South Pole; high _____). The complementary angle of a _____ is called the colatitude.
a. Latitude0
b. Thing
c. Undefined
d. Undefined

145. _____ is an adjective usually refering to being in the centre.
a. Central0
b. Thing
c. Undefined
d. Undefined

146. In geometry, two lines or planes if one falls on the other in such a way as to create congruent adjacent angles. The term may be used as a noun or adjective. Thus, referring to Figure 1, the line AB is the _____ to CD through the point B.
a. Perpendicular0
b. Thing
c. Undefined
d. Undefined

147. A _____ is traditionally an infinitesimally small change in a variable.
a. Thing
b. Differential0
c. Undefined
d. Undefined

148. A _____ is a mathematical equation for an unknown function of one or several variables which relates the values of the function itself and of its derivatives of various orders.
a. Differential equation0
b. Thing
c. Undefined
d. Undefined

149. _____ is defined as the rate of change or derivative with respect to time of velocity.
a. Acceleration0
b. Thing
c. Undefined
d. Undefined

150. In geometry, _____ lines are two lines that share one or more common points.
a. Thing
b. Intersecting0
c. Undefined
d. Undefined

151. In mathematics and its applications, a _____ is a system for assigning an n-tuple of numbers or scalars to each point in an n-dimensional space.
   a. Coordinate system0
   b. Concept
   c. Undefined
   d. Undefined

152. A _____ given two distinct points A and B on the _____, is the set of points C on the line containing points A and B such that A is not strictly between C and B.
   a. Ray0
   b. Thing
   c. Undefined
   d. Undefined

Chapter 9. Differential Equations

1. A _____ is traditionally an infinitesimally small change in a variable.
   a. Differential0
   b. Thing
   c. Undefined
   d. Undefined

2. A _____ is a mathematical equation for an unknown function of one or several variables which relates the values of the function itself and of its derivatives of various orders.
   a. Differential equation0
   b. Thing
   c. Undefined
   d. Undefined

3. _____ is a mathematical subject that includes the study of limits, derivatives, integrals, and power series and constitutes a major part of modern university curriculum.
   a. Calculus0
   b. Thing
   c. Undefined
   d. Undefined

4. In mathematics, the _____(e) for L-functions are a class of summation formulae, expressing sums taken over the complex number zeroes of a given L-function, typically in terms of quantities studied by number theory by use of the theory of special functions.
   a. Explicit formula0
   b. Thing
   c. Undefined
   d. Undefined

5. A _____ is an abstract model that uses mathematical language to describe the behavior of a system. Eykhoff defined a _____ as 'a representation of the essential aspects of an existing system which presents knowledge of that system in usable form'.
   a. Thing
   b. Mathematical model0
   c. Undefined
   d. Undefined

6. The _____ is a measurement of how a function changes when the values of its inputs change.
   a. Thing
   b. Derivative0
   c. Undefined
   d. Undefined

7. The mathematical concept of a _____ expresses the intuitive idea of deterministic dependence between two quantities, one of which is viewed as primary and the other as secondary. A _____ then is a way to associate a unique output for each input of a specified type, for example, a real number or an element of a given set.
   a. Function0
   b. Thing
   c. Undefined
   d. Undefined

8. In mathematics, two quantities are called _____ if they vary in such a way that one of the quantities is a constant multiple of the other, or equivalently if they have a constant ratio.
   a. Proportional0
   b. Thing
   c. Undefined
   d. Undefined

9. A _____ is a special kind of ratio, indicating a relationship between two measurements with different units, such as miles to gallons or cents to pounds.
   a. Thing
   b. Rate0
   c. Undefined
   d. Undefined

Chapter 9. Differential Equations

10. In sociology and biology a _____ is the collection of people or organisms of a particular species living in a given geographic area or space, usually measured by a census.
    a. Thing
    b. Population0
    c. Undefined
    d. Undefined

11. _____ is change in population over time, and can be quantified as the change in the number of individuals in a population per unit time.
    a. Thing
    b. Population growth0
    c. Undefined
    d. Undefined

12. Initial objects are also called _____, and terminal objects are also called final.
    a. Thing
    b. Coterminal0
    c. Undefined
    d. Undefined

13. _____ are the basic objects of study in graph theory. Informally speaking, a graph is a set of objects called points, nodes, or vertices connected by links called lines or edges.
    a. Graphs0
    b. Thing
    c. Undefined
    d. Undefined

14. In mathematics, an inequality is a statement about the relative size or order of two objects. For example 14 > 10, or 14 is _____ 10.
    a. Greater than0
    b. Thing
    c. Undefined
    d. Undefined

15. In mathematics, a _____ may be described informally as a number that can be given by an infinite decimal representation.
    a. Thing
    b. Real number0
    c. Undefined
    d. Undefined

16. A _____ is 360° or 2δ radians.
    a. Turn0
    b. Thing
    c. Undefined
    d. Undefined

17. In mathematics and the mathematical sciences, a _____ is a fixed, but possibly unspecified, value. This is in contrast to a variable, which is not fixed.
    a. Constant0
    b. Thing
    c. Undefined
    d. Undefined

18. Pierre François _____ was a mathematician and a doctor in number theory from the University of Ghent in 1825.
    a. Verhulst0
    b. Person
    c. Undefined
    d. Undefined

19. The _____ is the total number of human beings alive on the planet Earth at a given time.
    a. World population0
    b. Thing
    c. Undefined
    d. Undefined

Chapter 9. Differential Equations

20. In mathematics, _____ growth occurs when the growth rate of a function is always proportional to the function's current size.
    a. Thing
    b. Exponential0
    c. Undefined
    d. Undefined

21. An _____ is a combination of numbers, operators, grouping symbols and/or free variables and bound variables arranged in a meaningful way which can be evaluated..
    a. Thing
    b. Expression0
    c. Undefined
    d. Undefined

22. _____ is the ability to hold, receive or absorb, or a measure thereof, similar to the concept of volume.
    a. Capacity0
    b. Concept
    c. Undefined
    d. Undefined

23. _____ usually refers to the biological _____ of a population level that can be supported for an organism, given the quantity of food, habitat, water and other life infrastructure present.
    a. Carrying capacity0
    b. Thing
    c. Undefined
    d. Undefined

24. The _____, the average in everyday English, which is also called the arithmetic _____ (and is distinguished from the geometric _____ or harmonic _____). The average is also called the sample _____. The expected value of a random variable, which is also called the population _____.
    a. Mean0
    b. Thing
    c. Undefined
    d. Undefined

25. A _____ is a symbolic representation denoting a quantity or expression. It often represents an "unknown" quantity that has the potential to change.
    a. Variable0
    b. Thing
    c. Undefined
    d. Undefined

26. In mathematics, an _____ is any of the arguments, i.e. "inputs", to a function. Thus if we have a function f(x), then x is a _____.
    a. Independent variable0
    b. Thing
    c. Undefined
    d. Undefined

27. In mathematics, a _____ is the end result of a division problem. It can also be expressed as the number of times the divisor divides into the dividend.
    a. Thing
    b. Quotient0
    c. Undefined
    d. Undefined

28. The _____ is a method of finding the derivative of a function that is the quotient of two other functions for which derivatives exist.
    a. Thing
    b. Quotient rule0
    c. Undefined
    d. Undefined

Chapter 9. Differential Equations

29. In mathematics, the concept of a _____ tries to capture the intuitive idea of a geometrical one-dimensional and continuous object. A simple example is the circle.
    a. Curve0
    b. Thing
    c. Undefined
    d. Undefined

30. In mathematics, _____ are the intuitive idea of a geometrical one-dimensional and continuous object.
    a. Thing
    b. Curves0
    c. Undefined
    d. Undefined

31. In mathematics, in the field of differential equations, an initial value problem is a differential equation together with specified value, called the _____, of the unknown function at a given point in the domain of the solution.
    a. Thing
    b. Initial condition0
    c. Undefined
    d. Undefined

32. The _____ refers to a relationship between the duration of learning or experience and the resulting progress
    a. Thing
    b. Learning curve0
    c. Undefined
    d. Undefined

33. In mathematics, the _____ f is the collection of all ordered pairs . In particular, graph means the graphical representation of this collection, in the form of a curve or surface, together with axes, etc. Graphing on a Cartesian plane is sometimes referred to as curve sketching.
    a. Thing
    b. Graph of a function0
    c. Undefined
    d. Undefined

34. Sir Isaac _____, was an English physicist, mathematician, astronomer, natural philosopher, and alchemist, regarded by many as the greatest figure in the history of science
    a. Newton0
    b. Person
    c. Undefined
    d. Undefined

35. _____ is a physical property of a system that underlies the common notions of hot and cold; something that is hotter has the greater _____.
    a. Thing
    b. Temperature0
    c. Undefined
    d. Undefined

36. Leonhard _____ was a pioneering Swiss mathematician and physicist, who spent most of his life in Russia and Germany.
    a. Euler0
    b. Person
    c. Undefined
    d. Undefined

37. In geometry, a line _____ is a part of a line that is bounded by two end points, and contains every point on the line between its end points.
    a. Segment0
    b. Concept
    c. Undefined
    d. Undefined

Chapter 9. Differential Equations

38. _____ is often used to describe the measurement of the steepness, incline, gradient, or grade of a straight line. The _____ is defined as the ratio of the "rise" divided by the "run" between two points on a line, or in other words, the ratio of the altitude change to the horizontal distance between any two points on the line.
    a. Thing
    b. Slope0
    c. Undefined
    d. Undefined

39. A _____ is a part of a line that is bounded by two end points, and contains every point on the line between its end points.
    a. Line segment0
    b. Thing
    c. Undefined
    d. Undefined

40. A _____ is a graphical tool to qualitatively visualize, or aid in numerical approximation of, solutions to differential equations.
    a. Slope field0
    b. Thing
    c. Undefined
    d. Undefined

41. In mathematics, the _____ of a coordinate system is the point where the axes of the system intersect.
    a. Origin0
    b. Thing
    c. Undefined
    d. Undefined

42. _____ is the difference of electrical potential between two points of an electrical or electronic circuit, expressed in volts
    a. Thing
    b. Voltage0
    c. Undefined
    d. Undefined

43. _____ is a term used to characterize electrical devices, such as voltaic cells, thermoelectric devices, electrical generators and transformers, and even resistors.
    a. Thing
    b. Electromotive force0
    c. Undefined
    d. Undefined

44. The _____, in practice often shortened to amp, is a unit of electric current, or amount of electric charge per second.
    a. Amperes0
    b. Thing
    c. Undefined
    d. Undefined

45. In physics, _____ is an influence that may cause an object to accelerate. It may be experienced as a lift, a push, or a pull. The actual acceleration of the body is determined by the vector sum of all forces acting on it, known as net _____ or resultant _____.
    a. Thing
    b. Force0
    c. Undefined
    d. Undefined

46. A _____ is the result of the addition of a set of numbers. The numbers may be natural numbers, complex numbers, matrices, or still more complicated objects. An infinite _____ is a subtle procedure known as a series.
    a. Thing
    b. Sum0
    c. Undefined
    d. Undefined

Chapter 9. Differential Equations

47. The ratio of the magnetic flux to the current is called the _____, or more accurately self-_____ of the circuit.
    a. Thing
    b. Inductance0
    c. Undefined
    d. Undefined

48. In economics, economic _____ is simply a state of the world where economic forces are balanced and in the absence of external influences the values of economic variables will not change.
    a. Thing
    b. Equilibrium0
    c. Undefined
    d. Undefined

49. _____ is a function whose values do not vary and thus are constant.
    a. Thing
    b. Constant function0
    c. Undefined
    d. Undefined

50. The _____ of measurement are a globally standardized and modernized form of the metric system.
    a. Thing
    b. Units0
    c. Undefined
    d. Undefined

51. The word _____ comes from the Latin word linearis, which means created by lines.
    a. Linear0
    b. Thing
    c. Undefined
    d. Undefined

52. A _____ is a first degree polynomial mathematical function of the form: f(x) = mx + b where m and b are real constants and x is a real variable.
    a. Linear function0
    b. Thing
    c. Undefined
    d. Undefined

53. _____ is a branch of mathematics concerning the study of structure, relation and quantity.
    a. Concept
    b. Algebra0
    c. Undefined
    d. Undefined

54. A _____ is an instrument used in geometry technical drawing and engineering/building to measure distances and/or to rule straight lines.
    a. Thing
    b. Ruler0
    c. Undefined
    d. Undefined

55. A _____ is a negotiable instrument instructing a financial institution to pay a specific amount of a specific currency from a specific demand account held in the maker/depositor's name with that institution. Both the maker and payee may be natural persons or legal entities.
    a. Check0
    b. Thing
    c. Undefined
    d. Undefined

56. _____ are a measure of time.
    a. Thing
    b. Minutes0
    c. Undefined
    d. Undefined

57. Mathematical _____ is used to represent ideas.

a. Thing
b. Notation0
c. Undefined
d. Undefined

58. _____ was a German mathematician and philosopher. He invented calculus independently of Newton, and his notation is the one in general use since.
   a. Leibniz0
   b. Person
   c. Undefined
   d. Undefined

59. _____ named in honor of the 17th century German philosopher and mathematician Gottfried Wilhelm Leibniz, was originally the use of expressions such as dx and dy and to represent "infinitely small" or infinitesimal increments of quantities x and y, just as Äx and Äy represent finite increments of x and y respectively.
   a. Thing
   b. Leibniz notation0
   c. Undefined
   d. Undefined

60. _____ is the path a moving object follows through space.
   a. Projectile motion0
   b. Thing
   c. Undefined
   d. Undefined

61. In geometry, the _____ of an object is a point in some sense in the middle of the object.
   a. Thing
   b. Center0
   c. Undefined
   d. Undefined

62. In Euclidean geometry, a _____ is the set of all points in a plane at a fixed distance, called the radius, from a given point, the center.
   a. Thing
   b. Circle0
   c. Undefined
   d. Undefined

63. In mathematics, _____ is synonymous with perpendicular when used as a simple adjective that is not part of any longer phrase with a standard definition. It means at right angles. It comes from the Greek á½€Ï Î¸Ï ÏŒÏ, orthos, meaning "straight", used by Euclid to mean right; and Î³Ï‰Î½Î¯Î± gonia, meaning angle. Two streets that cross each other at a right angle are _____ to one another.
   a. Thing
   b. Orthogonal0
   c. Undefined
   d. Undefined

64. In mathematics, a _____ is a family of curves in the plane that intersect a given family of curves at right angles.
   a. Orthogonal trajectory0
   b. Thing
   c. Undefined
   d. Undefined

65. _____ Any process by which a specified characteristic usually amplitude of the output of a device is prevented from exceeding a predetermined value.
   a. Limiting0
   b. Thing
   c. Undefined
   d. Undefined

66. In geometry and trigonometry, a _____ is defined as an angle between two straight intersecting lines of ninety degrees, or one-quarter of a circle.

Chapter 9. Differential Equations

a. Thing
c. Undefined

b. Right angle0
d. Undefined

67. _____ means "constancy", i.e. if something retains a certain feature even after we change a way of looking at it, then it is symmetric.
   a. Symmetry0
   c. Undefined

   b. Thing
   d. Undefined

68. An _____ is a straight line around which a geometric figure can be rotated.
   a. Thing
   c. Undefined

   b. Axis0
   d. Undefined

69. _____ of a two-dimensional figure is a line such that, if a perpendicular is constructed, any two points lying on the perpendicular at equal distances from the _____ are identical.
   a. Axis of symmetry0
   c. Undefined

   b. Thing
   d. Undefined

70. In mathematics, the _____ is a conic section generated by the intersection of a right circular conical surface and a plane parallel to a generating straight line of that surface. It can also be defined as locus of points in a plane which are equidistant from a given point.
   a. Thing
   c. Undefined

   b. Parabola0
   d. Undefined

71. In statistics, a _____ measure is one which is measuring what is supposed to measure.
   a. Thing
   c. Undefined

   b. Valid0
   d. Undefined

72. In mathematics, the multiplicative inverse of a number x, denoted $1/x$ or x^{-1}, is the number which, when multiplied by x, yields 1. The multiplicative inverse of x is also called the _____ of x.
   a. Thing
   c. Undefined

   b. Reciprocal0
   d. Undefined

73. In trigonometry, the _____ is a function defined as $\tan x = \sin x / \cos x$. The function is so-named because it can be defined as the length of a certain segment of a _____ (in the geometric sense) to the unit circle. In plane geometry, a line is _____ to a curve, at some point, if both line and curve pass through the point with the same direction.
   a. Thing
   c. Undefined

   b. Tangent0
   d. Undefined

74. _____ has two distinct but etymologically-related meanings: one in geometry and one in trigonometry.
   a. Thing
   c. Undefined

   b. Tangent line0
   d. Undefined

75. In botany, _____ are above-ground plant organs specialized for photosynthesis. Their characteristics are typically analyzed by using Fiobonacci's sequences.

160 *Chapter 9. Differential Equations*

    a. Thing
    b. Leaves0
    c. Undefined
    d. Undefined

76. In chemistry, a _____ is substance made by combining two or more different materials in such a way that no chemical reaction occurs.
    a. Thing
    b. Mixture0
    c. Undefined
    d. Undefined

77. _____ is a kind of property which exists as magnitude or multitude. It is among the basic classes of things along with quality, substance, change, and relation.
    a. Amount0
    b. Thing
    c. Undefined
    d. Undefined

78. The plus and _____ signs are mathematical symbols used to represent the notions of positive and negative as well as the operations of addition and subtraction.
    a. Thing
    b. Minus0
    c. Undefined
    d. Undefined

79. The _____ or kilogramme is the SI base unit of mass. It is defined as being equal to the mass of the international prototype of the _____.
    a. Thing
    b. Kilogram0
    c. Undefined
    d. Undefined

80. A _____ is a function that assigns a number to subsets of a given set.
    a. Measure0
    b. Thing
    c. Undefined
    d. Undefined

81. In the scientific method, an _____ (Latin: ex-+-periri, "of (or from) trying"), is a set of actions and observations, performed in the context of solving a particular problem or question, in order to support or falsify a hypothesis or research concerning phenomena.
    a. Thing
    b. Experiment0
    c. Undefined
    d. Undefined

82. In classical geometry, a _____ of a circle or sphere is any line segment from its center to its boundary. By extension, the _____ of a circle or sphere is the length of any such segment. The _____ is half the diameter. In science and engineering the term _____ of curvature is commonly used as a synonym for _____.
    a. Radius0
    b. Thing
    c. Undefined
    d. Undefined

83. In mathematics, a _____ is the set of all points in three-dimensional space (R^3) which are at distance r from a fixed point of that space, where r is a positive real number called the radius of the _____. The fixed point is called the center or centre, and is not part of the _____ itself.
    a. Sphere0
    b. Thing
    c. Undefined
    d. Undefined

84. _____ is a process of combining or accumulating. It may also refer to:

Chapter 9. Differential Equations 161

a. Thing
b. Integration0
c. Undefined
d. Undefined

85. _____ is a differential equation together with specified value, called the initial condition, of the unknown function at a given point in the domain of the solution.
   a. Initial value problem0
   b. Thing
   c. Undefined
   d. Undefined

86. _____ is the property of a physical object that quantifies the amount of matter and energy it is equivalent to.
   a. Mass0
   b. Thing
   c. Undefined
   d. Undefined

87. _____ of an object is its speed in a particular direction.
   a. Velocity0
   b. Thing
   c. Undefined
   d. Undefined

88. _____ is defined as the rate of change or derivative with respect to time of velocity.
   a. Thing
   b. Acceleration0
   c. Undefined
   d. Undefined

89. The _____ of a solid object is the three-dimensional concept of how much space it occupies, often quantified numerically.
   a. Volume0
   b. Thing
   c. Undefined
   d. Undefined

90. A _____ is a movement of an object in a circular motion. A two-dimensional object rotates around a center (or point) of _____. A three-dimensional object rotates around a line called an axis. If the axis of _____ is within the body, the body is said to rotate upon itself, or spin—which implies relative speed and perhaps free-movement with angular momentum. A circular motion about an external point, e.g. the Earth about the Sun, is called an orbit or more properly an orbital revolution.
   a. Thing
   b. Rotation0
   c. Undefined
   d. Undefined

91. In mathematics, the word _____ is used informally to refer to certain distinct bodies of knowledge about mathematics.
   a. Theoretical0
   b. Thing
   c. Undefined
   d. Undefined

92. The population _____ is the total number of human beings alive on the planet Earth at a given time.
   a. Thing
   b. Of the world0
   c. Undefined
   d. Undefined

93. _____ is the pressure at some point withig the fluid
   a. Thing
   b. Water pressure0
   c. Undefined
   d. Undefined

Chapter 9. Differential Equations

94. In business, particularly accounting, a _____ is the time intervals that the accounts, statement, payments, or other calculations cover.
   a. Thing
   b. Period0
   c. Undefined
   d. Undefined

95. In mathematics, a _____ is a quadric surface, with the following equation in Cartesian coordinates: $(x/_a)^2 + (y/_b)^2 = 1$.
   a. Cylinder0
   b. Thing
   c. Undefined
   d. Undefined

96. In mathematics, _____ occurs when the growth rate of a function is always proportional to the function's current size.
   a. Exponential growth0
   b. Thing
   c. Undefined
   d. Undefined

97. The _____ of a ring R is defined to be the smallest positive integer n such that $n\,a = 0$, for all a in R.
   a. Thing
   b. Characteristic0
   c. Undefined
   d. Undefined

98. Richard Dagobert _____ was a leading German and Jewish American mathematician. He worked mainly in abstract algebra, but made important contributions to number theory. He was the founder of modular representation theory.
   a. Person
   b. Brauer0
   c. Undefined
   d. Undefined

99. _____, Greek for "knowledge of nature," is the branch of science concerned with the discovery and characterization of universal laws which govern matter, energy, space, and time.
   a. Physics0
   b. Thing
   c. Undefined
   d. Undefined

100. _____ is the fee paid on borrowed money.
   a. Thing
   b. Interest0
   c. Undefined
   d. Undefined

101. A _____ are accounts maintained by commercial banks, savings and loan associations, credit unions, and mutual savings banks that pay interest but can not be used directly as money by, for example, writing a cheque.
   a. Savings account0
   b. Thing
   c. Undefined
   d. Undefined

102. _____ studies and addresses the ways in which individuals, businesses, and organizations raise, allocate, and use monetary resources over time, taking into account the risks entailed in their projects
   a. Thing
   b. Finance0
   c. Undefined
   d. Undefined

103. In mathematics, a _____ is a constant multiplicative factor of a certain object. The object can be such things as a variable, a vector, a function, etc. For example, the _____ of $9x^2$ is 9.

Chapter 9. Differential Equations

a. Thing
b. Coefficient0
c. Undefined
d. Undefined

104. _____ is one of the most important functions in mathematics. A function commonly used to study growth and decay
a. Exponential function0
b. Thing
c. Undefined
d. Undefined

105. _____ is a subset of a population.
a. Thing
b. Sample0
c. Undefined
d. Undefined

106. _____ or investing is a term with several closely-related meanings in business management, finance and economics, related to saving or deferring consumption.
a. Investment0
b. Thing
c. Undefined
d. Undefined

107. _____ is a radiometric dating method that uses the naturally occurring isotope carbon-14 to determine the age of carbonaceous materials up to about 60,000 years.
a. Radiocarbon dating0
b. Thing
c. Undefined
d. Undefined

108. In geometry and physics, _____ are half-lines that continue forever in one direction.
a. Thing
b. Rays0
c. Undefined
d. Undefined

109. _____ is the process in which an unstable atomic nucleus loses energy by emitting radiation in the form of particles or electromagnetic waves.
a. Thing
b. Radioactive decay0
c. Undefined
d. Undefined

110. In geometry, an _____ of a triangle is a straight line through a vertex and perpendicular to (i.e. forming a right angle with) the opposite side or an extension of the opposite side.
a. Altitude0
b. Concept
c. Undefined
d. Undefined

111. An _____ is the fee paid on borrow money.
a. Interest rate0
b. Concept
c. Undefined
d. Undefined

112. In mathematics, an _____, mean, or central tendency of a data set refers to a measure of the "middle" or "expected" value of the data set.
a. Average0
b. Concept
c. Undefined
d. Undefined

Chapter 9. Differential Equations

113. The _____ of a function is an extension of the concept of a sum, and are identified or found through the use of integration.
   a. Integral0
   b. Thing
   c. Undefined
   d. Undefined

114. In elementary algebra, an _____ is a set that contains every real number between two indicated numbers and may contain the two numbers themselves.
   a. Thing
   b. Interval0
   c. Undefined
   d. Undefined

115. The _____ of an object is the extra energy which it possesses due to its motion.
   a. Kinetic energy0
   b. Thing
   c. Undefined
   d. Undefined

116. A _____ consists of one quarter of the coordinate plane.
   a. Thing
   b. Quadrant0
   c. Undefined
   d. Undefined

117. In astronomy, geography, geometry and related sciences and contexts, a plane is said to be _____ at a given point if it is locally perpendicular to the gradient of the gravity field, i.e., with the direction of the gravitational force at that point.
   a. Thing
   b. Horizontal0
   c. Undefined
   d. Undefined

118. _____ is a a point on a curve at which the tangent crosses the curve itself.
   a. Thing
   b. Inflection point0
   c. Undefined
   d. Undefined

119. _____ is a synonym for information.
   a. Thing
   b. Data0
   c. Undefined
   d. Undefined

120. _____ of a population is the number of childbirths per 1,000 persons per year
   a. Birth rate0
   b. Thing
   c. Undefined
   d. Undefined

121. The _____ is the total number of human beings alive on the planet Earth at a given time.
   a. Population of the world0
   b. Thing
   c. Undefined
   d. Undefined

122. In mathematics, a _____ is the result of multiplying, or an expression that identifies factors to be multiplied.
   a. Thing
   b. Product0
   c. Undefined
   d. Undefined

123. _____ is a special mathematical relationship between two quantities. Two quantities are called proportional if they vary in such a way that one of the quantities is a constant multiple of the other, or equivalently if they have a constant ratio.

a. Thing
b. Proportionality0
c. Undefined
d. Undefined

124. A _____ models the S-curve of growth of some set P. The initial stage of growth is approximately exponential; then, as saturation begins, the growth slows, and at maturity, growth stops.
a. Thing
b. Logistic function0
c. Undefined
d. Undefined

125. In algebra, the _____ decomposition or _____ expansion is used to reduce the degree of either the numerator or the denominator of a rational function.
a. Partial fraction0
b. Thing
c. Undefined
d. Undefined

126. A _____ is a function that repeats its values after some definite period has been added to its independent variable.
a. Periodic function0
b. Thing
c. Undefined
d. Undefined

127. A _____ function is a function for which, intuitively, small changes in the input result in small changes in the output.
a. Event
b. Continuous0
c. Undefined
d. Undefined

128. _____ is a function that is chosen to facilitate the solving of a given ordinary differential equation. Consider an ordinary differential equation of the form
a. Thing
b. Integrating factor0
c. Undefined
d. Undefined

129. In mathematics, _____ is an elementary arithmetic operation. When one of the numbers is a whole number, _____ is the repeated sum of the other number.
a. Multiplication0
b. Thing
c. Undefined
d. Undefined

130. A _____ is an equation in which each term is either a constant or the product of a constant times the first power of a variable.
a. Thing
b. Linear equation0
c. Undefined
d. Undefined

131. _____ is a notation for writing numbers that is often used by scientists and mathematicians to make it easier to write large and small numbers.
a. Scientific notation0
b. Thing
c. Undefined
d. Undefined

132. _____ is the transport of people on a trip/journey or the process or time involved in a person or object moving from one location to another.

a. Travel0
b. Thing
c. Undefined
d. Undefined

133. In mathematics, a _____ is a two-dimensional manifold or surface that is perfectly flat.
   a. Plane0
   b. Thing
   c. Undefined
   d. Undefined

134. In common philosophical language, a proposition or _____, is the content of an assertion, that is, it is true-or-false and defined by the meaning of a particular piece of language.
   a. Statement0
   b. Concept
   c. Undefined
   d. Undefined

135. _____ was an Austrian-born biologist known as one of the founders of general systems theory.
   a. Von Bertalanffy0
   b. Person
   c. Undefined
   d. Undefined

136. A _____ is a statement or claimt that a particular event will occur in the future in more certain terms than a forecast.
   a. Prediction0
   b. Thing
   c. Undefined
   d. Undefined

137. A _____ consists either of a suggested explanation for a phenomenon or of a reasoned proposal suggesting a possible correlation between multiple phenomena.
   a. Thing
   b. Hypothesis0
   c. Undefined
   d. Undefined

138. In epidemiology, an _____ is a disease that appears as new cases in a given human population, during a given period, at a rate that substantially exceeds with is "expected," based on recent experience.
   a. Thing
   b. Epidemic0
   c. Undefined
   d. Undefined

139. _____ is mass m per unit volume V.
   a. Density0
   b. Thing
   c. Undefined
   d. Undefined

140. In geometry, two lines or planes if one falls on the other in such a way as to create congruent adjacent angles. The term may be used as a noun or adjective. Thus, referring to Figure 1, the line AB is the _____ to CD through the point B.
   a. Perpendicular0
   b. Thing
   c. Undefined
   d. Undefined

Chapter 10. Parametric Equations and Polar Coordinates

1. A _____ is a value used to represent a certain population characteristic. Because of the impracticality of measuring an entire population to determine this value, parameters are usually estimated.
   a. Parameter10
   b. 15 theorem
   c. Undefined
   d. Undefined

2. The very fact that we are measuring objects with respect to some characteristic implies that the objects differ in that characteristic; or stated in another way, that the characteristic can take on a number of different values. These properties or characteristics of an object that can assume two or more different values are referred to as a _____.
   a. Variable10
   b. 15 theorem
   c. Undefined
   d. Undefined

3. A _____ is a number or variable, or the product or quotient of a number or variable.
   a. Term10
   b. Concept
   c. Undefined
   d. Undefined

4. A _____ goes up and down or from North to South.
   a. Thing
   b. Vertical line10
   c. Undefined
   d. Undefined

5. An _____ is represented by two expressions that have the same value.
   a. Equation10
   b. Thing
   c. Undefined
   d. Undefined

6. A _____ is an undefined term. However, it is often thought of as a series of points. A _____ has one dimension - length. A _____ is either named by a lower case letter or by two points on the _____.
   a. Thing
   b. Line10
   c. Undefined
   d. Undefined

7. A _____ is a relation where every x value has one and only y value.
   a. Function10
   b. Thing
   c. Undefined
   d. Undefined

8. A _____ is an undefined term. We can think of it as a series of lines having 2 dimensions, width and length.
   a. Plane10
   b. Thing
   c. Undefined
   d. Undefined

9. A _____ is an undefined term. We usually represent this by a dot, but a _____ actually has no dimension. A capital letter names any _____.
   a. Thing
   b. Point10
   c. Undefined
   d. Undefined

10. The graph of a quadrataic equation is a symmetric curve called a _____.
    a. Thing
    b. Parabola10
    c. Undefined
    d. Undefined

11. A _____ is a series of points the same distance from a given point, called the center.

a. Circle10
b. Thing
c. Undefined
d. Undefined

12. The word _____ can have three meanings: In _____ theory, a _____ is an abstract object consisting of vertices (or nodes) and edges (or arcs) between pairs of vertices. The _____ of a function f : X ¨ Y is the set of all pairs (x,f(x)) The _____ of a relation, a generalisation of the _____ of a function.
   a. Concept
   b. Graph10
   c. Undefined
   d. Undefined

13. The _____ is the distance around a closed curve. _____ is a kind of perimeter.
   a. Circumference10
   b. Concept
   c. Undefined
   d. Undefined

14. The point of intersection of the horizontal and vertical axes in the rectangular coordinate plane is the _____. It is is expressed as the ordered pair (0,0).
   a. Concept
   b. Origin10
   c. Undefined
   d. Undefined

15. The _____ of a circle is the distance from the center to the circle.
   a. Radius10
   b. Thing
   c. Undefined
   d. Undefined

16. An _____ is one of the number lines found on the rectangular coordinate system. The x asis is the horizontal number line while the y _____ is the vertical number line.
   a. Thing
   b. Axis10
   c. Undefined
   d. Undefined

17. A piece of a circle is called an _____.
   a. Thing
   b. Arc10
   c. Undefined
   d. Undefined

18. A _____ is a piece of a line. The _____ has definite length and is named by the two endpoints.
   a. Thing
   b. Line segment10
   c. Undefined
   d. Undefined

19. Any polygon that has 3 sides is called a _____.
   a. Thing
   b. Triangle10
   c. Undefined
   d. Undefined

20. The _____ is the given point all the points of the circle come from.
   a. Thing
   b. Center of a circle10
   c. Undefined
   d. Undefined

21. A _____ is a well-defined collection of objects considered as a whole.

Chapter 10. Parametric Equations and Polar Coordinates

a. Set10
b. Thing
c. Undefined
d. Undefined

22. An _____ is composed of two rays that have a common endpoint, called the vertex. Each _____ is named by a lower case letter or by one point from each ray and the vertex inbetween. _____ a might be the same _____ as _____ ABC.
   a. Angle10
   b. Thing
   c. Undefined
   d. Undefined

23. A _____ is a quotient of numbers, like 3⁄4, or more generally, an element of a quotient field.
   a. Concept
   b. Fraction10
   c. Undefined
   d. Undefined

24. _____ is any number that multiples to get a product..
   a. Factor10
   b. Thing
   c. Undefined
   d. Undefined

25. When a number in decimal form does not repeat nor terminate, it is an _____. Pi and the square root of 7 are example s of an _____.
   a. Irrational number10
   b. Thing
   c. Undefined
   d. Undefined

26. An _____ is any process or study, which results in the collection of data, the outcome of which is unknown. In statistics, the term is usually restricted to situations in which the researcher has control over some of the conditions under which the _____ takes place.
   a. ACTRAN
   b. Experiment10
   c. Undefined
   d. Undefined

27. _____ is a central branch of mathematics, developed from algebra and geometry, and built on two major complementary ideas, differential _____ and integral _____.
   a. Calculus10
   b. Concept
   c. Undefined
   d. Undefined

28. The _____ refers to the amount of change in Y for a 1 unit change in X or is the ratio of the rise over the run; or in-other-words, the rate of change in the predicted value as a function of a change in the predictor variable.
   a. Slope10
   b. Thing
   c. Undefined
   d. Undefined

29. A _____ is the relationship between two quantities. It is expressed as the quotient of two numbers, or as two numbers separated by a colon (pronounced "to"). A number that can be written as a _____ of two integers is a rational number.
   a. Thing
   b. Ratio10
   c. Undefined
   d. Undefined

30. _____ measure how long something is.

a. Length10 b. Thing
c. Undefined d. Undefined

31. Any number that is divisible by 2 is an _____ number.
a. Thing b. Even10
c. Undefined d. Undefined

32. _____ means to multiply by 2.
a. Thing b. Twice10
c. Undefined d. Undefined

33. In a large distribution of data it is often easier to understand the data if it is grouped into intervals where each _____ can contain more than one data value. Distributions are often reduced to 10 to 20 intervals.
a. ACTRAN b. Interval10
c. Undefined d. Undefined

34. An _____ is an indication of the value of an unknown quantity based on observed data. More formally, an _____ is the particular value of an estimator that is obtained from a particular sample of data and used to indicate the value of a parameter.
a. ACTRAN b. Estimate10
c. Undefined d. Undefined

35. A quadrilateral with opposite sides equal and parallel and containing all right angles is called a _____.
a. Rectangle10 b. Thing
c. Undefined d. Undefined

36. _____, or less commonly, denary, usually refers to the base 10 numeral system.
a. Decimal10 b. Concept
c. Undefined d. Undefined

37. The _____ of a number is the number that makes a sum zero. In most cases, this means just to change the sign. 3 is the _____ of -3.
a. Event b. Opposite10
c. Undefined d. Undefined

38. An _____ is two numbers, where the first number represents a value on the horizontal axis, and the second number represents a value on the vertical axis, such as (x,y).
a. Ordered pair10 b. Concept
c. Undefined d. Undefined

39. When a divisor does not divide into the dividend evenly, the left over number is called the _____. In most cases, we would write this as a fraction by putting the _____ over the divisor.
a. Remainder10 b. Thing
c. Undefined d. Undefined

40. A _____ is the answer in multiplication, or an expression that identifies factors to be multiplied

Chapter 10. Parametric Equations and Polar Coordinates

171

a. Product10
b. Thing
c. Undefined
d. Undefined

41. In a proportion the "middle" values are often referred to as the _____.
a. Means10
b. Thing
c. Undefined
d. Undefined

42. The most important measure of central tendency, and one of the basic building blocks of all statistical analysis, is the arithmetic _____. It is simply the sum of all the set of values divided by the number of values involved. It can also be called the average.
a. Mean10
b. Thing
c. Undefined
d. Undefined

43. Any angle that equals 90 degrees is called a _____. This angle also forms perpendicular lines.
a. Thing
b. Right angle10
c. Undefined
d. Undefined

44. _____ are intuitively defined as numbers that are in one-to-one correspondence with the points on an infinite line—the number line. The term "real number" is a retronym coined in response to "imaginary number". _____ may be rational or irrational; algebraic or transcendental; and positive, negative, or zero. _____ measure continuous quantities. They may in theory be expressed by decimal fractions that have an infinite sequence of digits to the right of the decimal point; these are often (mis-)represented in the same form as 324.823211247... (where the three dots express that there would still be more digits to come, no matter how many more might be added at the end).
a. Concept
b. Real numbers10
c. Undefined
d. Undefined

45. There are properties of objects that do assume one and only value, and we refer to these characteristics as _____. _____, then, are the invariables that differentiate one class of objects from another.
a. Constants10
b. 15 theorem
c. Undefined
d. Undefined

46. A number that does not change in value in a given situation is a _____.
a. Constant10
b. 15 theorem
c. Undefined
d. Undefined

47. _____ is a branch of mathematics which studies structure and quantity. It may be roughly characterized as a generalization and abstraction of arithmetic, in which operations are performed on symbols rather than numbers. It includes elementary _____, taught to high school students, as well as abstract _____ which covers such structures as groups, rings and fields. Along with geometry and analysis, it is one of the three principal branches of mathematics.
a. Algebra10
b. Concept
c. Undefined
d. Undefined

48. The outcome of a trial is called the _____.
a. Event10
b. ACTRAN
c. Undefined
d. Undefined

Chapter 10. Parametric Equations and Polar Coordinates

49. A _____ is a concrete example of an item or a specification against which all others may be measured. For example, there are "primary standards" for length, mass (see Kilogram _____), and other units of measure, kept by laboratories and standards organizations.
   a. Standard10
   b. Concept
   c. Undefined
   d. Undefined

50. A _____ is the point that occurs whenever two lines, line segments, or rays meet. The _____ of an angle is very important.
   a. Thing
   b. Vertex10
   c. Undefined
   d. Undefined

51. Addition (or summation) is one of the basic operations of arithmetic. In its simplest form, addition combines two numbers, the augend and addend, into a single number, the _____. Adding more numbers can be viewed as repeated addition. (Repeated addition of the number one is the most basic form of counting.) By extension, the addition of zero numbers, one number, or infinitely many numbers can be defined.
   a. Sum10
   b. Concept
   c. Undefined
   d. Undefined

52. A quadrilateral with 4 equal sides and all right angles is called a _____.
   a. Square10
   b. Thing
   c. Undefined
   d. Undefined

53. The _____ is the point where a graph intersects the x-axis and is found by letting y = 0 and then solving for the x-value.
   a. Thing
   b. X-intercept10
   c. Undefined
   d. Undefined

54. The _____ is t the point where a graph intersects the y-axis and is found by setting x = 0 and then sovling for the y-value.
   a. Y-intercept10
   b. Thing
   c. Undefined
   d. Undefined

55. In experiments, a _____ is something that researchers administer to experimental units.
   a. 15 theorem
   b. Treatment10
   c. Undefined
   d. Undefined

56. The answer to subtraction is called the _____.
   a. Thing
   b. Difference10
   c. Undefined
   d. Undefined

57. The _____ of a circle is a chord that goes through the center.
   a. Diameter10
   b. Thing
   c. Undefined
   d. Undefined

58. The bottom part of any fraction represents the number of pieces in one whole unit. This bottom part is called the _____.

Chapter 10. Parametric Equations and Polar Coordinates

a. Thing
b. Denominator10
c. Undefined
d. Undefined

59. The top part of the fraction is called the _____. It could also be called the dividend, but _____ is preferred.
   a. Numerator10
   b. Thing
   c. Undefined
   d. Undefined

60. By _____ we mean collecting observations made upon our environment -- observations, which are the results of measurements using clocks, balances, measuring rods, counting operations, or other objectively defined measuring instruments or procedures. _____ may mean simply counting the number of times a particular property occurs.
   a. Data10
   b. 15 theorem
   c. Undefined
   d. Undefined

61. The lowest number in a list of values is called the _____.
   a. Thing
   b. Minimum10
   c. Undefined
   d. Undefined

62. The highest number in a list of values is called the _____.
   a. Maximum10
   b. Thing
   c. Undefined
   d. Undefined

63. The _____ is often confused with the median. The Median is a statistic for the distribution whereas the _____ provides a statistic for an interval; it is the center of the interval; the arithmetic average of the upper and lower limits.
   a. Midpoint10
   b. 15 theorem
   c. Undefined
   d. Undefined

Chapter 11. Infinite Sequences and Series

1. A _____ is a relation where every x value has one and only y value.
   a. Function11
   b. Thing
   c. Undefined
   d. Undefined

2. Addition (or summation) is one of the basic operations of arithmetic. In its simplest form, addition combines two numbers, the augend and addend, into a single number, the _____. Adding more numbers can be viewed as repeated addition. (Repeated addition of the number one is the most basic form of counting.) By extension, the addition of zero numbers, one number, or infinitely many numbers can be defined.
   a. Concept
   b. Sum11
   c. Undefined
   d. Undefined

3. A _____ is a number or variable, or the product or quotient of a number or variable.
   a. Term11
   b. Concept
   c. Undefined
   d. Undefined

4. _____ is any number that multiples to get a product..
   a. Thing
   b. Factor11
   c. Undefined
   d. Undefined

5. Whenever a number is written in exponential expression, the exponent can also be called a _____.
   a. Thing
   b. Power11
   c. Undefined
   d. Undefined

6. A _____, also referred to as a universe, is any well-defined collection of things. By well-defined we mean that the members of the _____ are spelled out, or an unequivocal statement is made as to which things belong in it and which do not.
   a. 15 theorem
   b. Population11
   c. Undefined
   d. Undefined

7. _____, or less commonly, denary, usually refers to the base 10 numeral system.
   a. Concept
   b. Decimal11
   c. Undefined
   d. Undefined

8. A _____ is an undefined term. However, it is often thought of as a series of points. A _____ has one dimension - length. A _____ is either named by a lower case letter or by two points on the _____.
   a. Line11
   b. Thing
   c. Undefined
   d. Undefined

9. In a large distribution of data it is often easier to understand the data if it is grouped into intervals where each _____ can contain more than one data value. Distributions are often reduced to 10 to 20 intervals.
   a. ACTRAN
   b. Interval11
   c. Undefined
   d. Undefined

10. The word _____ can have three meanings: In _____ theory, a _____ is an abstract object consisting of vertices (or nodes) and edges (or arcs) between pairs of vertices. The _____ of a function f : X ¨ Y is the set of all pairs (x,f(x)) The _____ of a relation, a generalisation of the _____ of a function.

Chapter 11. Infinite Sequences and Series

a. Graph11
b. Concept
c. Undefined
d. Undefined

11. An _____ is represented by two expressions that have the same value.
    a. Thing
    b. Equation11
    c. Undefined
    d. Undefined

12. _____ is a quick way of adding identical numbers. For example, the sum 7 + 7 + 7 can be found by multiplying 3 times 7. This model is reflected in the use of the word times as a synonym for multiplied by. The resuult of multiplying numbers is called a product. The numbers being multiplied are called factors.
    a. Concept
    b. Multiplication11
    c. Undefined
    d. Undefined

13. An _____ combines numbers, operators, and/or variables but contains no equal or inequality sign.
    a. Expression11
    b. Thing
    c. Undefined
    d. Undefined

14. In a proportion the "middle" values are often referred to as the _____.
    a. Thing
    b. Means11
    c. Undefined
    d. Undefined

15. The most important measure of central tendency, and one of the basic building blocks of all statistical analysis, is the arithmetic _____. It is simply the sum of all the set of values divided by the number of values involved. It can also be called the average.
    a. Mean11
    b. Thing
    c. Undefined
    d. Undefined

16. A _____ is a well-defined collection of objects considered as a whole.
    a. Thing
    b. Set11
    c. Undefined
    d. Undefined

17. Any set of ordered pairs is called a _____.
    a. Relation11
    b. Thing
    c. Undefined
    d. Undefined

18. When something occurs once a year it is said to occur _____.
    a. Thing
    b. Annually11
    c. Undefined
    d. Undefined

19. The amount of money paid for borrowing or investing money is called the _____. There are two main kinds of _____ called simple _____ and compound _____.
    a. Thing
    b. Interest11
    c. Undefined
    d. Undefined

20. Any number that is divisible by 2 is an _____ number.

Chapter 11. Infinite Sequences and Series

a. Thing
b. Even11
c. Undefined
d. Undefined

21. Whenever a number is not divisible by 2, then it is called an _____ number.
a. Odd11
b. Thing
c. Undefined
d. Undefined

22. The _____ are on the right of the zero on the number line. Although they can have the + sign, it is usually left out.
a. Thing
b. Positive numbers11
c. Undefined
d. Undefined

23. The _____ is another name for the average of a series of numbers. It is found by adding all the numbers together and then divide by the number of numbers.
a. Thing
b. Arithmetic mean11
c. Undefined
d. Undefined

24. A statistic calculated by multiplying the data values together and taking the N-th root of the result., the _____ is often used as a measure of central tendency for skewed distributions.
a. Geometric mean11
b. 15 theorem
c. Undefined
d. Undefined

25. _____ or arithmetics (from the Greek word áñéèìüò = number) in common usage is a branch of (or the forerunner of) mathematics which records elementary properties of certain operations on numerals, though in usage by professional mathematicians, it often is treated as a synonym for number theory.
a. Concept
b. Arithmetic11
c. Undefined
d. Undefined

26. The answer to subtraction is called the _____.
a. Difference11
b. Thing
c. Undefined
d. Undefined

27. A _____ is a quotient of numbers, like 3⁄4, or more generally, an element of a quotient field.
a. Fraction11
b. Concept
c. Undefined
d. Undefined

28. A _____ is the relationship between two quantities. It is expressed as the quotient of two numbers, or as two numbers separated by a colon (pronounced "to"). A number that can be written as a _____ of two integers is a rational number.
a. Thing
b. Ratio11
c. Undefined
d. Undefined

29. Any polygon that has 3 sides is called a _____.
a. Triangle11
b. Thing
c. Undefined
d. Undefined

30. _____ consist of the positive natural numbers (1, 2, 3, ...), their negatives (−1, −2, −3, ...) and the number zero.

Chapter 11. Infinite Sequences and Series

a. Concept
b. Integers11
c. Undefined
d. Undefined

31. _____ means to multiply by 2.
    a. Thing
    b. Twice11
    c. Undefined
    d. Undefined

32. A _____ is a series of points the same distance from a given point, called the center.
    a. Thing
    b. Circle11
    c. Undefined
    d. Undefined

33. The _____ of a circle is the distance from the center to the circle.
    a. Thing
    b. Radius11
    c. Undefined
    d. Undefined

34. At times we must contend with variables that assume a large number of values. In this case it is typical to create _____ of values of the variable and then make a frequency tally of the number of observations falling within each interval. As is the case with any data reduction technique, detail is lost.
    a. Intervals11
    b. ACTRAN
    c. Undefined
    d. Undefined

35. _____ measure how long something is.
    a. Length11
    b. Thing
    c. Undefined
    d. Undefined

36. A quadrilateral with 4 equal sides and all right angles is called a _____.
    a. Thing
    b. Square11
    c. Undefined
    d. Undefined

37. _____ are intuitively defined as numbers that are in one-to-one correspondence with the points on an infinite line—the number line. The term "real number" is a retronym coined in response to "imaginary number". _____ may be rational or irrational; algebraic or transcendental; and positive, negative, or zero. _____ measure continuous quantities. They may in theory be expressed by decimal fractions that have an infinite sequence of digits to the right of the decimal point; these are often (mis-)represented in the same form as 324.823211247... (where the three dots express that there would still be more digits to come, no matter how many more might be added at the end).
    a. Real numbers11
    b. Concept
    c. Undefined
    d. Undefined

38. An _____ is any process or study, which results in the collection of data, the outcome of which is unknown. In statistics, the term is usually restricted to situations in which the researcher has control over some of the conditions under which the _____ takes place.
    a. ACTRAN
    b. Experiment11
    c. Undefined
    d. Undefined

39. A triangle with all sides of equal length is called an _____.

Chapter 11. Infinite Sequences and Series

a. Equilateral triangle11
b. Thing
c. Undefined
d. Undefined

40. An _____ is an indication of the value of an unknown quantity based on observed data. More formally, an _____ is the particular value of an estimator that is obtained from a particular sample of data and used to indicate the value of a parameter.
    a. Estimate11
    b. ACTRAN
    c. Undefined
    d. Undefined

41. A quadrilateral with opposite sides equal and parallel and containing all right angles is called a _____.
    a. Thing
    b. Rectangle11
    c. Undefined
    d. Undefined

42. An _____ is a point at the end of a line segment.
    a. Thing
    b. Endpoint11
    c. Undefined
    d. Undefined

43. A number that is raised to a power, or _____ of an exponential function. This finds common use, for example, in the depiction of numbers, for instance, 10 is the _____ used in the decimal system, whereas 2 is the _____ in the binary numeral system.
    a. Thing
    b. Base11
    c. Undefined
    d. Undefined

44. Any time one number is on the left side of another number on a number line, the first number is _____ the second number. The symbol for this is <.
    a. Thing
    b. Less than11
    c. Undefined
    d. Undefined

45. When a divisor does not divide into the dividend evenly, the left over number is called the _____. In most cases, we would write this as a fraction by putting the _____ over the divisor.
    a. Remainder11
    b. Thing
    c. Undefined
    d. Undefined

46. The _____ is often confused with the median. The Median is a statistic for the distribution whereas the _____ provides a statistic for an interval; it is the center of the interval; the arithmetic average of the upper and lower limits.
    a. Midpoint11
    b. 15 theorem
    c. Undefined
    d. Undefined

47. In statistics an arrangement of values of a variable showing their observed or theoretical frequency of occurrence is called a _____.
    a. Distribution11
    b. 15 theorem
    c. Undefined
    d. Undefined

Chapter 11. Infinite Sequences and Series

48. A _____ is a concrete example of an item or a specification against which all others may be measured. For example, there are "primary standards" for length, mass (see Kilogram _____), and other units of measure, kept by laboratories and standards organizations.
   a. Standard11
   b. Concept
   c. Undefined
   d. Undefined

49. The bottom part of any fraction represents the number of pieces in one whole unit. This bottom part is called the _____.
   a. Denominator11
   b. Thing
   c. Undefined
   d. Undefined

50. The top part of the fraction is called the _____. It could also be called the dividend, but _____ is preferred.
   a. Numerator11
   b. Thing
   c. Undefined
   d. Undefined

51. The _____ of a number is the distance between zero and the number on the lnumber line.
   a. Absolute value11
   b. Concept
   c. Undefined
   d. Undefined

52. _____ is the process by which sample data are used to indicate the value of an unknown quantity in a population.
   a. Estimation11
   b. ACTRAN
   c. Undefined
   d. Undefined

53. If one number is to the right of another number on the number line, this number is _____ the number on the left. The symbol that is used is >.
   a. Greater than11
   b. Thing
   c. Undefined
   d. Undefined

54. A number that does not change in value in a given situation is a _____.
   a. 15 theorem
   b. Constant11
   c. Undefined
   d. Undefined

55. A _____ is the answer in multiplication, or an expression that identifies factors to be multiplied
   a. Thing
   b. Product11
   c. Undefined
   d. Undefined

56. A _____ is a multiplicative factor of a certain object such as a variable (for example, the coefficients of a polynomial), a basis vector, a basis function and so on. Usually, the objects and the coefficients are indexed in the same way, leading to expressions such as $a_1x_1 + a_2x_2 + a_3x_3 + \ldots$ where a_n is the _____ of the variable x_n for each $n = 1, 2, 3, \ldots$
   a. Concept
   b. Coefficient11
   c. Undefined
   d. Undefined

57. There are properties of objects that do assume one and only value, and we refer to these characteristics as _____. _____, then, are the invariables that differentiate one class of objects from another.

Chapter 11. Infinite Sequences and Series

a. Constants11
b. 15 theorem
c. Undefined
d. Undefined

58. The very fact that we are measuring objects with respect to some characteristic implies that the objects differ in that characteristic; or stated in another way, that the characteristic can take on a number of different values. These properties or characteristics of an object that can assume two or more different values are referred to as a _____.
   a. 15 theorem
   b. Variable11
   c. Undefined
   d. Undefined

59. The _____ of a graph or equation is the set of all the possible x values.
   a. Domain11
   b. Thing
   c. Undefined
   d. Undefined

60. A _____ is a class of simple functions where they are constructed using only multiplication and addition of terms.
   a. Thing
   b. Polynomial11
   c. Undefined
   d. Undefined

61. A _____ is an undefined term. We usually represent this by a dot, but a _____ actually has no dimension. A capital letter names any _____.
   a. Thing
   b. Point11
   c. Undefined
   d. Undefined

62. The Greek letter _____ indicates summation.
   a. Sigma11
   b. 15 theorem
   c. Undefined
   d. Undefined

63. _____ is a branch of mathematics which studies structure and quantity. It may be roughly characterized as a generalization and abstraction of arithmetic, in which operations are performed on symbols rather than numbers. It includes elementary _____, taught to high school students, as well as abstract _____ which covers such structures as groups, rings and fields. Along with geometry and analysis, it is one of the three principal branches of mathematics.
   a. Concept
   b. Algebra11
   c. Undefined
   d. Undefined

64. _____ is a central branch of mathematics, developed from algebra and geometry, and built on two major complementary ideas, differential _____ and integral _____.
   a. Concept
   b. Calculus11
   c. Undefined
   d. Undefined

65. The point of intersection of the horizontal and vertical axes in the rectangular coordinate plane is the _____. It is is expressed as the ordered pair (0,0).
   a. Origin11
   b. Concept
   c. Undefined
   d. Undefined

66. A _____ is simply a polynomial with two terms such as this example: 2x + 7.

Chapter 11. Infinite Sequences and Series 181

    a. Binomial11
    b. Thing
    c. Undefined
    d. Undefined

67. _____ is the study of quantity, structure, space, and change. Historically, _____ developed from counting, calculation, measurement, and the study of the shapes and motions of physical objects, through the use of abstraction and deductive reasoning.
    a. Mathematics11
    b. Concept
    c. Undefined
    d. Undefined

68. An _____ is one of the number lines found on the rectangular coordinate system. The x asis is the horizontal number line while the y _____ is the vertical number line.
    a. Axis11
    b. Thing
    c. Undefined
    d. Undefined

69. A measure of variability, the _____ is the distance from the lowest to the highest score.
    a. Range11
    b. 15 theorem
    c. Undefined
    d. Undefined

70. A _____ is a number that when multiplied by a given number gives you one. This is also called multiplicative inverse.
    a. Thing
    b. Reciprocal11
    c. Undefined
    d. Undefined

71. A _____ contains at least one squared term.
    a. Thing
    b. Quadratic11
    c. Undefined
    d. Undefined

72. The _____ of a number is the number that makes a sum zero. In most cases, this means just to change the sign. 3 is the _____ of -3.
    a. Event
    b. Opposite11
    c. Undefined
    d. Undefined

73. By _____ we mean the cumulative frequency, counting in from the nearer end.
    a. Depth11
    b. 15 theorem
    c. Undefined
    d. Undefined

74. An _____ is composed of two rays that have a common endpoint, called the vertex. Each _____ is named by a lower case letter or by one point from each ray and the vertex inbetween. _____ a might be the same _____ as _____ ABC.
    a. Thing
    b. Angle11
    c. Undefined
    d. Undefined

75. The same statistical principles apply to the evaluation of observed _____ between sets of data. The field of statistics provides the necessary techniques for making statements of our certainty that there are real as opposed to chance _____.

Chapter 11. Infinite Sequences and Series

    a. 15 theorem   b. Differences11
    c. Undefined   d. Undefined

76. _____, the height of the curve for a given value of X; closely related to the probability of an observation in an interval around X.
    a. Density11   b. 15 theorem
    c. Undefined   d. Undefined

77. _____ is the result of assigning numbers to objects to abstractly represent the objects or characteristics of the objects.
    a. 15 theorem   b. Measurement11
    c. Undefined   d. Undefined

78. The highest number in a list of values is called the _____.
    a. Thing   b. Maximum11
    c. Undefined   d. Undefined

79. Sometimes, when a fraction is converted to a decimal, one or more digits occurs over and over. This is called a _____. One-third becomes .333333... and is an example of a _____.
    a. Thing   b. Repeating decimal11
    c. Undefined   d. Undefined

80. A _____ occurs in a right triangle and is the side opposite the right angle. It will also be the longest side of a right triangle.
    a. Thing   b. Hypotenuse11
    c. Undefined   d. Undefined

ANSWER KEY

Chapter 1

1. b	2. a	3. a	4. b	5. a	6. b	7. b	8. a	9. a	10. b
11. a	12. a	13. b	14. b	15. b	16. b	17. a	18. b	19. b	20. a
21. b	22. b	23. b	24. a	25. a	26. b	27. a	28. a	29. b	30. b
31. a	32. b	33. b	34. a	35. a	36. b	37. a	38. a	39. a	40. a
41. a	42. a	43. b	44. a	45. a	46. b	47. a	48. a	49. a	50. b
51. a	52. b	53. b	54. a	55. a	56. b	57. b	58. b	59. a	60. a
61. b	62. a	63. a	64. a	65. a	66. b	67. a	68. a	69. b	70. a
71. a	72. a	73. b	74. a	75. a	76. b	77. b	78. a	79. b	80. a
81. a	82. a	83. a	84. b	85. b	86. a	87. b	88. a	89. b	90. b
91. b	92. b	93. b	94. b	95. b	96. b	97. b	98. b	99. a	100. b
101. a	102. b	103. b	104. b	105. a	106. a	107. a	108. b	109. b	110. a
111. a	112. a	113. a	114. a	115. a	116. b	117. b	118. a	119. b	120. b
121. a	122. a	123. a	124. b	125. a	126. b	127. a	128. a	129. a	130. b
131. a	132. b	133. b	134. b	135. b	136. a	137. a	138. a	139. b	140. b
141. a	142. b	143. a	144. b	145. b	146. a	147. a	148. a	149. b	150. b
151. b	152. b	153. a	154. b	155. b	156. a	157. a	158. a	159. b	160. b
161. a	162. a	163. b	164. a	165. a	166. b	167. b	168. b	169. b	170. a
171. b	172. a	173. a	174. b	175. a	176. b	177. a	178. a	179. a	180. a
181. b	182. a	183. b	184. b	185. a	186. b	187. a			

Chapter 2

1. a	2. a	3. b	4. b	5. b	6. b	7. b	8. a	9. a	10. b
11. a	12. b	13. b	14. a	15. b	16. b	17. b	18. b	19. b	20. b
21. a	22. b	23. a	24. a	25. a	26. b	27. a	28. b	29. b	30. a
31. a	32. a	33. b	34. b	35. a	36. b	37. b	38. a	39. a	40. a
41. b	42. a	43. a	44. a	45. b	46. a	47. b	48. b	49. b	50. a
51. a	52. b	53. a	54. a	55. b	56. b	57. b	58. b	59. b	60. b
61. b	62. b	63. b	64. a	65. b	66. b	67. a	68. b	69. b	70. b
71. a	72. a	73. b	74. b	75. a	76. a	77. b	78. a	79. b	80. a
81. b	82. b	83. b	84. b	85. a	86. b	87. b	88. b	89. a	90. b
91. a	92. b	93. b	94. b	95. b	96. a	97. a	98. a	99. b	100. b
101. b	102. b	103. a	104. a	105. b	106. b	107. b	108. b	109. a	110. b
111. b	112. a	113. b	114. a	115. b	116. a	117. b	118. b	119. b	120. b
121. a	122. a	123. b	124. b	125. a	126. a	127. b	128. a	129. b	130. a
131. a	132. b	133. a	134. a	135. a	136. a	137. a	138. b	139. a	140. b
141. b	142. b								

Chapter 3

1. b	2. a	3. b	4. a	5. a	6. a	7. b	8. a	9. a	10. a
11. a	12. a	13. b	14. a	15. b	16. b	17. a	18. b	19. b	20. b
21. a	22. b	23. a	24. b	25. a	26. a	27. a	28. b	29. b	30. b
31. a	32. a	33. a	34. b	35. a	36. b	37. a	38. b	39. b	40. b
41. b	42. b	43. b	44. b	45. a	46. a	47. b	48. b	49. a	50. a
51. b	52. a	53. b	54. a	55. a	56. a	57. a	58. b	59. a	60. a
61. b	62. a	63. a	64. a	65. a	66. a	67. b	68. a	69. b	70. b
71. b	72. b	73. b	74. a	75. a	76. a	77. a	78. b	79. a	80. a
81. b	82. a	83. b	84. a	85. a	86. b	87. b	88. b	89. b	90. b
91. b	92. b	93. b	94. a	95. b	96. a	97. b	98. a	99. a	100. a
101. a	102. b	103. b	104. b	105. a	106. a	107. a	108. a	109. b	110. a
111. a	112. b	113. b	114. a	115. a	116. b	117. b	118. b	119. b	120. b
121. b	122. b	123. a	124. b	125. b	126. b	127. b	128. b	129. a	130. a
131. a	132. a	133. a	134. b	135. a	136. a	137. a	138. a	139. b	140. b
141. b	142. b	143. a	144. a	145. a	146. b	147. b	148. a	149. b	150. a
151. b	152. a	153. a	154. a	155. b	156. b	157. a	158. a	159. b	160. b
161. a	162. a	163. a	164. b	165. a	166. a	167. a	168. b	169. b	170. b
171. a	172. a	173. b	174. a	175. a	176. b	177. a	178. b	179. b	180. a
181. a	182. b	183. a	184. a	185. b	186. a	187. a	188. a	189. b	190. a
191. a	192. b	193. a	194. b	195. a	196. a	197. a	198. b	199. b	200. a
201. a	202. a	203. a	204. a	205. a	206. b	207. b	208. b	209. b	210. a
211. b	212. b	213. b	214. b	215. a	216. a	217. a	218. a	219. b	220. a
221. b	222. b	223. a	224. b	225. b	226. a	227. b	228. a	229. a	230. b
231. b	232. b	233. b	234. b	235. a	236. a				

ANSWER KEY

Chapter 4

1. b	2. b	3. b	4. a	5. a	6. b	7. a	8. b	9. a	10. b
11. a	12. a	13. a	14. a	15. b	16. a	17. a	18. b	19. a	20. a
21. b	22. a	23. b	24. a	25. a	26. b	27. b	28. a	29. a	30. a
31. b	32. a	33. b	34. b	35. b	36. a	37. a	38. b	39. b	40. a
41. a	42. a	43. a	44. a	45. b	46. a	47. a	48. a	49. b	50. b
51. a	52. a	53. a	54. a	55. a	56. a	57. b	58. b	59. b	60. a
61. a	62. a	63. b	64. b	65. a	66. a	67. b	68. b	69. b	70. a
71. b	72. a	73. a	74. a	75. b	76. a	77. a	78. a	79. a	80. a
81. a	82. b	83. b	84. a	85. a	86. a	87. b	88. a	89. b	90. b
91. a	92. a	93. a	94. a	95. a	96. a	97. b	98. b	99. b	100. a
101. b	102. b	103. b	104. b	105. b	106. b	107. b	108. a	109. a	110. a
111. a	112. a	113. b	114. a	115. b	116. a	117. a	118. b	119. a	120. a
121. a	122. b	123. b	124. b	125. a	126. b	127. b	128. a	129. a	130. a
131. b	132. a	133. b	134. b	135. a	136. b	137. b	138. b	139. a	140. a
141. b	142. a	143. b	144. a	145. b	146. b	147. a	148. a	149. a	150. b
151. a	152. b	153. a	154. a	155. a	156. b	157. b	158. b	159. b	160. b
161. a	162. a	163. b	164. b	165. a	166. b	167. b	168. b	169. a	170. a
171. b	172. a	173. a	174. a	175. a	176. a	177. a	178. b	179. a	180. b
181. a	182. a	183. b	184. a	185. b	186. a	187. a	188. b	189. b	190. b
191. a	192. a	193. b	194. b	195. b	196. a	197. a	198. a	199. a	200. a
201. a	202. b	203. a	204. b	205. b	206. a	207. b	208. a	209. a	210. a
211. a	212. a	213. b	214. b	215. a	216. a	217. a	218. a	219. a	220. b
221. b	222. a	223. a	224. b	225. a	226. b	227. b	228. b	229. a	230. a
231. a	232. a	233. b	234. a	235. b	236. a	237. a			

Chapter 5

1. b	2. b	3. b	4. b	5. a	6. b	7. a	8. a	9. a	10. a
11. b	12. b	13. a	14. a	15. a	16. b	17. b	18. b	19. a	20. b
21. b	22. b	23. a	24. a	25. b	26. b	27. a	28. b	29. b	30. a
31. a	32. a	33. a	34. a	35. b	36. b	37. b	38. b	39. a	40. b
41. a	42. b	43. a	44. a	45. a	46. b	47. b	48. b	49. b	50. b
51. a	52. b	53. a	54. b	55. b	56. a	57. a	58. b	59. b	60. a
61. a	62. a	63. a	64. b	65. a	66. b	67. a	68. b	69. a	70. a
71. b	72. a	73. a	74. b	75. b	76. b	77. b	78. b	79. a	80. a
81. a	82. a	83. a	84. a	85. a	86. a	87. a	88. b	89. a	90. a
91. b	92. b	93. b	94. a	95. b	96. a	97. a	98. b	99. b	100. a
101. b	102. b	103. a	104. b	105. b	106. b	107. a	108. b	109. b	110. a
111. a	112. a	113. a	114. b	115. b	116. a	117. b	118. b	119. b	120. a
121. a	122. a	123. a	124. a	125. a	126. a	127. b	128. a	129. a	130. a
131. a	132. b	133. a	134. a	135. a	136. b	137. b	138. a	139. a	140. b
141. a	142. a	143. a	144. b	145. a	146. b	147. b	148. b	149. a	150. a
151. a	152. a	153. a	154. b	155. b	156. a				

Chapter 6

1. b	2. b	3. b	4. a	5. b	6. a	7. a	8. a	9. b	10. b
11. b	12. a	13. b	14. b	15. a	16. b	17. a	18. b	19. a	20. a
21. b	22. b	23. a	24. b	25. b	26. a	27. a	28. b	29. b	30. a
31. a	32. a	33. a	34. b	35. a	36. b	37. a	38. b	39. b	40. a
41. b	42. a	43. a	44. b	45. b	46. b	47. a	48. b	49. b	50. b
51. b	52. b	53. a	54. a	55. b	56. a	57. a	58. a	59. b	60. a
61. a	62. a	63. a	64. b	65. b	66. a	67. b	68. b	69. a	70. a
71. a	72. b	73. b	74. b	75. a	76. b	77. a	78. a	79. a	80. a
81. b	82. b	83. a	84. a	85. a	86. a	87. b	88. a	89. b	90. b
91. b	92. b	93. a	94. b	95. b	96. b	97. b	98. a	99. a	100. a
101. b	102. a	103. a	104. a	105. a	106. a	107. b	108. b	109. a	110. b
111. a	112. a	113. a							

Chapter 7

1. b	2. b	3. a	4. b	5. b	6. b	7. a	8. b	9. a	10. a
11. a	12. a	13. a	14. b	15. b	16. a	17. a	18. b	19. b	20. a
21. b	22. b	23. b	24. b	25. b	26. b	27. a	28. a	29. b	30. a
31. a	32. a	33. a	34. a	35. b	36. b	37. b	38. a	39. a	40. a
41. b	42. a	43. a	44. a	45. a	46. b	47. b	48. a	49. b	50. b
51. b	52. a	53. a	54. a	55. b	56. a	57. a	58. b	59. a	60. b
61. b	62. a	63. a	64. b	65. b	66. b	67. a	68. a	69. a	70. a
71. a	72. b	73. a	74. a	75. b	76. b	77. b	78. b	79. b	80. a
81. a	82. a	83. b	84. b	85. a	86. a	87. b	88. a	89. b	90. a
91. a	92. a	93. a	94. a	95. a	96. a	97. b	98. a	99. b	100. a
101. a	102. b	103. a	104. b	105. b	106. a	107. a	108. a	109. a	110. a
111. b	112. b	113. a	114. b	115. a	116. a	117. b	118. b	119. a	120. a
121. b	122. b	123. b	124. a	125. a	126. b	127. b	128. a	129. a	130. b
131. b	132. a	133. a	134. b	135. a	136. b	137. a	138. b	139. b	140. b
141. a	142. a	143. b	144. b	145. a	146. b	147. a	148. b	149. b	150. a
151. a	152. a	153. a	154. a	155. b	156. b	157. b	158. a	159. a	160. b
161. b	162. a	163. b	164. b	165. b	166. a				

ANSWER KEY

Chapter 8

1. a	2. a	3. a	4. b	5. a	6. b	7. b	8. a	9. a	10. b
11. b	12. a	13. b	14. a	15. b	16. a	17. a	18. b	19. b	20. a
21. a	22. b	23. a	24. a	25. a	26. a	27. b	28. a	29. b	30. a
31. b	32. b	33. b	34. a	35. a	36. b	37. b	38. a	39. a	40. a
41. b	42. a	43. b	44. b	45. a	46. b	47. b	48. a	49. b	50. a
51. b	52. a	53. b	54. a	55. a	56. a	57. b	58. b	59. a	60. b
61. b	62. a	63. b	64. b	65. b	66. b	67. a	68. a	69. b	70. a
71. b	72. b	73. b	74. a	75. b	76. b	77. b	78. b	79. b	80. a
81. a	82. a	83. b	84. a	85. b	86. b	87. b	88. b	89. a	90. a
91. b	92. a	93. a	94. b	95. a	96. a	97. a	98. b	99. a	100. b
101. a	102. a	103. b	104. b	105. a	106. b	107. b	108. a	109. a	110. a
111. a	112. a	113. a	114. b	115. b	116. b	117. b	118. b	119. b	120. a
121. a	122. a	123. a	124. a	125. b	126. a	127. b	128. a	129. a	130. b
131. b	132. b	133. b	134. b	135. a	136. a	137. b	138. b	139. b	140. b
141. a	142. b	143. b	144. a	145. a	146. a	147. b	148. a	149. a	150. b
151. a	152. a								

Chapter 9

1. a	2. a	3. a	4. a	5. b	6. b	7. a	8. a	9. b	10. b
11. b	12. b	13. a	14. a	15. b	16. a	17. a	18. a	19. a	20. b
21. b	22. a	23. a	24. a	25. a	26. a	27. b	28. b	29. a	30. b
31. b	32. b	33. b	34. a	35. b	36. a	37. a	38. b	39. a	40. a
41. a	42. b	43. b	44. a	45. b	46. b	47. b	48. b	49. b	50. b
51. a	52. a	53. b	54. b	55. a	56. b	57. b	58. a	59. b	60. a
61. b	62. b	63. b	64. a	65. a	66. b	67. a	68. b	69. a	70. b
71. b	72. b	73. b	74. b	75. b	76. b	77. a	78. b	79. b	80. a
81. b	82. a	83. a	84. b	85. a	86. a	87. a	88. b	89. a	90. b
91. a	92. b	93. b	94. b	95. a	96. a	97. b	98. b	99. a	100. b
101. a	102. b	103. b	104. a	105. b	106. a	107. a	108. b	109. b	110. a
111. a	112. a	113. a	114. b	115. a	116. b	117. b	118. b	119. b	120. a
121. a	122. b	123. b	124. b	125. a	126. a	127. b	128. b	129. a	130. b
131. a	132. a	133. a	134. a	135. a	136. a	137. b	138. b	139. a	140. a

Chapter 10

1. a	2. a	3. a	4. b	5. a	6. b	7. a	8. a	9. b	10. b
11. a	12. b	13. a	14. b	15. a	16. b	17. b	18. b	19. b	20. b
21. a	22. a	23. b	24. a	25. a	26. b	27. a	28. a	29. b	30. a
31. b	32. b	33. b	34. b	35. a	36. a	37. b	38. a	39. a	40. a
41. a	42. a	43. b	44. b	45. a	46. a	47. a	48. a	49. a	50. b
51. a	52. a	53. b	54. a	55. b	56. b	57. a	58. b	59. a	60. a
61. b	62. a	63. a							

Chapter 11

1. a	2. b	3. a	4. b	5. b	6. b	7. b	8. a	9. b	10. a
11. b	12. b	13. a	14. b	15. a	16. b	17. a	18. b	19. b	20. b
21. a	22. b	23. b	24. a	25. b	26. a	27. a	28. b	29. a	30. b
31. b	32. b	33. b	34. a	35. a	36. b	37. a	38. b	39. a	40. a
41. b	42. b	43. b	44. b	45. a	46. a	47. a	48. a	49. a	50. a
51. a	52. a	53. a	54. b	55. b	56. b	57. a	58. b	59. a	60. b
61. b	62. a	63. b	64. b	65. a	66. a	67. a	68. a	69. a	70. b
71. b	72. b	73. a	74. b	75. b	76. a	77. b	78. b	79. b	80. b